The Chosen Tongue

The Negro in Literature

General Editor, J. Saunders Redding

The Chosen Tongue

English Writing in the Tropical World

Gerald Moore
School of African and Asian Studies
University of Sussex

J. & J. HARPER EDITIONS
HARPER & ROW, PUBLISHERS
NEW YORK AND EVANSTON

First published in England by Longmans, Green and Co Ltd 1969
THE CHOSEN TONGUE by Gerald Moore

© Gerald Moore 1969

First J. & J. Harper Edition 1970

Library of Congress Catalog Card Number: 77-97058

Contents

Plates

Between pages 88 and 89

Contents

Acknowledgements

We are grateful to the following for permission to reproduce copyright material.

Jonathan Cape Ltd for extracts from 'As John to Patmos', 'Prelude', and 'To a Painter in England' from *In a Green Night* by Derek Walcott, and for extracts from 'The Castaway', 'The Whale, His Bulwark', 'Crusoe's Journal', 'The Almond Trees', 'A Village Life', 'Crusoe's Island', 'Missing the Sea', and 'The Voyage Up River' from *The Castaway* by Derek Walcott; Jonathan Cape Ltd and the executors of Roger Mais' estate for extracts from *The Hills were Joyful Together* by Roger Mais; André Deutsch Ltd for extracts from *The Year at San Fernando* by Michael Anthony, and an extract from *Danda* by Nkem Nwankwo; East African Publishing House for extracts from *Song of Lawino* by Okot p'Bitek; Faber & Faber Ltd for extracts from *Palace of the Peacock*, and extracts from *The Whole Armour* both by Wilson Harris; Harper & Row Inc. for extracts from *Banjo* by Claude McKay, Copyright 1929 by Harper & Brothers, renewed 1957 by Hope McKay Virtue; William Heinemann Ltd for extracts from *Arrow of God* by Chinua Achebe; Hogarth Press Ltd and the author's literary estate for extracts from *Morning at the Office* by Edgar Mittelholzer; Michael Joseph Ltd for extracts from *Of Age and Innocence*, *The Emigrants*, and *In the Castle of my Skin* all by George Lamming; Longmans, Green & Co. Ltd for extracts from *A Few Nights and Days* by Mbella Sonne Dipoko; MacGibbon & Kee Ltd for extracts from *The Last Enchantment* by Neville Dawes, and extracts from *The Lonely Londoners* by Samuel Selvon (published by Mayflower Books); author, and Methuen & Co. Ltd for extracts from 'Civilian and Soldier' and 'Massacre October '66' from *Idanre* by Wole Soyinka; the proprietors of *New Zealand Monthly Review* for an extract from *Not By Wind Ravaged* by Hone Tuwhare from issue dated September 1960; author's executors for extracts from *Limits*, *Distances*, *Heavensgate*, 'Come Thunder' and 'Elegy for Alto' all by Christopher Okigbo; Oxford University Press for extracts from *Masks* by Edward Brathwaite, and for extracts from 'The Dust', 'Folkways', 'New World A-Comin', 'Epilogue', 'Emigrants', 'Postlude', 'South', 'Journeys', and 'Prelude' from *Rights of Passage* by Edward Brathwaite, and for extracts from *A Dance of the Forests* by Wole Soyinka; and Martin Secker & Warburg Ltd for an extract from *The Wild Coast* by Jan Carew.

We have been unable to trace the copyright holders of the following:

Acknowledgements

'Outcast' from *Selected Poems* by Claude McKay, *Epitomé* by U. Tam'si, 'The Years Behind', 'My God of Songs Was All', and 'Weaverbird' all from *Rediscovery* by George Awoonor-Williams, 'My Sounds Begin Again' and 'Somehow We Survive' from *Sirens, Knuckles, Boots* by Dennis Brutus, 'Elegy' by Mazisi Kunene, and *We are Going* by Kath Walker, and would appreciate any information that would enable us to do so.

The publishers would like to acknowledge the following sources for photographs used in this book:

J. Allen Cash for cover photograph; Anne Bolt for plates 1 and 2; Camera Press for plate 3; Paul Popper for plates 5 and 6; Radio Times Hulton Picture Library for plate 4. Plates 7, 8a and b are from photographs by the author.

Introduction

The English language advanced step by step with the expansion of the imperial frontiers. As these have contracted again, a process which began with the American Revolution in 1776 and is not yet completed, the language has generally remained behind to make its own way in countries no longer politically subject to England. Since the seventeenth century, successive generations of writers have struggled to accommodate English to the expression of values, climates, landscapes and historical experiences quite different from those which originally shaped it: all, that is to say, have been engaged in using English to define cultures not English, or no longer English. This book will be concerned with writers who, in addition to this, are themselves of non-English stock, for many of whom this language is not the obvious or the imperative choice. But first it will be necessary to look briefly at the historical process by which English came to assume such importance in the definition of new nationalisms and in the total literary expression of the modern world.

The establishment of the precarious little English colony at Jamestown, Virginia, in 1607 announced the opening of a migration which continues to this day. The "assisted immigrants" who crowd hopefully aboard the white liners at Tilbury, bound for the Antipodes, are pebbles in a stream of white colonization that has scarcely slackened in three hundred and fifty years. This great expansion of the English-speaking peoples beyond their native island led to the establishment in North America, Australia, New Zealand and parts of South Africa of large communities who not only shared English as a mother-tongue but remained for a long period predominantly British in stock, in culture and in orientation.

This process, so familiar to every Englishman, coincided and partly intermingled with another, even more massive migration. In the year 1619, one year before the sailing of the *Mayflower*, a Dutch vessel landed twenty African men and women upon Jamestown Quay. These were not slaves, since slavery did not yet exist in Virginia, but booty from a Spanish slaver which the Dutch had captured on the high seas. Nearly fifty years were to elapse before Negro slavery became a recognized institution in the North American colonies. Meanwhile the plantation and development of the Americas remained throughout a joint enterprise of Africans and Europeans in which the African, most notably south of latitude 37°N, was frequently the major partner. That obscure landfall at Jamestown, so seldom noticed in the history books, was quite as momentous for the future of the Americas as the arrival of the *Mayflower* fifteen months later. But whereas the uprooted Englishman was able to retain his name, religion, language and some living contact with his mother culture, the enslaved African was all too often robbed of precisely these things. Utterly severed from his old world, he found himself without rights or status in the new. All the devices which make for continuity in the human family, tribe or race were deliberately stripped from him, so that he might become a chattel devoid of social connections. The emergence of distinctive Afro-American cultural achievements in jazz, folk-lore, blues, spiritual, calypso, work-song, ballad and many other forms was brought about in the teeth of these obstacles. If the slave was defined by nothing else, he found a measure of collectivity in his very exclusion from the society of the white and the free.

The Atlantic slave trade, which forcibly transported at least twenty million human beings from Africa to the Americas and endured for some three centuries and a half, was accompanied and followed by the conquest and colonization, first of the West Indies, then of India and South East Asia, and finally of Africa itself. But this was to be colonization in a new sense, foreign to the concepts of Greek or Roman. It did not necessarily involve thorough-going cultural penetration or the plantation of permanent and substantial white settlements on the conquered soil. Vast countries like Burma were administered for sixty years by a handful of transient officials who made the minimum of impact upon its life, while many small West Indian islands boasted a white population composed of overseers and soldiers, safeguarding the profits of landlords who never left London. It was, unlike the white migration referred to earlier, an imperialism essentially military and exploitative, rather than ethnic or even cultural. The tenuous administrations presided over communities which throughout remained overwhelmingly non-English in ethnic stock, social habits and language.

Nevertheless the language did slowly make its way into the life of these tropical communities, inhabiting climates and landscapes infinitely removed from its origin. In the British West Indies, as successive waves of African, Indian and Chinese immigration spent themselves upon the shore, forgetting in a generation or two the very provinces whence they had come, English in a variety of dialect forms gradually established itself as the unique language of the region. In Asia and Africa it became, at least temporarily, the language of government, of higher education and, more important still, of higher status. In Asia, however, the withdrawal of imperial control revealed how precarious the situation of the language really was. The volume of literary activity in languages such as Bengali, Tamil, Gujarati, Malay and Urdu, together with the gradual decline of English usage in public life, suggests that ultimately the imperial language may prove as marginal as the English presence itself; whilst in tropical Africa only the recent spread of mass education has offered it the possibility of escape from an equally marginal role. For historical experience confirms that a language which remains the property of a small élite cannot provide the basis for a national culture. A recent parallel would be the use of French by polite society in nineteenth century Russia.

The development of various overseas literatures in English, a development which began in the seventeenth century and has been gaining momentum ever since, can only usefully be considered by taking these historical processes into account. The beginnings of a literature in North America, as later in Australasia and South Africa, were strictly provincial in character. Not only was the culture described essentially a transplanted British culture, but the immediate physical environment of the writer was still seen as something exotic, mysterious and untamed. Hence the landscape was to the writer a continual reminder of his own strangeness. The aboriginal inhabitants, where they still existed, challenged him by their complete identification with an environment that also challenged him. For there was as yet no sense that he had in any way been made or shaped by the physical presence of the land or climate around him.

Whilst sometimes celebrating his own freedom from the dogmas and archaic laws of Europe, the American writer of this period frequently envies the larger freedom of the 'savage' who, far beyond the boundaries of the settled areas, ranges over the continent he has inherited and from which even extermination cannot entirely drive his presence. Here is an early North American traveller, William Bartram, describing an ascent of the Altamaha River in the 1770's:

> I ascended this beautiful river, on whose fruitful banks the generous and true sons of liberty securely dwell, fifty miles above the white settlements ... [Allured by] the sublime enchanting scenes of primitive nature ... and visions of terrestrial happiness. ... How happily situated is this retired spot of earth! What an elysium it is! Where the Seminole, the naked red warrior roams at large, and after the vigorous chase retires from the scorching heat of the meridian sun. Here he reclines and reposes under the odoriferous shades of Zanthoxylon, his verdant couch guarded by the Deity; Liberty, and the Muses, inspiring him with wisdom and valour whilst the balmy zephyrs fan him to sleep.[1]

This is the pure essence of colonial literature, the romanticism of the outsider which was to remain an ingredient in American writing for almost another century. We can speak of the emergence of an autonomous American or Australian or South African literature only when an acceptance, a deep and intimate awareness, of his present world begins to infuse the writer's work. Fenimore Cooper, writing sixty years after Bartram, still sees America as a virgin wilderness, gradually encroached upon by the white settlements. These settlements still, to some extent, symbolize an alien and intrusive element. For Cooper, the red man, though fast disappearing, is still the real owner of the land of America. He is the master of a lore which can be known only by those who have lived for centuries in daily intimacy with beast, tree, weather, water and rock. Of his white characters, only the old scout Hawk-Eye, who is culturally almost an Indian, glimpses this knowledge. The others become tyros the instant they step out of the settlements into the rough bosom of America.

Cooper's attitude towards the Indians also exposes the

1 *Travels of William Bartram* (New York, Dover, 1928), p. 64.

characteristic ambivalence of the colonial expatiating on 'native' virtues and weaknesses. Those who are loyal to their new masters are allowed to possess great qualities. Those who prefer to remain aloof or to fight for their liberty are invariably cruel, vengeful and devilish. Even a good shot becomes a 'treacherous aim'. His pages abound with phrases such as these: 'the characteristic cunning of the savage'; 'it would have exceeded the credulity of even a native to have doubted any longer'; and, anticipating the apologetics of the coming century of imperialism, 'it is not always easy to deal with an Indian as you would with your fellow Christian.'

Whitman is the first American poet whose work carries, however crudely at times, the whole sense of America and of being an American. Whitman sees America not as exotic or unknown, but as unique in its vast energy and democratic faith. He exults, as an American, in this uniqueness. In fiction we shall have to look as late as Mark Twain to find any expression of comparable sureness, for Melville seems almost frightened of what he sees in America, and his writing is a kind of perpetual setting out for the seas and the islands where he can confront this fear alone. It is the ocean, rather than the prairie, which supplies his images of grandeur. By contrast, Huck Finn and Nigger Jim never need to look beyond America in order to define themselves. Indeed, America itself is much too vast for their comprehension. The great river is their sufficient world, dividing as it does the slave shore from the free, and flowing with infinite grandeur towards a rumoured coast which faces, not Europe, but Mexico.

To create the literary image of this contained and self-sufficient America some two hundred and fifty years of settlement and expansion had been demanded. It will be revealing now to look at some of the other shores of the world where substantial colonies of English-speaking settlers were establishing themselves.

The first landmark in the naturalization of English writing to South Africa was set up by a young governess called Olive Schreiner. Her *Story of an African Farm*, written in the late 1870's, proved in many ways a false dawn. She gives us a feeling of the insistence of earth and sky in a landscape without detail or near horizons, and of what William Plomer calls 'the constriction of the great open spaces'. She defines the plight of women, indeed of all sensitive and rounded souls, in a narrow, severe and authoritarian society, continually punishing itself in punishing the humanity of those around it. But her confrontation with the denial at the heart of Boer society, her great cry for personal emancipation, drowns out her awareness of the coming struggle between black and white, each striving to stamp its image upon the flow of South Africa's destiny. For her, the 'natives' never really move into the foreground; they remain part of the furniture of the plains around her, but they do not people the human drama at the centre of her writing. And if this is true of Olive Schreiner, we are scarcely likely to find a wider human concern in the following years, as the tradition of Cape Liberalism which she represented is driven backward step-by-step by militant Afrikanerdom. The South African tragedy had already greatly darkened by the time William Plomer erected the second landmark in his novel *Turbott Wolfe*, published in 1925. Like *The Story of an African Farm*, this is the first work of a very young writer; Olive Schreiner was nineteen when she began her book, and Plomer's was written between the ages of nineteen and twenty-one, when he was working at a lonely trading-post in Zululand.

Plomer is no less aware than Schreiner of all that is crushed down in the white man's nature by the spiritual, mental and physical *laager* in which he forces himself to live. Turbott Wolfe's love for the African girl Nhliziyombi is most tenderly and movingly evoked, but the fear which makes him turn aside from it, thus failing both himself and Africa, is not denied. His final comment is 'She knew and I knew.'[1] Yet Plomer goes beyond this and shows us in Mabel van der Horst both a prophetess of the wrath to come and a woman with the courage and humanity to love, be loved, and live the consequences. Mabel is a Boer girl who marries a young African teacher at the end of the novel, an action which Wolfe reluctantly accepts as a counterpoint to his own failure to stretch out his hand and draw Nhliziyombi from dream into reality.

The other day I heard a young exponent of Black Power tell his cringing white audience:

"The white man is dead. He died at Hiroshima. He died at Nagasaki. He died at Sharpeville."

---

1 *Turbott Wolfe* (London, Hogarth Press, 1965 edition), p. 190.

He meant that the white man must learn, slowly and painfull
to be simply a man. It was with a thrill of surprise that I fou
almost exactly the same words given to Mabel van der Horst
more than forty years ago. Asked to expound her views on the
native question, she explodes:

> 'What the hell *is* the native question? You take away the black
> man's country, and, shirking the future consequences of your
> action, you blindly affix a label to what you know (and fear) the
> black man is thinking of you—'the native question'. Native
> question, indeed! My good man, there is no native question.
> It isn't a question. It's an answer. I don't know whether people are
> wilfully blind, that they can't see what's coming. The white
> man's as dead as a doornail in this country. . . . All this Empire-
> building's a blooming blind alley. We think we're invincible
> because we can fly round the world in an aeroplane, and because
> we can send our silly voices flying round the world by wireless.
> Wait a little, the black man will break our areoplanes, and the
> yellow man will effectually silence even our loudest loudspeakers.
> The strength of the natives is in their weakness.'[1]

Vietnam, as well as the turn of events in Southern Africa, has
given these words a new resonance. But South Africa was not
to follow the path towards a whole humanity indicated by
Plomer as the only way out of her nightmare. The events of the
last forty years have alienated every South African writer of any
compassion or sensitivity from the society developing around him.
Most of them have taken refuge in exile, others are prematurely
dead, banned or in prison. Nadine Gordimer, the only white
English writer of real stature still working in the Republic,
finds herself forced to write for an overseas audience, owing to
the total banning of all her recent books within South Africa.
No matter where he lives, the South African writer cannot
address his own people in freedom.

An exile mentality cannot produce a national literature.
Nor can a chronically divided and embattled society. If there
is one characteristic that all South African writers, of whatever
class or colour, have in common, it is a kind of struggling,
semi-articulate patriotism; a common feeling, however throttled
back by the frustration of human instinct and often by self-
hatred also, that South Africa, if only it could be otherwise,

---

1 *Ibid.*, p. 137.

is incomparably the finest country in the world to live in. But only when the South African writer can again work among his own people and address them in freedom can the task of building a truly national literature be resumed.

Australians, despite the ballads of the bush-whackers, have taken longer to come to terms with their own haunting, bleak interior. D. H. Lawrence's *Kangaroo* (1924), the work of a visitor, was one of the first attempts to capture in literature the unique sense of antiquity that hangs about the Australian landscape, peopled as it is with great waddling lizards, strange birds and leaping marsupials, beset with forests that look like artists' impressions of the Carboniferous Age. This is pre-eminently a land which challenges the invader by its vast indifference to his presence. The accommodation of white men to this strange continent was not bought by the plantation of its coastal fringes, but by those who crossed the mountains and died, like Burke, in the furnace of its inner heart. Only in the past thirty years or so have Australian artists been able to confront the harsh reality of that inner heart and make it their own. Sydney Nolan and Arthur Boyd have done in paint what Patrick White consciously set out to do in a book like *Voss*. Yet even for them every stone and tree of the land is not stamped with associations, as it is for the vanishing remnants of the aboriginal Australians. The aboriginal poet can still up-stage them, for only his people have learnt to live here with nothing to help them but their hands. Thus the poet Kath Walker, in the best work of a very uneven collection, can write as she looks at the deserted *bora* ground:

> We are as strangers here now, but the white
> > tribe are the strangers.
> We belong here, we are of the old ways.
> We are the corroborree and the bora ground,
> We are the old sacred ceremonies, the laws
> > of the elders . . .
> We are the past, the hunts and the laughing
> > games, the wandering camp fires,
> We are the lightning-bolt over Gaphembah Hill
> Quick and terrible,
> And the Thunderer after him, that loud fellow,
> We are the quiet daybreak paling the dark lagoon.
> We are the shadow-ghosts creeping back as the camp
> > fires burn low.

We are nature and the past, all the old ways.
Gone now and scattered.
The scrubs are gone, the hunting and the laughter.
The eagle is gone, the emu and the kangaroo are
     gone from this place.
The bora ring is gone.
The corroborree is gone.
And we are going.[1]

Yet Kath Walker's poem, too, is part of the new life acquired by English half a world away from Stratford. And because she writes in English, a dialogue is joined where before there was neither comprehension nor communication.

The challenge of the Maoris living in their midst, together with a prolonged obsession with 'the old country', have prevented the New Zealanders, despite their lusher and more welcoming pastures, from producing any work as yet which has really impressed the presence of their country upon the world. If the Maori cannot be driven out, forgotten or largely exterminated, then the white New Zealander must find some means of sharing in his spiritual possession of the land. The obvious method, large-scale intermarriage, has not been chosen. But until the challenge has been met the white New Zealander will continue to reflect in his writing a sense of being the alien and the newcomer that he is.

The emergence of a new generation of Maori poets writing in English can only reinforce this feeling of exclusion and strengthen the Maori challenge. Whereas the American today, over most of the continent, has only the beautiful names of his states and rivers to remind him of those he has dispossessed, the New Zealander must face many thousand living reminders who are beginning to find their voices and celebrate audibly their love and understanding of the land they were the first to find.

The Maori poet Hone Tuwhare, gazing at the eroded hillsides of the Reserves, sees a spiritual desolation expressed in the physical. Offering himself with love to the brief renewal of the land:

Distribute my nakedness

---

1 *We are Going* (Brisbane, 1963).

he still knows that one mortal dust is no better than another; all must return without distinction to the impartial earth:

> Deep scarred
>> not by wind ravaged nor rain
>> nor the brawling stream:
>>> . . .
> O voiceless land, let me echo your desolation
>> the mana of my house has fled and the marae is
>> but a paddock of thistle
>> I come to you with a bitterness that only your
>> dull folds can soothe[1]
>>> . . . .

Here again the dialogue is joined after a hundred years drowned by the voice of the newcomer. Out of this dialogue a truly national literature may soon spring.

The situation of the West Indian writer differs markedly from those we have been considering, yet it does share common elements of their dilemmas. Thus, whether his ancestors be from Africa, India, Europe or China, or any mixture of these, he has to learn the shape and feeling of his new Caribbean environment and make himself a part of it. He also, unless he is a fairly new arrival, has English as his mother tongue; albeit an English stamped by the islands, with many structures, sequences and words derived from non-English sources. For the vast majority of West Indians today, of whatever colour, English is their sole language, and it is through English alone that they can hope to define themselves and their society.

Challenging the importance of these common elements is the fact that the West Indian will probably be either largely or entirely of non-British stock. His culture and social habits, though heavily permeated with British and American influences, are really an amalgam of many things, some avowed and others unavowed. The black West Indian writer, especially if he comes from the poorer, rural areas of the islands, will probably find many elements from African religions, foods, languages, folk-lore, music and cultural values still working within the texture of his society. Some sociologists have identified the common law marriages of the islands as an adaptation of African social customs. The man who distributes his favours

---

1 'Not by wind ravaged', *New Zealand Monthly Review*, September 1960.

and his children among several separate households is practising a form of dispersed polygamy. Similar co of influence can be found in Trinidad East Indian society, genially satirized in V. S. Naipaul's early novels, or among the Chinese and Indian social groups in Guyana.

The task of the West Indian writer who seeks to establish himself within his Caribbean environment is thus more complex than that which typically faced the colonial white writer in North America or elsewhere. The Caribbean situation marks a sort of half-way house between the white colonial writer who is struggling to become national, and the other great stream of English writing overseas. This other stream stems from people (for the most part in Africa and India, but also to be found in South-East Asia and the Middle East) who are wholly indigenous in stock and in their early cultural environment, but who through education, travel, and the influences to which these have exposed them have become fully familiar with English and have chosen it, either in orthodox or dialect form, as the medium for their writing.

For this third group of writers, the task is complicated by two entirely new factors. Firstly, they have to define and describe in English, cultures of which that language and its traditional associations form only a superficial part, if any part at all. Secondly, the English speech given to their characters (which, for the dramatist, means the whole of his text) can be no more than an equivalent for the words, tones and rhythms in which their originals habitually speak. If we admit that its language is the deepest and fullest expression of any culture, the magnitude of the task facing these English writers of the Third World can be realized. 'To speak a language,' said Frantz Fanon, 'is to assume a world, a culture.'[1] A whole generation of writers is striving to disprove his words. The success they attain, even if not complete, is likely to enlarge and enrich the medium even more than the work of those whose path to expression has been more direct.

Where the common speech is not simply a dialect of English, however, but another language altogether, the writer who works in English finds himself in a rather anomalous position with regard to what would normally be his immediate public.

---

[1] 'Le noir et le langage', *Peau Noire, Masques Blancs* (Paris, Seuil, 1952), p. 50.

It is true that as this public progressively acquires some knowledge of English, through education and contact, his works will become accessible to more and more of them. But, whereas the West Indian writer may be strengthening and enriching the local vernacular by giving it new patterns of literary expression, the African or Indian writer in English can only enrich the language in which he works. Hence his own mother tongue, the tongue in constant use by those immediately around him, enjoys no refreshment from the activities of its own sons and, without such refreshment, may gradually weaken and deteriorate.

The West African writer occupies a position of singular linguistic complexity in this regard. His native languages offer no discernible alternative to English as a nationally unifying form of expression, let alone a pan-African one. Yet they are still very much a part of the living texture of his society, still the medium in which most popular discussion or celebration takes place. Alongside these there exists, in the various forms of coastal pidgin and in Krio, a distinctive and popular form of English-derived speech, Africanized in its grammar, its intonation and rhythm and in much of its vocabulary. Yet 'deep' pidgin will prove to be as restricting, from the point of view of audience, as a single tribal vernacular. It will be largely unintelligible to English-speaking communities outside the Guinea coast and may even present difficulties for many of the writer's own countrymen; especially those from the far interior, where pidgin has never really taken root. If he is to use it, therefore, he will probably do so in a modified form, which 'suggests' pidgin rather than actually being it. Finally, he has at his disposal the various forms of generally accepted English usage; formal, colloquial, rhetorical, commercialized 'pop', and so forth. A writer of skill and resource, such as the Nigerian dramatist Wole Soyinka, may make use of virtually all these types and levels of expression within the compass of a single work, thereby bringing them into a controlled relationship with each other. Thus the very range of choice, instead of merely perplexing the writer, can be turned to creative use.

The situation in most of East, Central and South Africa differs from this in certain respects. Partly owing to the generally later contact with English speech, no creolized version of the language has emerged on that side of the continent. In some respects Swahili enjoys the sort of position in East Africa that pidgin English partly enjoys in the West. Although it has an ancient literary tradition and is the native language of certain peoples along the East African coast, it exists over wide areas in a debased form as a *lingua franca* used side-by-side with the vernacular. There is, therefore, a discernible alternative to English for both national and neighbourly international communication. Swahili, being essentially a Bantu language containing many common root words and a familiar grammatical system, could be spread fairly easily throughout Central and South Africa, if policies favouring this development were ever introduced. For the moment, it is only in East Africa proper (Tanzania, Kenya and Uganda) that the writer's palette extends from his tribal vernacular, through Swahili, to the varieties of recognized English usage mentioned above. Southwards of Tanzania the choice tends to be a stark one between Standard English and a tribal vernacular. though the major Southern African vernaculars do cover substantial areas and populations.

Logically, a study of this kind could extend from Hong Kong and the Philippines, via Malaysia and Ceylon, to the Indian subcontinent, Africa and the Caribbean. All these areas are tropical; all are inhabited predominantly by people of non-European stock; all have fallen at some period under the sway of English-speaking rulers; all have had educational systems penetrated to a greater or lesser extent by English; and all have produced creative writers working in English. To cast the net so wide would be to risk diffusion of effect rather than comprehensiveness. It would involve an attempt at cultural and historical evaluation of many societies infinitely varied, complex and remote from one another. It would also carry the danger of equating literatures whose English area is small, recent and peripheral, such as India or Ceylon, with others where it is most or the whole of what is available in print. By confining this study to the English writing of tropical Africa and the Caribbean, as I propose to do, a much greater degree of coherence can be attained. Quite apart from their common use of English, these areas have direct historical, cultural and ethnic links with one another too obvious to need labouring here. It may, however, be worth stressing that the traffic has by no means been one-way only. As early as 1835 free negroes in the New World were themselves making trading voyages to Africa. Many returned voluntarily to live in African cities like Lagos, Porto Novo and Cape Coast. Others, like the Maroons forcibly deported from Jamaica after the Second Maroon War, were washed back to Africa by the storm of their vicissitudes. West Indian missionaries were active on the Guinea coast from the mid-nineteenth century onwards, to be followed shortly by a small army of clerks, craftsmen, lawyers, doctors, journalists and teachers. Even Nigeria's engine-drivers were at one time recruited from the West Indies. Today, a substantial number of Africa's university teachers are likewise 'revenants' from the Caribbean. Consequently, there is a considerable body of Caribbean literature specifically concerned, not just with nostalgia for a lost Africa, but with the actual impact and experience of modern Africa. More recently, certain African writers have begun to interest themselves in the history and literature of the West Indies, with results that must soon affect both criticism and literature in Africa itself.

The density and antiquity of these connections across the Atlantic basin would itself justify an attempt to study the area as a whole. But there is an even stronger reason for making such a study today, for any writer who successfully encounters the English language with the headlong charge of his own living shifts and extends that language for anyone, anywhere, who uses it.

Unlike the writers of the white dominions, those of Africa and the Caribbean are by no means convinced that they belong, spiritually and intellectually, to the West. The brilliant preaching of Frantz Fanon, powerfully reinforced by the practical example of Maoism and Castroism, has imprinted upon many the concept of a Third World, largely coloured and almost universally poor, whose interests and aspirations are inimical to those of the West and the Russian East, both envisaged as white blocs of immense military and economic power. This power they will use to keep the Third World, strong at present only in numbers, in a proper state of subservience. The English language, like the French and the Spanish, still spans this terrifying gulf opening across the world, but precious little else does. The prospect of an all-out race war must frighten many who ponder the real implications of Vietnam and the mounting crisis in Southern Africa.

This book will not concern itself with the oft-repeated question 'Ought these people to write in English?'. Such questions are properly the concern of journalism. The concern of criticism rests with what is, and this concern is perfectly echoed by Chinua Achebe in his reply to that very question: 'I have been given this language and I intend to use it.'[1] Likewise, we have been given this literature and we intend to examine it.

---

1 In 'English and the African Writer', Kampala, *Transition* 18, 1965.

Part One
The Islands

Chapter 1
Discovery

So I shall voyage no more from home; may I speak here.

Derek Walcott*

It was to the islands of the New World that the first dark voyagers came. There is reason to believe that at least one officer of African descent sailed with Columbus on his first voyage. And long before the sixteenth century was out Africans both slave and free had been carried to many of the Caribbean islands, whilst the indigenous Arawaks of the Greater Antilles were already far gone towards extinction. But though Africans may have been present at the very first landfall on the islands and were certainly prominent in their exploration and early settlement, that is not the sort of discovery with which we are concerned in this chapter. Discovery in the cultural sense comes with the realization that one is neither a rootless being devoid of identity, nor a lost son of Africa or Asia, but a man made and shaped by this island now. In West Indian literature this species of discovery has come about only during the past twenty years, some four and a half centuries after Columbus landed in Jamaica. And it was in Jamaica that the first announcement of this discovery was made, with the publication of V. S. Reid's novel *New Day* in 1947.

This novel rests upon a single proposition; that Jamaica has a history. This history is distinct from that of its various racial groups separately viewed. No group of people, however polyglot, can inhabit an island through four hundred and fifty years of turbulence and change without forming a history

---

* The sources of all quotations at the head of chapters in this work are given at the end of the book.

and culture uniquely their own. It follows that there is such a creature as a Jamaican, and that we can only get to know him by looking at his island and following its story.

This central proposition is built into the structure of Reid's novel, for the life of a single man, his narrator, bridges the bloody Morant Bay Rebellion of 1865 and the new constitution of 1944. The first event signalled the abolition of representative government after more than two hundred years, the second announced its return. As the old man compares these events in his mind, relating them to one another and to the larger history of the island, the lineaments of Jamaica begin to emerge. For the constitution abolished in 1865, though offering a measure of local autonomy, gave government into the hands of the white plantocracy. Slavery, which had effectively ended only twenty-seven years before, still left its mark upon every aspect of society, still manipulated attitudes and motives, still pushed events towards the culmination of the Rebellion itself. The constitution which returned in 1944 held the promise, at least, of government based on consent; the consent of that vast despised majority which had been as powerless under the intervening eighty years of crown colony rule as it was under the old regime of the planters.

Reid's book, written so soon after the latter event, is not concerned to ask whether that promise has been fulfilled. It announces by its very title a hope only, but a hope which had not been there before at any time in the island's history.

Yet the importance of *New Day* does not rest only on its central concern with Jamaica and its people. The same new confidence that dictated its theme extends into the style itself, for the whole book is couched in the form of a long monologue by the aged narrator as the crowds celebrating their new measure of freedom surge under his window. Hence it is written throughout in a style approximating to Jamaican country dialect of the mid-nineteenth century. To use this style of speech even for dialogue, except to produce comical 'quashi' (country bumpkin) effect, was effrontery enough to the delicate colonial sensibility which rotated around wistful connections with 'Home' and garden parties at King's House. To write an entire book in this despised dialect, albeit spoken habitually by nine-tenths of the population, and in off-moments by the rest, was radical indeed.

Here is the old man beginning to carry us back into the menacing atmosphere of the parish of St. Thomas a few days before the Rebellion broke out. Yet what he recovers first from the debris of memory is the breaking of a bright morning over that sodden impoverished earth. We notice the characteristic repetition of the verb root, transposed from West African speech, and the use of English archaisms like 'a-drown', 'day-cloud' and the delightful 'kitty-up' which remind us that the English settlers of seventeenth century Jamaica and Barbados have left many distinctive regional marks upon the popular speech of the islands:

> Is remember I remember one August morning when rain was a-drown the earth. For two weeks now the sun had no' shone. Black is the morning, black the evening, and Mas'r God's heaven does no look on us at all. Yallahs and Morant Bay and Plantain Garden rivers heavy so, until you do not know where rivers end and land begins. That was the time when an alligator swam clear up to the barrack and took away my friend Timothy's bro'. Then there was dirging down at the barracks. Day in, day out, you heard it through the rain, a mark-time with the drip, drip, drip of *guinep* and mango trees weeping.
>
> Then one morning when day-cloud was peeping, I woke and did no' hear the rain. Creeping out o' my kitty-up, I went to the door and pulled the latch-wood—Wayah!
>
> Look there! Is no' that Mas'r God's heaven looking down on us again?[1]

The extent to which Reid has modified his rendering of dialect, so as to reduce visual irritation and slowness in apprehension for the general reader of English, may be seen by looking at a passage of any typical Jamaican country story recorded, not in phonetic script, but in ordinary Roman:

> Ol' Witch razor mout' tu'n over. Ol' Witch gi' out, 'Bway, whe' you come from, torment me so?' Boy said 'Hi, Nana! When me to home, when me yawzy bite me, it is de bigges' barrow me mamma got, kill him an' tek de blood wash me.' An' Ol' Witch kill a barrow an' wash him, an' de boy gone to bed, gone sleep.[2]

---

1 *New Day*, English edition (London, Heinemann, 1950), p. 37.
2 'Andrew and his Sisters' in *Memoirs of the American Folk-lore Society*, Vol. XVII, 1924.

Such a comparison makes it clear that Reid has in effect composed a musical script with dialect features. For the purposes he set out to achieve, anything more documentary would have been self-defeating and might well have reinforced the existing prejudice against the literary use of dialect rather than diminishing it.

Obvious though it may be to date the appearance of a new West Indian literature from the publication of *New Day*, it is probably just also. Recognition is due to some earlier works such as Mittelholzer's *Corentyne Thunder* (1941), but it was with *New Day* that a new generation of West Indian writers really began the task of breaking free from the colonial cocoon and flying with wings of their own, in a distinctly tropical sky.

There are, of course, dissentients even now. It is not entirely surprising that it was those of negro extraction who led the movement towards a new regional consciousness centred in the West Indies themselves, and not in some dim anterior condition alleged to be Africa, India, China or England. Not only are those of African descent an overwhelming majority of the area's population, especially in Jamaica and all the smaller islands, but by and large they have been there longest, thereby shedding most of the associations, other than colour, which might tie them to an identifiable culture, religion or language rooted elsewhere. Hence it is equally unsurprising to find a writer like V. S. Naipaul ridiculing the whole idea of a West Indian history, or a West Indian anything else. For Naipaul is a Trinidad East Indian who grew up in a community whose older members still spoke, thought and worshipped in terms of India, remembering the very villages from which they came. Massive Indian immigration continued into Trinidad and Guyana until 1917, so that many are still living who remember another life and another land. Yet Naipaul himself admits that this dense pattern of associations with India is rapidly disappearing among the younger generations. Indeed, this process of 'Creolization' is one of the principal themes of his novels and it is a process he generally laments, since he sees it as one of loss rather than transition. The positive point about this transition had already been made by another Trinidad Indian writer, Samuel Selvon, in his very first book. In *A Brighter Sun* (1952), Selvon shows how his young hero Tiger and his bride Urmila, East Indians both and of orthodox Hindu background are quite naturally befriended by their Creole (African) neighbours, Joe and Rita, when they move into a new district, away from the strict social rituals of their own family groups. Visiting relatives may glower and protest, but Tiger is not prepared to reject those who have shown him real generosity, who share his youth and his poverty. Hindu religious rituals and social taboos have less and less meaning for him. The English dialect of Trinidad has become his language, and his life is shaped by its brash energy and jazzy tempo, rather than by any real consciousness of Mother India. Their parents merely live in Trinidad, but Tiger and Urmila have become Trinidadians.

Yet Naipaul does not seem to recognize that people like these will soon need to define a West Indian existence, call it nationalism or what you will, quite as urgently as their Creole compatriots. For he has written as recently as 1961:

> How can the history of this West Indian futility be written? . . . The history of the islands can never be satisfactorily told. Brutality is not the only difficulty. History is built around achievement and creation; and nothing was created in the West Indies.[1]

Here Naipaul is surely confusing a purely personal rejection with a historical fact. Many might think that this kind of total rejection of what and where one is, once so common in the West Indies, can only become a sickness of the spirit. From this sickness the society as a whole seems to be making a slow but miraculous recovery. The salient impression upon the outsider who looks at West Indian achievement in literature, music, dance, drama and art over the past twenty years is precisely of intense creativity. But Naipaul also challenges the product:

> Living in a borrowed culture, the West Indian, more than most, needs writers to tell him who he is and where he stands. Here the West Indian writers have failed. Most have so far only flattered the prejudices of their race or colour groups. With two or three exceptions, the West Indian writer has so far avoided the American Negro type of protest writing, but his aims have been equally propagandist: to win acceptance for his group.[2]

The charge is singularly unfair. It is possible to read an early

---

1 *The Middle Passage* (London, Deutsch, 1962), pp. 28–9.
2 *Ibid.*, p. 68.

novel of Selvon's without even guessing the race of the author himself. The same cannot be said of early Naipaul, the Naipaul of *The Mystic Masseur* (1957) or *The Suffrage of Elvira* (1958), which, witty and accomplished as it is, remains firmly rooted and confined in a Trinidad East Indian society. But even if the charge were justified, would not the writer's aim to 'win acceptance for his group' look rather different if that group happened to be the vast majority of his island's population, as with the black Jamaican for example? Here was a majority whose claim to be in any way representative of Jamaica had been constantly ridiculed by the tiny coloured and white élite, clinging to the coat-tails of colonial officialdom. It was this élite, and not the Jamaican masses, whose culture was truly 'borrowed' and provincial. Surely for the black Jamaican to win acceptance for his group was, in these circumstances, to win acceptance for the reality of Jamaican life itself? Any true West Indian nationalism must ultimately learn to ignore colour, but before it can do this it must take cognizance of the objective fact that most West Indians are more or less black. This fact alone, the implications of which were so long ignored, will influence decisively the nature of the culture now emerging. For, even if the West Indies had created nothing else, they have certainly created a people; a people, moreover, forged from the most diverse of elements in the most tragic of circumstances.

New Day taught West Indians to look at their past in more positive terms; to see it as one of constant struggle and protest rather than of passive endurance. Jamaica alone experienced dozens of courageous slave rebellions, as well as two substantial and protracted wars against the Maroons. The suffering and privation of rural life also gave rise to violent movements in more recent years. Such a movement forms the subject of Andrew Salkey's first novel *A Quality of Violence*, set in a remote district of Jamaica in 1905. Here it is drought which is driving the peasants to extremity and many of them seek the outlet of violent religious excitement in the syncretic cult of Pocomania. Ma Johnson, the leader of the cult, finally dominates the action of the novel by her willingness to die, stoned by her own followers, in order that the kind of power she represents may live. Writers like Reid, Salkey and Roger Mais (in his last novel, *Black Lightning*) have given a strong rural dimension to the Jamaican novel, reminding us how explosions of terrible energy can pass across the face of those verdant, peaceful-looking hills. In its totally different way, another novel published soon after *New Day* contributed to the exploration of West Indian reality. Whereas the action of *New Day* is rooted in the life of the newly-emancipated black peasantry of nineteenth century rural Jamaica, Edgar Mittelholzer's *A Morning at the Office* (1950) is concerned with a cross-section of contemporary Trinidad society in the urban, commercial world of Port of Spain. Compared with the warm romanticism of Reid's hero and treatment, Mittelholzer's method is deliberately clinical. He confines his narrative to the events of a single morning in the office of Essential Products Limited, but he constantly escapes from these limits both spatially and temporally by giving us glimpses of the past lives of his characters, their daydreams, aspirations and sneaking fears. Furthermore, he adopts the technique of 'telescopic objectivity' propounded by one of them, a writer who visits the office during the day and is perhaps to some extent a flattering self-portrait. His formula requires the novelist to explore the history of certain selected objects which surround the lives of his characters. These can be 'dynamic' objects, like the table-leg which sends out a rough hand to clasp Miss Henery's thigh in the midst of her erotic reverie; or 'static' objects, which are only important because of their past significance in their owners' lives, like Sidney Whitmer's nib, which has left the realm of his personal affairs but continues to trouble the relationship between Jagabir, the East Indian accountant, and Mary, the Creole cleaner. Tracing the careers of such objects is another of the devices by which Mittelholzer escapes from the strait limits of his morning.

This clinical approach enables him to be didactic from time to time about West Indian society, since he is laying it bare for our enlightenment. Thus Mittelholzer, as omniscient author, weaves together the separate anxieties of the fearful Jagabir, the ambitious young Creole office boy Horace Xavier and the tearful, loquacious Mary. Their common insecurity does not unite them; often it sets them tearing at each other in dumb hatred and mutual contempt:

> His [Jagabir's] ears were perpetually on the alert, for the fear was always with him that, despite his efficiency as a book-keeper, he would one day be thrown out. He had been brought up to feel that an East Indian's place was in the Field. . . . An office

was meant for white people and good-class coloured people. He considered his officiousness justified, it was his defence against possible attack and the ejection that might result from such an attack.

Horace, who had merely glanced up at his approach continued to read. He too, did not like Mr. Jagabir. From the first day he had come to work at the office Mr. Jagabir had begun to nag at him. Horace considered him a mean, quarrelsome man.

'You might say morning, Xavier,' said Mr. Jagabir. Horace, prepared for this, looked up. 'Who? Me? I thought it was your place to say morning. You come in and find me here.' There was no respect in his voice as would have been the case with another member of staff.

Mr. Jagabir hesitated, unsure of himself, then said: 'I'm your superior'.

'If you were the king it was your place to tell me morning when you come in and find me here'. Mr. Jagabir did not argue. He suddenly knew he had erred. The boy was probably right.... Frowning heavily, he went to his desk.... On his way he gave Mary a swift sideways glance. Horace's rebuke still moved like a pebble in his chest, and he was very much aware that he was guilty of a second breach of good manners in refraining from saying good morning to Mary. A feeling of frustration and resentment tightened his inside, and he told himself he had every right to ignore Mary. She was an insolent woman. She hated him—as all the rest of them hated him. Because he was an Indian, because he was the son of indentured coolies, they all looked on him as dirt.[1]

This jangling of enclosed fears, hostilities and anxieties continues throughout the morning. Occasionally Mittelholzer as commentator is even more specific about the categories within which virtually all his characters feel compelled to operate. Thus he interrupts an account of Miss Henery's contemplation of a suitor and his claims to remark:

as a member of the West Indian coloured middle-class, she conceived of human hair in terms of 'good' and 'bad'— sometimes 'good' and 'hard'; 'good' hair is hair that is European in appearance: 'bad' or 'hard' hair is hair of the kinky, Negroid type.[2]

The emergence of Mittelholzer as lecturer introducing West

---

1 *A Morning at the Office* (London, Hogarth, 1950; Penguin edition, 1964), pp. 27-8.   2 *Ibid.*, p. 59.

Indian society to a supposedly foreign public is sometimes irritating. Nevertheless, he never steps from lecturing into preaching: his comment on this farrago of hair-splitting prejudice is confined to the single word 'human', which can be left to set up its own reverberation. He does not protest, he describes. Consequently, such words as 'kinky', 'Negroid', 'black', 'coloured', 'coolie', 'white', occur in almost every paragraph, like some kind of dreadful stammer which must be employed before any person can be registered by his neighbours as existing at all. It is true that Mittelholzer gives us a two-layered map (in full-colour and class) of Trinidad society which would be of assistance to any enterprising tourist. But by being ruthlessly direct in the description of what many West Indians take for granted, and assume to be so taken everywhere, he prepares that groundwork of reality from which alone any new integrated vision of West Indian humanity can spring. The effect of the novel is not ultimately depressing, partly because Mittelholzer is a compassionate surgeon, who pities as he dissects; partly because a strong vein of humour flows through the whole book. And the novelist does offer us one character, the gentle Miss Bisnauth, who refuses to think ill of anybody, who transcends the anxieties which confine everyone else to their own shade of skin and insists on living in a world of people. In this way, she serves to show us how dreadfully imprisoning such a social order is, how it restricts acquaintance, corrupts judgement, limits choice, dictates action. Another character, Mrs. Hinckson, has glimpses of this truth also, but is unable to grasp it. In her quiet style, it is Edna Bisnauth who points the way towards a new definition of personality which only a rejection of these old categories, by setting people free, can make possible.

The nature of Mittelholzer's purpose in this book dictates a spare, analytical style, confining itself to the exposure of motives, the linking of people with objects, and the bare bones of a narrative structure. His tone is deliberately cool and carefully detached. But his purpose also enables him to register the various levels of speech within the office, and how these are imposed as much by the expectations of others as by differences of opportunity and education. Thus Mary plays her 'black-momma' part in the accepted manner with lines like these:

'Ow boy! It's not for want o' trying. You know how often Ah

talk to Richard! Oh, God! Ah weary talking, weary, weary. And he leading his brudder astray—dat's de hurtful part'[1]

The 'posh' coloured folk like Miss Henery, Mrs. Hinckson and Pat Lorry sedulously avoid anything that savours of dialect, especially in the presence of their supposed inferiors. Jagabir hovers linguistically, as he does socially, uncertain where to settle. But he puts on a special East Indian voice when he is in his most insinuating and ingratiating manner, as when he mutters to Miss Henery, *à propos* of Horace:

> 'Dat boy got too much on his mind that he shouldn't got. ... Lil' half-penny black boy like dat to mek out he in love wid a big-family lady like Mrs. Hinckson. He properly rude.'[2]

Language, then, is one of the instruments with which people try to plot their own positions on Mittelholzer's map of Trinidad society. Along with skin-colour, it is the focus of some of their strongest taboos, tensions and patterns of inhibited response. This is especially true in an urban office like the scene of the novel, which throws together people who might successfully avoid much social contact outside, and so be relieved of the necessity to demonstrate continually their precise social station to those imagined as above or below them.

Novels set in a more socially and racially homogeneous environment open up to the writer an easier prospect of escaping from realistic rapportage and a freer use of language, since he is not concerned with making discriminations within his group. This freedom is fully exploited by George Lamming in his first, semi-autobiographical novel *In the Castle of My Skin* (1953), which centres around his growth from the ages of nine to eighteen in a small Barbados village.

Lamming's discovery of his childhood world, which forms one of the most beautiful and original books yet produced by the West Indies, is not effected by the sort of clinical analysis offered by Mittelholzer. Rather, he shows us the gradual unfolding and flowering of an adolescent sensibility, interwoven movement by movement with changes in the life of the village around. These changes are felt and observed by others even more than by the narrator himself. Thus it is not only the process of growing that distances the boy from the innocence of childhood,

---

1 *Ibid.*, p. 22.   2 *Ibid.*, p. 84.

but the actual disintegration of his childhood world as he moves through and beyond it.

This poignant intricacy of effect is achieved partly by Lamming's deliberate crumbling of time into fragments, which are then re-arranged by association with particular objects or experiences, not in accordance with any strict chronological scheme. We are often not sure, if we pause to ask, just how old the narrator is at a particular moment, or how much time has gone by since the last cluster of memory was explored. Each moment enjoys an autonomy and completeness of its own, like a movement in music. One sequence in the novel begins with his burying a pebble in the beach sand, in the hope of finding it there next day and achieving one victory over 'envious and calumniating Time'. But on the morrow, although he finds the marked place and burrows there, the stone has gone. His desolation at this images the sense, growing ever stronger through the book, that life is a continued process of goodbyes to moments and people that we shall never see again. So he writes, following upon the discovery of the pebble's disappearance:

I tried to recall when this feeling had started, but that seemed useless. . . . You couldn't bear the thought of seeing things for the last time, and things included people, objects and situations. . . . I remembered vaguely that something used to happen when as a small boy I rode in a bus and reviewed the objects and people as they glided by. The shop and that lamp-post and the man who stood at the corner blank and impersonal. It seemed that the bus was steady while they slipped past, and I wondered whether I would see them again. . . . I experienced the feeling in a high degree when I left the village school; and in the circumstances there was no reason to be sorry. . . . Yet the feeling was there. I was seeing the village school for the last time. The teachers shook my hand and wished me the best of luck. And I was left with the intolerable feeling that they had somehow gone for ever. I recalled the lamp-posts and the shops and the man at the corner, and I knew that the feeling was not new. . .

Later, when Trumper came to say that he was going to America I couldn't bear to look him straight in the face. . . . He left on a wet morning three years before I left the High School; and although an important difference in our fortunes had forced us apart I went to see him off. We stood on the pier together and watched the ship which was anchored in the distance.

> There were hundreds of them leaving for America, and I saw them all less real than Trumper but with the same sickness, which the feeling brought on. It seemed I wasn't going to see any of those faces again. . . . I started to think of the High School and what had happened to all of us in the intervening years; and suddenly as if by an inner compulsion my mind went back to the spot under the grapeleaf and the pebble which I had seen for the last time. I ducked my head in the water and come up wet and refreshed.
>
> It was a year or two after the riots and I was eleven. . . .[1]

These few paragraphs, growing out of a single moment of time to which the last sentences return us, roam backwards to a childhood recollection of the writer's first awareness of this intense mortality within experience, then forwards to the leaving of the village school; forwards again (beyond the pebble's moment) to his friend Trumper's departure, then back to the central episode of the vain search for the pebble. Only then, four pages into the new chapter, does Lamming establish the period of this episode ('a year or two after the riots'), for the pebble's importance as an object resides not only in itself but in its ability to set memory and imagination moving freely in time. Mittelholzer had attempted an evocation of the history and significance of certain objects in *A Morning at the Office*, but did not sustain it through the book. Lamming, by rooting their power to move him and us in the rendering of certain childhood experiences, is able to trace the progress of time's sickness through objects as well as through people. He does this not only with the pebble but with the dark mysterious woods around the white landlord's house, which were later felled to leave a bare and startled landscape; or with the railway where the boys once took their nails to be beaten into blades by the passing trains, which was later torn up for wartime scrap.

It is an elegiac childhood on which change has cast its sadness from the first and which sustains its note into the last sentences of the book:

> The earth where I walked was a marvel of blackness and I knew in a sense more deep than simple departure I had said farewell, farewell to the land.[2]

---

1 *In the Castle of my Skin* (London, Michael Joseph, 1953), pp. 215–16.
2 *Ibid.*, p. 303.

The book begins with a great flood, announcing the ninth birthday of the fatherless only child who looks out upon the waste of waters carrying everything away. So the flood becomes the first great climacteric announcing change. We are told nothing of what preceded it. At this time the social and physical geography of the village still reflects the age of plantation slavery in which Barbados was founded. The house of the English landlord on the hill, shrouded by its woods, looks out over the little field-patches and hovels of its tenantry. To them the landlord is still the only real source of power and authority, but the flood costs him money and begins the slow process of his disengagement. As the landlord's power wanes it is replaced by that Mr. Slime, an ex-teacher who builds up his position through a Penny Bank, a Friendly Society, a trade union, and finally in island politics. The village has supported Slime without really comprehending his goals, but he uses their painfully-saved pennies to buy them out and sell off the land under their feet to the 'big-shot Coloureds' from the neighbouring and expanding suburbs. Slime is the type of every corrupt popular demagogue who had risen to power in the modern West Indies. He knows how to exploit the resentments of others because he is himself genuinely resentful. His type of leadership, even when crooked, may have something to offer the urban worker in need of organization, but it holds nothing for the ruined peasantry. Abandoned by their old paternal overlords (who also feel abandoned, because their former pre-eminence is going) and betrayed by their new leaders, the emigrant ship is all that awaits them now.

The flood is followed by the waterfront strike, the strike by the riot and British naval intervention (we are now in the late 'thirties), the riot by the war with its tree-felling and metal-scrapping, the war by the big landgrab and the enforced departures. Around these events George Lamming and his friends Trumper, Bob and Boy Blue, weave their own pattern of adventure—swimming, running, exploring, hunting for crabs, creeping into the landlord's garden by night to watch the white folks dancing. George's admission to High School gradually forces the four friends apart, Trumper departing to America and the other two into the police force. At the end of the book, George is leaving for a teaching post in Trinidad; but it is Trumper, newly returned from America, who already has a larger experience of the world to offer. Trumper had discovered his race by leaving the obscuring intimacy of the island for the impersonal jungle of America. In Barbados the whites are few and aloof, unable to penetrate the dense solidarity of the black masses; hence overt racial insults are kept to a minimum. Being black is almost a condition of being Barbadian, scarcely needing definition in terms of an opposed system of power and values. America has changed all that. Trumper plays George a record in the local rumshop:

> 'You know the voice?' Trumper asked. He was very serious now. I tried to recall whether I might have heard it. I couldn't. 'Paul Robeson' he said. 'One o' the greatest o' my people.'
> 'What people?' I asked. I was a bit puzzled.
> 'My people,' said Trumper. His tone was insistent. Then he softened into a smile. I didn't know whether he was smiling at my ignorance, or whether he was smiling at his satisfaction with the box and the voice and above all Paul Robeson.
> 'Who are your people?' I asked him. It seemed a kind of huge joke.
> 'The Negro race,' said Trumper. The smile had left his face and his manner had turned grave again. I finished my drink and looked at him . . .[1]

Lamming's many English voices in this story of 'Little England' embrace not only the tender evocative prose of his narrative and the groping dialogue of the boys as they struggle with new levels of experience, but the free surrealistic flow of Pa's dream and the vigorous dialect of the shoemaker threatened with eviction. The old man called Pa is not only the oldest person in the village and the repository of its vague traditions, but a link with Africa itself, the original home of its people. Dreaming on the night of his wife's death, he speaks of the land his imagination has painted to cradle itself in; here the highly alliterative and rhythmic language introduces a new theme in the complex musical structure of the whole work:

> time was I see by the sun how the season sail and the moon make warning what crops to expect. . . . Far and near there were neighbours who keep gods like my brother rear rabbits, and the answer was obedience to a question never asked. Sometimes they was glad and sometimes they was sad, but the gift of the gods

---

[1] *Ibid.*, p. 295.

was always good. When life leave the body and the corpse keep contract with the grave in the jungle the soul sail away above or below as the gods find fit. And the rest who remain give praise. In the land of the tribes 'twas the way of our neighbours . . .[1]

But to a younger generation, modern Barbados was the only reality that imagination could compass. Even the sharp pain of slavery had faded to the extent that the schoolboys debate whether it ever really existed on the island. And when the shoemaker, the village philosopher and a man born and bred there, is told to get himself and his shop off the land now suddenly and mysteriously bought by a total stranger, he can only round upon the bailiff in wounded incredulous rage:

> 'Respect for who?' . . . 'I've respect as when as I've got to have it, but for you, a two-colour shit-smelling bastard like you, what you' talkin' 'bout respect. An' if you don't get off this blasted land before I count ten, if by the time I count ten you ain't off this spot o' land they'll hang me, the law'll hang me!'[2]

Thus Lamming fills his story with the sound and rhythm of his people's speech, but he also exploits his freedom to escape from it into a personal narrative style of great flexibility and beauty. His presence in the book is more often as narrator than as actor; many scenes are described in which the young Lamming does not himself figure, and this assists the equality of balance between a story of individual growth and one of historical change objectively observed, a balance which lies at the heart of the book's whole structure.

Although Lamming often evokes moments of boyhood experience with great clarity and freshness, the aspects of his book which dwell upon the poetry of time and the processes of island history draw upon the consciousness and literary skill of the grown man. Alongside his book we may lay a more recent chronicle of boyhood, Michael Anthony's *The Year in San Fernando* (1965). Anthony's may seem the less ambitious of the two, since he attempts to describe the events and feelings of a single year in the life of a twelve-year old boy. We learn virtually nothing of the hero's past life and nothing whatever of his future, yet this twelfth year is clearly of such importance in the discovery of himself and his world that there is no sense of our wanting to know more. The young Francis is one of

---

1 *Ibid.*, p. 210.　　　　2 *Ibid.*, p. 234.

several children of a poor widow in the seaside village of
Mayaro, in Eastern Trinidad. He has never travelled far from
his home and knows no-one outside his village circle. Mr.
Chandles, an arrogant and spoilt young man from San
Fernando, is courting a local girl and suddenly proposes carrying Francis back with him to be a sort of servant-companion
to his mother and to have schooling at his expense. Naturally
the idea is fallen upon at Mayaro, although Francis himself has
very mixed feelings about leaving home. In the big 'upstair'
house at San Fernando he is baffled by the mysterious conduct
and hidden motives of the adults around him. Mr. Chandles
and his mother have frequent and bitter quarrels, centring
upon the division of her inheritance between him and his brother Edwin. Francis is also shocked to discover that Chandles
is having an affair with a beautiful girl called Julia, whilst
also sleeping with his fiancée Marva, from time to time, under
his mother's roof. Francis is himself fascinated by Julia, who
plays upon his own dawning sexuality with light and tender
flirtatiousness. The geography of the strange city is soon
charged with meaning for him; the street where Julia lives is by
turns a magnet and a route to be shunned, according to his
present feelings for her. The dark space underneath the
Chandles' house is his refuge whenever he is bruised by life,
until one night he disturbs Julia and Chandles kissing there.
Mount Naparima, which broods over the town, also has its
moods, changing ever as the seasons shift. The length of a
childhood year is fully measured by the cycle of ploughing,
growth, harvest and burning in the great canefields which
stretch for miles around the city. Anthony's simple but alert
style of narration captures all the hero's bewilderment and
insecurity, the slow growth of his affection for his moody and
mysterious employers, his growing conviction that his year of
momentous, trivial events is to be unique and that, at its end,
he will return to Mayaro for good.

In the midst of the year his mother comes to see him, but her
visit is soon over. After escorting her to the Mayaro bus he
walks slowly homewards, all the landscape of city, land and
season strangely orchestrating with his mood:

> The pavement along Romaine Street rose very prominently
> from the road and I was just faintly eased of my sadness and I
> stepped up onto the pavement then down to the pitch again and

I walked right down the street like that. In the little spaces between the houses I could see red flickers. They were 'burning-out'—the estate people were. I stood up to watch the fire when-ever I came to a little space, and I could hear the crackle and the way the flames roared in the wind. This was the last of the cane-fires, for the crop was nearly ended. Watching the fires had been a great attraction for me through all these months. They had started from far away in that great expanse of green. Now the fires were blazing out the last patch, near the town. I stood up at the big gap between the school and our house, and the fire I could see here stretched over some distance, and the flame-tongues licked the air, and they reddened a large part of the sky between the houses. Away over the brown open field I could see the dusk coming.[1]

Writing like this, never striving for big effects or *post hoc* finger-wagging, demands tact and imaginative integrity. These qualities are constantly displayed in Anthony's writing, though the apparent smallness of his themes has caused him to be attacked by many West Indian reviewers, looking perhaps for riots, sultry affairs and deeds of violence. Yet *The Year in San Fernando* does move towards a climax of its own. At the end of the year Chandles is to marry Marva and Francis is to go home for Christmas. But the old lady falls ill and dies, bringing the struggle between the Chandles brothers to a head. Edwin appears and tells Francis that it is he who will have the house now that his mother is gone. Francis, already sure that San Fernando has taught him all he is yet able to learn, senses that the adventure is over, and perhaps the first innocence of child-hood ended with it. He goes to the bedroom to bid farewell to the dying Mrs. Chandles and, as he goes towards the bus, forces himself to remember what he saw there:

In my mind I kept seeing what was stretched out there on the bed. That was what Mrs. Chandles looked like. Although she wasn't dead yet. They had already swept the room and arranged it so people could come in to see the dead. There was a white cloth bandaging her chin and tied in a bow at the top of her head. That was done so she wouldn't die with her mouth open. Then they wouldn't have to break it shut. But she was still gasping breathlessly.
I had not stayed long in the room. I had just looked at what

---

1 *The Year at San Fernando* (London, Deutsch, 1965), pp. 94-5.

was on the bed. The room had been clean and tidy and sweet with the smell of lavender water. I had told Mrs. Princet goodbye and I had watched Mrs. Chandles and said goodbye just for the sake of saying it. The elderly lady had come in then and she had said, 'Shake Mrs. Chandles' hand, you wouldn't see her again.' I had hesitated, and Mrs. Princet had said, 'Go on, shake it, shake hands,' and I had gone up to the bed and held Mrs. Chandles' hand. It felt just like any other hand. Only bony and small and very hot.[1]

Francis never seems more than twelve, but his year in San Fernando has taught him to look with less fear and more compassion at the unpredictable behaviour of adults. His discoveries, despite the excitements of travel, have been largely human ones.

The landscape of Anthony's novel is dominated by houses, streets and canefields. The literature of the smaller islands faces the sea; a larger, more commanding reality than land or city. The St. Lucian Derek Walcott, the outstanding West Indian poet of today, situates much of his poetry imaginatively right upon the beach, where land, sea and sky encounter each other. Walcott is the solitary man, the castaway, who must learn to know the island upon which chance and history have stranded him; but his eyes are ever fixed upon the sea which vomited him up. Thus he is both a spokesman for a generation endeavouring to throw off racial and colonial inhibitions in the search for a distinctly West Indian existence, and the great reminder of the loneliness imposed upon them by space and time. It is their very loneliness, their exclusion, which forces self-discovery upon them. It gives them also a certain stature.

Caribbean man is not crushed and diminished by life, as Walcott sees man to be in America. He is a second Adam, infinitely nearer to us than the first, whose world effectively begins with his first stranding upon these shores. Its earlier inhabitants, the vanished Caribs, belong to a mythical unfallen past. To the imagery of Genesis, Walcott adds that of Robinson Crusoe. Crusoe is seen ironically as a missionary, bringer of a word which is the English tongue, a tongue now forced to begin afresh the mastery of a green untamed world which refuses its metaphors. Extending the irony, Caribbean

---

1 *Ibid.*, p. 186.

man himself is seen as Crusoe's Friday. Crusoe came and went, but his 'pupil' still:

> devours the seascape for the morsel of a sail[1]

As the emptiness of the sea defines his loneliness, so its huge silence defines his humanity:

> If I listen I can hear the polyp build,
> The silence thwanged by two waves of the sea.
> Cracking a sea-louse, I make thunder split.[2]

This discovered humanity now seeks a human love. But though God has withdrawn, the memory of his love is recent and still imposes its scale upon his world. Walcott evokes God's relative nearness, the sense that he was once actually *there*, through the story of a beached whale. Man hacks the whale into gobbets, leaving himself with nothing but a memory and perhaps an outsize bone or two, but he cannot forget the morning when it lay like a breathing mountain upon the sands.

> Once I heard
> Of a baleine beached up the Grenadines, fleshed
> By derisive, antlike villagers: a prize
> Reduced from majesty to pigmy-size.
> Salt-crusted, mythological,
> and dead.
>
> And the boy who told me couldn't believe his eyes,
> and I believed him. When I was small
> God and a foundered whale were possible.
> Whales are rarer, God as invisible.
> Yet, through His gift, I praise the unfathomable,
> Though the boy may be dead, the praise unfashionable,
> The tale apocryphal.[3]

The elemental grandeur of sea and sky, the brilliance of leaf and flower, the vivid separate existence of a seashell or a piece of seawrack, form the landscape which Walcott impregnates with his awareness of a mythological past still shaping the present. In his vision a solitary black man on the beach, a fisherman perhaps, stands analogously for that fathering figure, blending elements of Adam, Columbus and Crusoe-Friday,

---

1 Title poem, *The Castaway* (London, Cape, 1965), p. 9.
2 *Ibid.*, p. 10.   3 *Ibid.*, 'The Whale, His Bulwark', p. 21.

who first brought these islands into the consciousness of the world. Walcott's castaway, with Crusoe as his mentor, learns with his hands and the simplest of tools to make of these islands a place to live in, a land not of exile but of origin, a New World. Perhaps because the reminders of arrival are so insistent in the islands, where the sea still washes up trees and plants from other lands, Walcott conveys this sense more sharply than any mainland poet of America, living or dead. In certain ways he speaks for the whole of American experience, often overlaid on the mainland by the newer imagery of the frontier and the urban wilderness:

> perched between ocean and green, churning forest
> the intellect appraises
> objects surely, even the bare necessities
>   of style are turned to use. . . .
> in a green world, one without metaphors,
>   like Christopher he bears
> in speech mnemonic as a missionary's
>   the Word to savages,
> Its shape an earthen water-bearing vessel's
>   whose sprinkling alters us
> into good Fridays who recite his praise,
>   parroting our master's
> style and voice, we make his language ours,
>   converted cannibals
> we learn with him to eat the flesh of Christ.[1]

The fine austerity and perfect formal control with which Walcott writes throughout *The Castaway* is something to which he has come by returning again and again, with a craftsman's patience, to his central themes. Despite his dexterity as an occasional, descriptive and narrative poet, it is the image of man alone on his tropical island which provides the continuing thread of his development. His early poems can bewitch by their sensuous beauty of surface, but their adjectival extravagance sometimes defeats itself and his fondness for the startling coinage often arouses echoes of Dylan Thomas. This weakness persists here and there into his first major collection, *In a Green Night* (1962). 'A City's Death by Fire' conveys much of his excited horror at the burning of Castries in 1948, but neverthe-

---

1 *Ibid.*, 'Crusoe's Journal', p. 51.

less irresistibly suggests Thomas's 'A Refusal to Mourn' by its use of such phrases as 'the churched sky,' 'the rubbled tales' and 'the hills were a flock of faiths'. In the same volume, however, we can see Walcott striving to discipline his exuberance, reaching towards the cool architecture of his present style. A few pages away from these gobbets of undigested Thomas, Walcott quietly and confidently places us in his familiar seascape:

> Meanwhile the steamers which divide horizons prove
> Us lost.
> Found only
> In tourist booklets, behind ardent binoculars,
> Found in the blue reflection of eyes
> That have known cities and think us here happy.[1]

To see how far he has advanced in economy and control in the few years since the appearance of his first locally-printed collection, *Poems*, it is only necessary to look at an early poem such as this:

> A morning, green as envy, rears
> On both sides of this dirt road, minatory
> Grasses, call them spears
> To sharpen the metaphor to the extraordinary.
> Next I should start
> With the long street and the vine-flowering house;
> But night like an undertaker's hearse
> Carries all under to the real estate.[2]

Here the tendency is towards brilliant display; the reader may be amazed, but he is not led into the centre of the poet's vision. Rather, he is left admiring the coruscations of its surface.

It is with *In a Green Night* that Walcott emerges clearly as an important poet; his growing mastery of rhythmic patterns and shifting internal rhymes lends to his poetry a new interest of texture, while the sympathy and humour with which he handles contrasts of climate, landscape and temperament continually lead us outwards from the islands in which his imagination has made its home. Walcott's delicate talent for

---

1 'Prelude', *In a Green Night* (London, Cape, 1962), p. 11.
2 'You Can't Go Home Again', *Poems* (Jamaica, City Printery, no date), p. 35.

friendship gives an extraordinary warmth to those poems in which he addresses people he loves who are now dwelling under other skies. He situates himself as much by these excursions to England, Greece or America as by positive statements of his own imaginative commitment to the West Indies:

> So I shall voyage no more from home; may I speak here.
> This island is heaven—away from the dust-blown blood of cities . . .
> For beauty has surrounded.
> Its black children, and freed them of homeless ditties.[1]

The castaway now embraces his destiny, his isolation in a new tropical world to be cultivated with words. He does not repine—as earlier West Indian writers often did—for some imagined homeland elsewhere. And this rooted quality, so strongly expressed in both Walcott's major collections, makes possible a humour and compassion denied to the wistful exile. So a dead friend remembered in white America is evoked in intensely-felt images of an alien world, with its endless fields and its own cold static beauty:

> No self-reflection lies
> within these silent, ice-blue irises,
> whose image is some snowlocked mountain lake
> in numb Montana.[2]

The perspective maintained throughout Walcott's mature work enables him to evoke memories or fancies of other lands and seasons without ever descending to that eagerly descriptive gazetteer-poetry, so common in modern collections, which is really a superior form of journalism. A painter friend who has returned to England is addressed in tones of affectionate commiseration for one now condemned to live on pale reminders of nature's full explosion and light:

> It is April and already no doubt for you,
> As the journals report, the prologues of spring
> Appear behind the rails of city parks,
> Or the late springtime must be publishing
> Pink apologies along the wet, black branch

---

1 'As John to Patmos', *In a Green Night*, p. 12.
2 'A Village Life', *The Castaway*, p. 17.

To men in overcoats, who will conceal
The lines of song leaping behind their pipes.[1]

Walcott is pre-eminently a lyrical rather than a narrative poet. Though his ear must record delicately enough the vigorous speech-habits of the islands, he prefers to report these in his plays, where he even gives snatches of dialogue in the French *patois* of St. Lucia. A dialect style lends itself more easily to dramatic ballad or song than to the complex and allusive manner of his major poems. In his sonnet sequence 'Tales of the Islands'[2] he has attempted here and there a muted use of dialect words and phrases—almost a stage direction for the reader—but the very paucity of these indicates that he is not seeking to develop dialect as a poetic language. Elsewhere he has written:

> ... the poet in the West Indies, exiled from a mythically fertile past, must first explore his origins before he can purify the dialect of the tribe.[3]

Both exploration and purification are evident in Walcott's remarkably consistent development over the past ten years, but the purification is not a matter of eliminating dialect features. It is rather a process of shedding literary influences which might tie the chosen language too closely to the misty northern island where it was first hammered into shape. The allusion to Mallarmé must be taken in this sense if we are to understand what Walcott is about. His raw material is the whole range of the English tongue as literature and speech have made it; an inclusive approach which relates his work both to the central traditions of the language and to the Caribbean environment that shapes his sensibility and supplies his major themes. When Walcott is away from the islands he writes of them with genuine longing, a genuine sense of loss. For him there are no pleasures of exile. The very smallness of scale which troubles and repels so many West Indian writers does not disturb the true solitary, for the ocean intrudes its own grandeur, and away from its roar he feels its 'deafening absence'.

So Caribbean man, 'the second Adam since the fall', need

---

1 'To a Painter in England', *In a Green Night*, p. 16.
2 *In a Green Night*.   3 *Trinidad Guardian*, 18 June 1962.

not forsake his island to escape his loneliness. It is through language, not physical departure, that he reaches out to address the world, announcing his membership of the human community that once denied it:

> Craftsman and Castaway
> All heaven in his head,
> He watched his shadow pray
> Not for God's love, but human love instead.[1]

Another island poet, Edward Brathwaite of Barbados, is seemingly more intent on developing a poetic language from the speech and song rhythms peculiar to the New World. In his long work *Rights of Passage* he specifically draws upon the rhythms of work-song, blues and jazz in various sections of the poem. He also writes several movements in deep dialect and others in a subdued version which retains a number of dialect features. In the 'deep' manner he writes the whole of the movement called 'The Dust', a conversation among women in the corner-shop, humorous and alive:

> doan fuhget 'bout 'de
> biscuit an sawlfish
> you daughter Marilyn
> come here an' say that you wish
> to tek out las' month!
> Mundee Dee Vee, uh settlin'
> up ev'ry brass pill an' pen-
> ny that owin' this shop, Miss
> Olive muh dear.[2]

The movement called 'Folkways' describes the endless travelling of the forever exiled negro in search of life and work. Writing with an ear always cocked to the idioms and rhythms of negro folk music, which has so movingly captured all that restlessness, Brathwaite composes lines full of the sick longing for departure:

> So come
> quick cattle
> train, lick
> the long

---

1 'Crusoe's Island', *The Castaway*, p. 55.
2 *Rights of Passage*, (London, Oxford University Press, 1967), p. 64.

```
rails: choo-
choo chatanoo-
ga, pick
the long
trail to town . . .

Ever seen
a   man
travel more
seen more
lands
than this poor
land—
less, harbour-
less spade?¹
```

The short lines and split words, used frequently through the poem, dictate a quick jazzy movement of the eye down the page, and an alert carrying of incomplete sound from line to line. Brathwaite's experimental devices include shifting the rhyming syllable backwards and forwards within the line, like this:

```
quick cattle
train, lick
```

as well as rhyming some words upon the first syllable instead of the last. Assonance, alliteration and onamatopœia are all called into play, so that the great forward impetus of the short verses is controlled by a considerable density of sonic texture. This is particularly evident in the passages of the poem concerned with action rather than reflection, such as that remembering the first coming of the slave-raiders into the forest villages of Africa, where the short 'i' sounds create a sense of strict inexorable doom:

```
Click lock
your fire-
lock fore-
arm fire-
arm flashed
fire and our firm
fleshed flame
```

---

1 *Ibid.*, pp. 32–3.

warm, fly
bitten warriors
fell. . . .
And the fire, our
fire, fashioning locks,
rocks darker than iron;
fire betrayed us once
in our village; now
in the forest, fire falls
us like birds, hot pods
in our belly. Fire
falls walls, fashions
These fire-
locks darker than iron,
And we filed down the path
linked in a new
clinked silence of iron.[1]

Whereas Walcott is centrally concerned with Caribbean man, with his present and his island world, Brathwaite is haunted by a vision of the historic destiny of the negro race, not only in the Caribbean but everywhere. His poem begins in the Sahara, all images of drought and sharp glitter, then moves into the damp silence of the forests, the savage encounter with the armed intruders, the enslavement and the passage to the New World —the last a literal image of hell. Later it picks up the cyclical rhythm which seems to dominate the literature of the islands, the cycle of Discovery, Departure and Return upon which Book One of the present work is based. But Brathwaite's discovery of the new island home lacks the joy which Walcott imparts to it. The negro islander soon finds himself facing a new exile, to the urban slums and savage discrimination of America and England. Finally he returns to the islands, only to confront once more their poverty, hopelessness and squalor. The long shadow of the U.S. Marines now lies over the whole archipelago, inhibiting the process of revolution which can alone redeem them.

In his later poem *Masks* (1968), Brathwaite does chronicle a kind of African homecoming, a personal exploration of what Africa was and is. But that poem, which is discussed in detail in Chapter Eight, also ends upon a note of departure. The histori-

---

1 *Ibid.*, pp. 8–10.

cal severance from Africa was, he implies, a final one. The West Indian can revisit it, draw strength and inspiration from it, but cannot, in the fullest sense, return.

Where Walcott, poet of seascape, rock and sunlight, cries 'home is here!', Brathwaite, poet of voyages, train-whistles and quaysides, replies, 'home is nowhere!' Unlike Noah, stepping out onto the new earth of Ararat, the black men finds:

> no dove
> to return with its love
> in the morning, no lover
> to call like a bird in the green.[1]

Both voices are necessary to our understanding; for if Walcott shows us how Caribbean man may learn to know and love his island, Brathwaite reminds us why he so often has to leave it.

---

1 *Ibid.*, p. 85.

Chapter 2
Departure

What do they hope for
What find there?

Edward Brathwaite

If the West Indian is a second Adam, cast out of his African paradise by the flaming sword of the slaver, then he is the inheritor and possessor of the new island world into which history has cast him. Like the biblical Adam, he might feel that little lift of hope and lonely freedom with which Milton closes his epic:

The world was all before them, where to chose
Their place of rest

Many West Indians, however, select their governing myth from a later chapter of the Bible. Finding themselves not only scattered and exiled, but also in bondage to alien taskmasters, they find their archetypes in the children of Israel under the lash of Egypt or Babylon. This vision of themselves enabled generations of American slaves to comprehend their suffering and to give the world one of its greatest canons of folk music and one of its most moving songs, 'Let my People go'.

The bondage of poverty, hunger and hopelessness is scarcely less painful than that of slavery itself. No single Act of Parliament, however, seems capable of abolishing it. It can be endured only if there is a belief in some kind of ultimate escape. Those inhabiting the higher fringes of misery may permit themselves to dream of escaping upwards, into that bourgeois colonial society whose stuffy values they already aspire to share. But for the great unleavened mass below them the only possible escape is outwards, to another destiny altogether. The Caribbean slave used to dream of returning after death to 'Guinea', the shadowy land of his ancestors where a place was still kept for him beside the fire. The gods who possessed him in moments of trance, who rode his body like divine horsemen, came from there and kept him perpetually linked to a home-land neither he nor perhaps his grandfather had ever seen. This hope of reunion with the tribe and the ancestors in death was the theme of much Caribbean poetry in the late nineteenth and early twentieth centuries, most notably in Haiti. It lingers still in the dreamy sonnets of the Jamaican Claude McKay, whose conventional romantic language is occasionally transfigured by the passage of some strong, clear emotion:

> Something in me is lost, forever lost,
> Some vital thing has gone out of my heart,
> And I must walk the way of life a ghost
> Among the sons of earth, a thing apart.
> For I was born, far from my native clime,
> Under the white man's menace, out of time.[1]

These words were written, ironically enough, in the new exile of Harlem or London where McKay spent most his adult life, and which proved the nearest that he or thousands of his compatriots would ever get to Africa. Here they confronted the white world on the starkest and coldest terms. Jamaica, though far from Africa, had at least been warm, fertile and pre-dominantly black.

McKay's poetry is filled with the conviction that slavery, exile and deprivation have permanently ruined the negro in the New World. Hence his isolation is not simply the result of discrimination or of mutable social practices, but is the logical expression of his historical despair. It cannot be cured by any mere juggling with the social mechanism; its very depth and intensity can only be gauged by those who share it:

> Only a thorn-crowned Negro and no white
> Can penetrate into the Negro's ken,
> Or feel the thickness of the shroud of night,
> Which hides and buries him from other men.[2]

That word 'buries' conveys all the weight of his despair. If he were merely hidden some amelioration might be dreamt of, but he is buried beyond the reach of any external emotion.

With the decline of simple, undemanding religious faith and the answering rise of millenarian expectations here on earth,

---

1 'Outcast', *Selected Poems of Claude McKay* (New York, Bookman Assoc. Inc., 1953).   2 *Ibid.*

the emphasis shifted from a reunion with the African ancestors in death to the hope of an actual physical return to Africa in the present life. Marcus Garvey, also a Jamaican, fired the souls of millions with this vision during his years in black America and carried it back to Jamaica when he returned there in 1928, after his vengeful prison sentence. After Garvey's death and the collapse of his airy schemes for a United States of Africa with himself as President, many turned their eyes towards the Rastafarian cult, also strongest in Jamaica. Among the urban poor of West Kingston, as indigent and abandoned as any in the Caribbean or Latin America, the cultists shone forth by reason of their dignity, their quiet confidence in an eventual salvation, their gentle watchword, 'Peace and love'. In the intensive new mythology they developed, Ras Tafari emerged as the true black god, long obscured from his children by the systematic lies of their white masters. Abraham, Garvey and others might be seen as his prophets sent before, but present hope was fastened upon the living Emperor, Haile Selassie, the Conquering Lion of Judah and direct descendant of Solomon and Sheba. He it was who would eventually come and, Joseph-like, lead them all out of bondage to their inheritance in Africa, known in the cult always as 'Ethiopia'. Haile Selassie's gallant fight against the white invaders of 1935 and his triumphant return to Addis Ababa (riding on a white horse) in 1941 all served to strengthen the vision and sharpen its immediacy. Among the ignorant and neglected denizens of the spreading shanty-towns this story hung together, impregnable to attack. All attempts to challenge either its accuracy or the feasibility of a mass return to Ethiopia could be dismissed as white propaganda, 'the lies of Babylon', designed to perpetuate their bondage. The Rastafarian cult, with its dignified withdrawal from the fawning rituals of colonial life, its stirring music and its visible black 'leader' on an ancient Christian throne in Africa, gave a purpose and a hope to many who could not have kept going without it:

> Dry bones in the valley,
> Dry bones in the valley,
> It all depend on them to come
> Walkin' in the valley of dry bones.[1]

---

1 From a Rastaferian hymn.

Beside this massive simplicity, how does one evaluate the patronizing sneers of their betters, or even the polite surprise of the Emperor himself?

The young Jamaican novelist Orlando Patterson offers this example of Rastafarian rhetoric in his novel about the Kingston slums, *The Children of Sisyphus* (1964):

> 'Me Brother, is hard to explain these mysteries, but as a Brethren you know the simple truth that man is God. The white man in him trickery create another God. Him say that that God live in the sky and him call up there heaven; then he say that when we dead we go to heaven if we do good. Of course this is the horrible trick he use to pacify us in this life while he rob us of all that belong to us an' live off the fat of the land himself. He tell us all kind o' nonsense about blessed are the poor for they shall inherit the Kingdom of Heaven. What Kingdom? The one in the sky, of course. But we know that the true God is Rastafari. . . . But there is another thing they hide from us. The most important of all. And that is that man is God. The spirit of Rastafari is invested in every one of us. Is just for us to find it. This, this, Brother is the wickedest sin that the white man commit on himself and us and the brown allies now perpetuate. For when they enslave us in this land of Babylon after taking us from the sweet heaven of Africa they not only enslave we body but also we mind.'[1]

Patterson's novel, like the earlier books of Roger Mais, presents the dilemma with which the Rastafarians confront the Jamaican novelist. Those who have nothing, whose ideas are apparently based on the wildest misrepresentation of contemporary reality, can nevertheless stand up and be men. They scorn the colonial pantomime through which their more successful compatriots seem compelled to move, sweating their way from garden party to garden party in tightly-fitting borrowed identities. Simply because they have nothing to lose, because they have a sustaining myth which is independent of the white men, the Rastafarians can refuse to play. Now that Haile Selassie has visited Jamaica, however, and has failed to usher in the promised millennium, it is possible that the movement will gradually run down, as Garvey's did. If so, it is likely to be replaced by something more secular and more overtly revolutionary.

Mais, a more powerful and accomplished novelist than

---

1 *Children of Sisyphus* (London, New Authors Ltd., 1964), pp. 49–50.

Patterson, has given an enduring account of the poorest stratum of Jamaican city life in *The Hills Were Joyful Together* (1953) and *Brother Man* (1954). But his characters do not dream of an ultimate escape from their bitter world, as Patterson's do. So intensely does Mais create his urban landscape, so completely does he infuse it with his tragic view of life, that his books scarcely touch upon the theme of departure, unless it be to another 'yard', to prison or to the mortuary. Though he experienced many years of exile himself, he presents his slum-dwellers only with the three more immediate alternatives which crowd upon their narrow existence: escape into the underworld, where they wage war upon society through a precise reversal of its values; escape through revivalist sects, with their emphasis on rhythmically-induced frenzy and possession; or escape into the aloof withdrawal of the Rastafarians.

The more literal modes of escape, to Panama, New York or Wolverhampton, usually involve the scraping together of more funds than Mais's characters ever seem possessed of. But the fact that so many West Indian writers are themselves exiles has not, as is sometimes assumed, cut them off from all the sources of their material. A good many of these sources crossed over in the same boat with them. A city like London or Birmingham has a far larger West Indian population than most of the smaller islands can boast of. This second diaspora of the negro (for most of these emigrants are of negro stock) is one of the major convulsions of West Indian history, and only by participating in it has the writer been able to chronicle it with real understanding. Just as the generation of Garvey and McKay were only able to discover the full meaning of their blackness by experiencing the stark embattlement of the races in America, so this new generation gropes towards a sense of being West Indian when a new uprooting forces a recognition of what they have in common.

Edward Brathwaite, in the movement of *Rights of Passage* entitled 'Emigrants', asks:

What do they hope for
What find there
these New World mariners
Columbus coursing Kaffirs?[1]

---

1 *Rights of Passage*, p. 51.

But a little later in the poem he depicts a cosmic restlessness, a fated disillusionment that can never be assuaged by the packing of a grip. There is, it seems, no home for the negro, once out of Africa, except the shifting one constructed by a dynamic acceptance of himself:

> Where then is the nigger's
> home?
>
> In Paris Brixton Kingston
> Rome?
>
> Here?
> Or in Heaven?
>
> What crime
> his dark
>
> dividing skin
> is hiding?
>
> What guilt
> now drives him
>
> on?
> Will exile never
>
> end?...[1]

Only by embracing this restlessness can the negro conceive it as a forward movement, as a condition of his being, as the pathway to a possible salvation. To stand still is to wilt and die. The search itself is what defines the race, giving it purpose and momentum and a dogged hope:

> shatter the door
> and walk
> in the morning
> fully aware
>
> of the future
> to come?
> There is no
> turning back.[2]

---

1 *Ibid.*, p. 78.   2 *Ibid.*, p. 86.

So Brathwaite walks out of his poem. Many novels of West Indian life, also, have ended with a gesture of departure, the setting forth from childhood's island which proves to be so much more than a simple voyage. Thus Naipaul ends his semi-autobiographical *Miguel Street* (1957) with a parting that proves final for him, but barely ripples the current of life for those he leaves behind. Returning to the city for a final hour because his flight has been delayed, he encounters a friend sauntering through the streets:

> All he said was, 'I thought you was in the air by this time'. I was disappointed. Not only by that cool reception. Disappointed because although I had been away, destined to be gone for good, everything was going on just as before, with nothing to indicate my absence.

Later he returns to the airport and offers only the briefest of farewells to his relatives, impatient to be gone:

> I left them all and walked briskly towards the aeroplane, not looking back, looking only at my shadow before me, a dancing dwarf on the tarmac.[1]

The eyes of the departing voyager are fixed on his own image, dancing ahead of him like an embodiment of all his hopes and ambitions for the new life of exile. The old life may not feel itself wounded or diminished, but in the mind of the voyager it is dethroned; it can never again be the unique centre of his experience.

If the last pages of Lamming's *In the Castle of my Skin* form the classic example of such island farewells, his second novel is the classic treatment of the process of departure itself. *The Emigrants* (1954) is a restless, anguished, inconclusive book, totally lacking the unity of vision and setting which characterized his chronicle of Barbadian childhood. Ultimately it leaves the reader troubled and dissatisfied yet suspecting that he was not intended to feel otherwise. Lamming unfolds his story in three long movements. The first, 'A Voyage', begins at the literal moment of sailing from the familiar pierhead into the blue horizon which has bounded all island experience hitherto. The second, 'Rooms and Residents', traces the separate destinies of the voyagers when they reach London and scatter through the

---

1 *Miguel Street* (London, Deutsch, 1959), p. 222.

dark, anonymous strangeness of the waiting city. In the last movement, 'Another Time', the web of relationship brings them all together again for a brief moment of crisis and failure before they scatter once more.

Of these three movements, 'Voyage' is undoubtedly the strongest and most effective. It is the movement which gathers up each emigrant from his separate consciousness and island, imposes briefly upon them all the iron unity of the ship itself, and carries them gradually further and further away from the warm familiar latitudes towards the faint promise and menace of England.

We first join the ship at Martinique as it wanders northward, seeking its passengers from island to island. For all of them, this adventure is something much more than a voyage; it is perhaps the decisive gesture of their lives. The rail of the ship is crowded with idlers, consuming those moments of mingled boredom and expectancy that precede a sailing. On the pierhead a band is playing, reminder of a grimmer imperialism than that they have left behind; for a party of black conscripts bound for the war in Indo-China has just been bundled abroad. The band is for them, as are the dark glistening faces, the scarves and brilliant handkerchiefs that fill the pierhead with a less ordered life. Suddenly the sad-sweet atmosphere of parting erupts in comedy. A Trinidadian passenger, belated by rum and the seductions of an exotic whoredom, rushes towards the rising gangway:

> The sailors had raised it halfway and stopped uncertain what orders they would receive. Then they lowered it to a few feet from the brink of the pier and the man scrambled up on all fours. He made an odd shape under the burden of luggage which he carried. He held an artificial crocodile under one arm. Two water coconuts were strung round his neck and a bottle of rum stuck out of each hip pocket. . . . The man had brought a temporary relief from the strain of the soldiers' departure. Everyone except the captain seemed to shake with laughter. . . .[1]

The Strange Man soon makes his peace with the captain (at the cost of his coconuts and crocodile) and lays aside his comic aspect to tell the narrator that two new passengers just

---

1 *The Emigrants* (London, Michael Joseph, 1954), p. 17.

brought aboard are going to France for trial and possible execution on a charge of treason. The whole scene thus darkens again and the bizarre episode of his appearance fades within it.

> Now there was nothing between the ship and its port of call but a partition of night. The city lights went on like candles at the Feast of Paschal and the ship drifted with the sad certainty of the music that told those soldiers there was no parting.[1]

This beautiful control of mood is maintained through all the early pages of the novel, as the passengers grope towards awareness of each other. If nothing in their past experience has bound them together, the act of embarkation does. The approach of that dim northern shore for which they are bound forces them to consider what they are. As they lie smoking in the narrow bunks below or saunter about the decks, their broken talk adjusts itself to the discovery of this fact. None is yet described as a West Indian, but they talk of what such an animal might be. The character, known simply as 'the Jamaican', a veteran of earlier visits to England and of three years in the RAF, uses imagery of atrocious vividness to present his own portrait of the type:

> ... hist'ry tell me that dese same West Indies people is a sort of vomit you vomit up. Was a long time back England an' France an' Spain an' all the great nations make a raid on whoever live in them islands. Whatever the book call them me no remember, but most o' them get wipe out. Then de great nations make plans for 'dese said islands. England, France, Spain, all o' them, them vomit up what they din't want, an' the vomit settle there in that dim Caribbean sea. It mix up with the vomit them make Africa vomit, an' the vomit them make India vomit, an' China an' nearly every race under de sun. An' just as vomit never get back in yuh stomach, these people, most o' them, never get back where they vomit them from. Them settle right there in that Caribbean Sea, and the great nations, England, and the rest ... them stir an' stir till the vomit start to take on a new life .... Now it explodin' bit by bit. It beginnin' gradjally to stir itself. ... It stirrin' itself but there ain't no pot. An' when the vomit is people them get confuse. ... When them stay back home in they little island them forget a little an' them remain vomit ... but when them go 'broad, them remember, or them get tol'

---

1 *Ibid.*, p. 20.

w'at is w'at, an' them start to prove, an' them give what them provin' a name. A good name. Them is West Indians.[1]

At the moment of their landfall in England, Lamming switches to an impressionist technique, blending exclamations by the emigrants themselves with observations and remarks of their fellow passengers as the train collects them all and rushes towards London. The quick sentences, antiphonal arrangement of speech on the page and constant changes of voice all help to produce a breathless eagerness and freshness of attack, quite different from the slow, doubtful and desultory conversations of the voyage. This arrival in London is really the climax of the whole novel:

> This is England. Look you just missed it. Ah, there again, there it is, the white horse. Gone. There ah, there it is. White against the grass. Who put it there. Look. There again. Ah, it's gone. Gone. All the buildings are solid here. These were not bombed. Or perhaps these were rebuilt. They have blocked out the white horse. Forever. The white horse is gone. Only the buildings now.
>
> How long you been sleepin'?
>
> WILL PASSENGERS KEEP THEIR HEADS WITHIN THE TRAIN
>
> Look partner dat's where they make the blades, partner, all yuh shavin' yuh say you shave you do cause o' that place. Look it, ol' man, they make yuh blades there.
>
> Ponds, ol' man, look Ponds. They make cream there. All those women back home depend on what happen in there. Look, Ponds Cream. Look Tornado you see that. Paint. They make paint there. Look, paint. . . .
>
> They make everything here on this side. All England like this.[2]

But this lyrical train journey into London is not only the climax of an illusion about England, the long-imagined cultural mother who rejects her woolly-headed children; it is the climax also of the process of collective self-discovery which the journey has imposed. From this point onward, Lamming makes full use of what Brathwaite has called his 'fragmentation' technique. The characters literally fly apart. The process is briefly arrested by the existence of a student hostel in Knightsbridge where some of them occasionally gather, and

---

1 *Ibid.*, pp. 65–6.   2 *Ibid.*, p. 119.

by the various involvements of this hostel group with an Englishman called Frederick, but it is rapid enough to have reduced them to almost complete isolation within two years of their arrival. The first-person narrator who was fitfully present in the early part of the novel also withdraws, so that the main body of the book is without a human focus. Collis, described simply as 'a writer', seems for a time likely to fill this role, but he remains a shadowy, mysterious figure, impinging little upon the lives of the others. During the long central movement of the book, 'Rooms and Residents', we see fragments of experience in these diverging lives before each wheels back into the darkness. And the bizarre nature of these fragments deepens the suspicion that the book itself is lunging off at a tangent from the real experience of England that Lamming must by this time have known. Frederick, the only Englishman who plays any part of importance, is almost a parody of the effete, impotent and bungling white liberal. His exorbitant English mistress Peggy not only performs sexual exhibitions in front of him with at least two of the black characters, but has Lesbian liaisons with two of the emigrant women, one of whom subsequently murders the other after a drunken homosexual orgy. Dickson, another of the West Indians, is inspected in the nude by his white landlady and her sister, after an elaborate charade designed to give him an erection. Policemen and drug convictions hover always in the background.

Into this welter of perversion and moral disintegration blunders the essentially innocent, uncomplicated figure of the Strange Man, the very person whose sudden appearance on the gangway at Martinique had brought a whiff of humane comedy into a painful situation. This time, he is accompanied by a group of fresh West Indian arrivals looking for beds, but this simple request falls strangely on the ears of those assembled at the nightclub where the final movement takes place. This nightclub, run by a man called the Governor, has to some extent replaced the hostel as an occasional meeting-place. An abortion is taking place upstairs and a man called Higgins is going quietly mad in the bar. But the woman whom the Strange Man produces to claim a bed turns out to be the Governor's long-lost, long-detested wife. He sprawls her with a single blow, scattering guests and immigrants alike into the night, ending the novel itself with his fist.

The Emigrants thus develops a tendency already present in Lamming's first novel, the building up of events and impressions around a situation existing in time, rather than around a single person or a closely related group of people. With *In the Castle of My Skin* this tendency is obscured by the relative dominance of the narrator, though several scenes take place in his absence. But even in that novel the narrator's existence is partially dependent on his membership of a group of boys who together establish the typicality of their story, a West Indian boyhood of thirty years ago. And it is their separate and differing destinies in later years which finally establish that very typicality. In *The Emigrants* Lamming cuts us adrift from any mooring, deliberately subjecting the reader to that process of stirring which the Jamaican describes during the voyage. But the stirring continues to the last page; realization of an identity as West Indians is farther away than ever; and this nightmare England, all jagged flashes and fragments, seems to deny the very existence of any recognizable human identity at all. As if to emphasize this, Frederick at the book's end is about to marry a fair-skinned mulatto girl whom he has jilted years before, under her earlier name, in Jamaica. His failure to recognize the jilted Ursula Bis in the new Una Solomon matches her own refusal to do so. The separation, the absence of love in Lamming's characters, becomes a universal rather than a West Indian condition. Everyone is adrift; only some new dark figures, formerly locked in their islands, have entered the current.

Chapter 3
Return

*And here you are now
back from their schools
with the bent mind
which alien tongues secure
to bind
our hands and youthful reaches*

Elliot Bastien

The return of the West Indian voyager to his island must be accomplished through perilous seas, ringed about with the reefs of cliché. To return at all is a deliberate act, a recognition of some claim which that patch of land, by its very narrowness, has established. The critic, like the writer before him, must strive to abjure statements about 'identity' and 'finding one's roots; phrases which have grown so slack through familiarity that they have lost the power to keep truth in sight.

The immediate effect of departure has been to focus the writer's attention upon himself; himself as an apparently detachable and autonomous unit suddenly removed from its background. But ultimately the experience of viewing that background over a distance of space and time proves as definitive of it as the initial shock of self-consciousness, administered by departure, was definitive of the individual. So, in course of time, a person somewhat more certain of who he distinctively is returns to a world which has been placed and limited by absence. The effect of the actual return is usually to disturb considerably both of these certitudes.

Edward Brathwaite, sojourning in the interior of Africa, finds himself yearning for the encompassing ocean, the consciousness of which is central to Caribbean experience. The wide brown rivers of Guinea cannot compensate for its absence. But as he gazes upon the waters of such a river, he suddenly feels the impulse of return moving within him. He marches south along its banks, and the sea, when he reaches it, is

43

recognisably the same ocean that washes about the island of home. Absence is eclipsed in its waters:

> We who are born of the ocean can never seek solace
> in rivers: their flowing runs on like our longing . . .
>
> But today I would join you, travelling river,
> borne down the years of your patientest flowing . . .
> and moving on through the plains that receive us,
> processioned in tumult, come to the sea.
>
> Bright waves splash up from the rocks to receive us,
> blue sea-shells shift in their wake
> and *there* is the thatch of the fisherman's house, the path
> made of pebbles, and look!
> Small urchins combing the beaches
> Look up from their traps to salute us
>
> They remember us just as we left them.
> The fisherman, hawking the surf on this side
> of the reef, stands up in his boat
> and halloos us: a starfish lies in its pool.
> And the gulls, white sails slanted seaward,
> fly into the limitless morning before us.[1]

So here on the distant shore of Africa we encounter the familiar fisherman, who strides like some indifferent god through the pages of West Indian literature. It is the same fisherman who admonishes the frightened boys in Lamming's *In the Castle of My Skin*, after one of them has accidentally tumbled into the surf; the same who rescues the sunstruck Alexander Blackman in Orlando Patterson's *An Absence of Ruins*; the same who stirred Philip Sherlock's imagination long ago, and who casually dominates the lonely beaches of Walcott's play *The Sea At Dauphin* or his latest poetry:

> There's nothing here
> this early;
> cold sand
> cold churning ocean, the Atlantic,
> no visible history,
> except this stand
> of twisted, coppery, sea-almond trees

---

1 *Rights of Passage*, (London, Oxford University Press, 1967), pp. 56–7.

their shining postures surely
bent as metal, and one
foam-haired, slat-grizzled fisherman,
his mongrel growling, twirling on a stick
he pitches him; its spinning rays
'no visible history'
until their lengthened shapes amaze the sun.[1]

For the fisherman, whose lore is ancient, savage and strong, is master of the ocean which limits the action and imagination of his fellows. Sentimentalized in much minor West Indian verse, he emerges with an undiminished primal force in the best writing. He alone, it seems, escapes a mentality still deeply marked by slavery and colonialism. He alone is freed from what Walcott has called 'the search for our own sadness'. He alone does not appear marooned by time on a shore that does not yet belong to him. And he is master of the element which defines, if nothing else does, the status of the Caribbean islander.

Yet a slight distinction must be attempted here, for it is pre-eminently the 'small-islander' who displays this oceanic sensibility. Just as the imagery of return for the Barbadian Brathwaite is naturally couched in terms of the open beach and the familiar caress of the waves, so the St. Lucian Walcott is troubled by the silence, behind which he hears the aching absence of the shock and thunder of the surf:

Something removed roars in the ears of this house . . .
A deafening absence, a blow.[2]

But the landscape of Trinidad, as we discover it in early Selvon, Naipaul and Anthony, is a landscape of great canefields, rivers, and blue mountains far away. It is the seasons of the sugar crop rather than the moods of the sea which dominate. Indeed, we are not conscious of the sea in any positive sense in *Mr. Biwas* or *A Brighter Sun*. And Jamaica, with its long steep mountains and shrouded valleys, offers a secret landscape framed by its own hills rather than by beach or breaking wave. Hence the return in Jamaican literature is often a return to the village; man facing, not the sea, but a hidden world he has abandoned. We

---

1 'The Almond Trees', in *The Castaway* (London, Cape, 1965), p. 36.
2 'Missing the Sea', in *The Castaway*, p. 24.

find this in the uneven but eloquent novel of Neville Dawes, *The Last Enchantment*, just as we find it in the early pages of *Les Gouverneurs de la Rosée* (1944), where Jacques Roumain returns his Haitian hero to the ruined village of his childhood.

The Last Enchantment is a book that constantly suffers from uncertainty of focus, veering abruptly from raw autobiography to a pretence of fictional detachment. But the deliberately un-realistic, generalized and symbolic tone in which Dawes presents the return of his hero Ramsay Tull results in the novel's most sustained piece of writing. Dawes, like Brathwaite, has lived for several years in Ghana, but we doubt whether the mere sight of an African beach, with its palm-thatched huts, leaning trees and dazzling sand, would suffice to remind him of home. The atmosphere of the village here evoked is separate, withdrawn and inward-looking:

> The island was a place of long monotonous hills and sealed-off villages in the hills, a few where a man, long-known and out of exile, could enter and draw his soul around him.
>
> To enter the village, walking, you crossed a simple bridge of planks and wooden rails over which the village 'warner' one morning prophesied death and destruction and in the evening a truck full of drunken innocents fell from that bridge thirty feet to the dry river-bed. You crossed the bridge carefully remembering not death but the presentiment of death the old toothless woman could smell on her blood. Then a steep gravel path to the sharp turn and the village gate. The river was there, a spring, a trickle waiting for drought, the sweet water you sucked through green pimento leaves; that perfumed water, your first sensuous thrill, taken for thirst but for ever, in memory, the sacrament of belonging. . . . Just at the entrance before the first turning it was dark and cool in spite of its place near the sun. The gate you opened to the village was the gate of your own astonishment at the tensions under which you had lived for twenty years away from yourself. Your village is always open and has many closed gates.[1]

Not, then, man perpetually facing the surf, and lost without its thunder in his ears, but man withdrawn into a place 'dark and cool,' protected by bridge, pathway and gate from strangers, communing quietly with its own fecund, leafy groves. In such a setting, after all, the Maroons successfully defended their

---

1 *The Last Enchantment* (London, MacGibbon and Kee, 1960), pp. 198–9.

freedom and their privacy against all comers for two hundred years.

The Last Enchantment is a book that continually shifts from first person narration, with its implied subjectivity, to third person narration, with its implied objectivity. The effect of this, whatever the intention, is to create a sense of restlessness and uncertainty in the reader; especially as the passages of first person narration are neither prepared for nor explained, and are apparently inserted at random into the novel's texture. Sometimes we are not even sure whether this intrusive voice is Ramsay Tull's or the author's. Hence the gentle certainty of this passage, which transcends these doubts both by its intimacy and its generality, begins to allay the restlessness engendered by the novel as a whole; just as the introduction of yet another voice, the second person, curiously helps to reconcile the stark opposition of first and third.

In the next few paragraphs of the novel Dawes continues to address the hero (or the reader), whilst remaining partially outside him. The movement continues upwards, through the village and the house that was home, to the very top of the mountain. Now we see, not just the village or the valley, but the whole width of the island, defined by the distant and silent ocean. Then abruptly we are aboard the steamer which is bringing Ramsay Tull back to Jamaica from Europe. The steamer has just raised upon the horizon the very hills on which we have been standing with the projected presence of the hero. And simultaneously we are back with third person, descriptive narration:

> It is the first houses that shock you. They wait to trap you into simplicity so with your city habit you prepare to close yourself like the shame-a-lady fern your feet are kicking into modesty. . . .
> Again, from the city, it is the village people you want to avoid for they link you to objects with a simplicity that breaks down twenty years of certainties and velleities and labyrinths of tentative selves . . .
> The impulse was to go higher, through the house and climb, past the barbecues, up into the coffee grove, steeply, breathless at the end of your last journey, towards the top of the hill and the giddy biblical church.
> On its steps you commanded the village and the island and the truth. . . . From this Tabernacle step a variety of colours returned and you saw that the island was purple-grey between

the green of the trees and the afternoon sun. A valley flowed away from you, all the way down the St. Ann red clay across the place-names of saviours, Sturge, Buxton, Wilberforce, across the Christian messages of Mr. Zion and Salem, to the sea. The sea stood up straight in a curve of bay ten miles across your need to remember how small the island was, how small you were; the sea that locked you in and made you a warm, realized thing. Looking at the sea there, through this window of half-return, *that* was life, the breakers you could not hear, the soft white stitches where the waves turn over, the miracle of the myth-enduring sea.

The sea's wash was controlled, answered, and soft as the ship slowed to take the pilot on board about three o'clock in the morning. Ramsay went on deck and saw the unbelievable island stretched out in that special Palisadoes before-day half-light . . .[1]

Here we get the nearest thing to an explanation of Dawes' purpose. The tentative nature of the novel's structure corresponds to that taking up and setting down of 'tentative selves'. We realize that Dawes has accomplished his return without shipwreck on the reefs of cliché, not by avoiding the question of identity, but by trying to build it into the structure of the book itself. The quality of the detail in this sequence of return— the 'soft white stitches' of the sea, the 'warm, realized thing' locked in by it, the movement from the half-light of the forest to the brilliant clarity of the mountain view and back to the faint glow of dawn—makes this the most sustained piece of writing in a book that remains memorable, despite the failure of much of its structural experiment and its too-overt political satire; the original targets of Dawes' wrath glare at us through the thinnest of disguises. Here, one suspects, it is the nature of the subject itself that forces Dawes to write at his best, for it is pre-eminently at the moment of return that the pressure of emergent individuality must meet that of place.

It is this pressure that is so often lacking in Naipaul's *The Middle Passage*. For Naipaul is by no means sure that he is a West Indian when he begins the book, and seems to be fairly convinced that he is not by the time he finishes it. The West Indies, we gather, is just not much of a place for a writer to come from. Therefore, like Henry James fleeing the cultural shallows of America, he had better abandon it. Significantly,

---

1 *Ibid.*, pp. 199–200.

Naipaul does not write an imaginative work of return, but a kind of travel book, except that no real traveller could be so disenchanted; that is the authentic note of the intimate. As Naipaul's ship touches the quayside, ending his ten year absence from Trinidad, all his dislike of the place comes flooding back:

> I had never examined this fear of Trinidad. I had never wished to. In my novels I had only expressed this fear; ... I knew Trinidad to be unimportant, uncreative, cynical. ... Power was recognized, but dignity was allowed to no-one. Every person of eminence was held to be crooked and contemptible. We lived in a society which denied itself heroes. ... Generosity— the admiration of equal for equal—was therefore unknown; it was a quality I knew only from books and found only in England.

As often with Naipaul, the readiness to wound is also a readiness to tell painful truths about society. The pity is that, at the moment of return, he has nothing else to tell. The scenes of his own childhood and youth evoke not a flicker of nostalgia or warmth. Has Mr. Biswas consumed it all?[1]

It is George Lamming, however, who has written the classic document of return, just as the first half of *The Emigrants* forms the classic document of departure. Lamming's third novel, *Of Age and Innocence*, is his most complete and comprehensive work of fiction to date.[2] Lamming does not simply offer us the return of the alienated hero to the island of his birth. Mark Kennedy, who at first seems likely to fulfil this role, is viewed with extraordinary detachment from the start, and as the action proceeds his ineffectuality gradually removes him from the centre of the reader's attention. For Mark does not return alone to San Cristobal, an imaginary West Indian island moving rapidly towards independence. On the same 'plane comes Isaac Shepherd, a socially humbler Negro of evangelical, opinionated stock, who is returning filled with an urgent sense of his own unique destiny as the saviour of San Cristobal. Shepherd's is the genuine political messianism which enabled Kwame Nkrumah to call his autobiography *Ghana*. His single-minded fanaticism, joined to a curious vein of tolerance and compassion in his quieter moments, contrasts acutely with the

---

1 V. S. Naipaul, *The Middle Passage* (London, Deutsch, 1962), p. 41.
2 London, Michael Joseph, 1958.

fastidious intellectual discrimination of Mark, who is returning with no special sense of mission, purpose, or even affection, to his native island.

Mark has left San Cristobal at the age of ten and has spent twenty years of wandering in Europe and America. With him come three English companions; Marcia, his mistress, completely absorbed in her love of him; and Bill and Penelope Butterfield, friends from the world of Hampstead and the BBC, who are joining the party from a vague sense of boredom with their own contentment. Mark, as the only black man among them and the only one who knows San Cristobal already, is a source of muted excitement and speculation to his companions. But, as usual, he gives nothing away. Brooding, sensitive and withdrawn by nature, he spends most of the flight reading his own private diaries and fighting off a premonition of disaster.

One other passenger of importance to the novel rides on the plane, young Rowley Crabbe, son of the English Police Commissioner in San Cristobal. All of these passengers are involved when Shepherd suffers some curious kind of seizure during the flight and interrogates them at pistol-point about the motives of their visit. He insults Penelope brutally, but says nothing to Mark, whom he recognizes from long ago. Finally, he falls helpless in a fit at the feet of the astonished pilot.

On arrival in San Cristobal, the main lines of the action rapidly emerge. The older generation, those who stand immediately to gain or lose by independence, are all prisoners of the past, unable to rid themselves entirely of hatreds, suspicions and prejudgments which cannot enrich the future. Shepherd is able briefly to allay some of these phobias among his followers, but only at the cost of increasing them among his enemies. The main protagonists, apart from Shepherd, are the politicians Singh and Lee, the Police Commissioner Crabbe and the spy and informer Baboo. The younger generation are totally uninterested in the racial distinctions and power-struggles which obsess others. They are inspired by a common mythology about the island's past and a common vision of brotherhood to combat the evils of its present. They are Singh and Lee, sons of the established Indian and Chinese leaders; Bob, the son of a Negro butcher; and Rowley Crabbe. These four boys are absorbed by the independent discovery of their island world, looking for continuity to the mythology bequeathed them by Ma Shepherd, the midwife who has presided at the birth of countless islanders. Ma Shepherd is a semi-symbolical figure, repository of all the ancient lore of San Cristobal, and disapproving in her conservative piety of her son's hectic career towards power. For Shepherd has assumed leadership of the island's nationalist movement almost from the moment of his return. He brings to it a new emphasis, shifting it from the old communalism represented by Singh's exclusively Indian party towards an ideal of non-racial unity in the fight for independence. The leadership of this new national movement is shared between Singh, Lee and himself. Both acknowledge Shepherd's ascendancy, and Singh develops a kind of fierce, possessive love for the man. Even on the 'plane, at the height of his frenzy, Shepherd has shown the outlines of his vision:

> You do not know San Cristobal, coming up by accident one morning from water, the tiny skull of a mountain top which was once asleep under the sea. Here Africa and India shake hands with China, and Europe wrinkles like a brow begging every face to promise love. The past is all suspicion, now is an argument that will not end, and tomorrow for San Cristobal, tomorrow is like the air in your hand. I know San Cristobal. It is mine, me divided in a harmony that still pursues all its separate parts. No new country, but an old old land inhabiting new forms of men who can never resurrect their roots and do not know their nature. Colour is their old and only alphabet. The whites are turning whiter, and the blacks are like an instinct which some voice, my voice, shall exercise . . .[1]

While leaders and followers grope towards unity from the habit of suspicion, the four boys seem to sieze it spontaneously. They form themselves into a secret society, pledged to help and support one another, and look for their common inspiration to the legend of the Tribe Boys, aboriginal inhabitants of the island whose last remnants committed communal suicide in a leap from Mount Misery rather than submit to the invading Bandit Kings and their swarming warrior Ants.[2] Ma Shepherd

---

1 *Of Age and Innocence*, p. 58.
2 San Cristobal is a composite island, with features carefully borrowed from here and there. The Tribe Boys evoke the memory of the last Caribs in Grenada who leapt from the Morne des Sauteurs in the 1650's, while their attackers may catch an echo of the Brigands' War of 1795, when Victor Hugues led revolutionary attacks on the British islands with black soldiers

tells the boys that the island was thrust up suddenly from the bottom of the sea and that its earth was subsequently swept by wind and fire. This legendary fire is perhaps a paradigm for the fires of the old slave revolts and heralds the beginning of a more polyglot West Indies, adding Indian and Chinese elements to the old stark confrontation of black and white. The elemental nature of the whole myth echoes Shepherd's belief that San Cristobal is 'an old old land inhabiting new forms of men.'

The boys themselves, who prove to be the only growing point in the book, have a clear sense of what their society promises:

> It seemed they had, in some way, surpassed their elders; so that they behaved, during these expeditions, as though they were no longer dependent on the decisions others were making for them. It had made their age irrelevant, compared with the wasted experience of those who were so much older. Sometimes they felt that the others would have to catch up on what they had already accomplished.[1]

But the boys too are to be touched by tragedy. In a plot of great complexity and violence, San Cristobal is brought to the edge of disintegration. Lamming's older characters are driven by a combination of conflicting ambitions, misunderstandings and recklessness into actions which destroy both their objectives and themselves. At the end of a few months, Shepherd and Crabbe have both been murdered, Singh and Lee stand under imminent sentence of death, whilst Rowley, Marcia and Penelope have all burnt to death in a disastrous fire at the madhouse and the whole island is groaning under martial law. The boys themselves even contribute, unwittingly, to bring about the fire which devours their hopes and one of their number.

The sequence of events which brings all this about cannot be unravelled here, but it is important to note certain characteristics of Lamming's mature technique in this novel. Firstly, it is those with relatively narrow vision and objectives who are most likely to act. This group includes Crabbe, who acts throughout

---

from Martinique. The volcanic explosiveness of San Cristobal suggests St. Vincent. Mount Misery, however, is in St. Kitts. In *Season of Adventure* (1960) Lamming lends the island qualities borrowed from Haiti and Trinidad as well.

1 *Ibid.*, p. 115.

with ruthless expediency to break the national leadership and maintain the imperial presence; Baboo, who murders Shepherd because he wants a fellow-Indian like Singh to seize the leadership, and who later murders Crabbe to conceal his earlier crime and ingratiate himself with what he judges to be the new power-group; and, to some extent, it includes Shepherd himself. For, although he acts initially with vision and purpose to capture the national movement and give it a valuable new emphasis, his messianic tendencies cause him to lose hold of reality at the moment of his triumph and so encompass his own destruction.

Contrasted with this group are the temporisers, forever trying to come to terms with situations created by other men. These include Flagstead, Bill's white friend in Radio San Cristobal, and Parevecino, the typical off-white colonial politician, always in and out of Government House. Singh and Lee also have affiliations with this group, since both are smaller men without Shepherd's inspiration to guide them.

Flagstead is a liberal apostate who nurses a reluctant admiration for Crabbe. The scene in which he outlines his new position to Bill, still angry and confused by the moral velleities and furtive skullduggery of the island's public life, is one of the most brilliant in the book:

> 'Places like San Cristobal lure you into a position which makes you a wholly different person ... once you're in the situation, you do find yourself playing some part which ultimately supports people like Crabbe. And there is nothing you can do. You can even justify it. ... I do believe that if certain people took over the Official Administration, they'd cut our throats,' he said, 'yours and mine, and every European in San Cristobal. You have to protect yourself against such a possibility. ... You seem justified in holding on, and if holding on means protecting yourself, you protect yourself. And you use power to do it. Shepherd and his group would do it too, if they were in the same situation.'[1]

Flagstead probably never realizes that it is precisely the sort of 'holding on' he advocates that raises the throat-cutting from a fantasy to an imminent probability.

Between these two groups and the boys' little society drift the

---

1 *Ibid.*, p. 223.

53

newcomers to San Cristobal, trying to get to grips with an exciting but disturbing environment. Mark is attracted by Shepherd's movement, but fails to tell his friends about his increasing involvement in it, victim as ever of his own chronic self-isolation. He is in any case only a trimming to Shepherd's platform, being far too fastidious for the political front-line. In the end he finds himself suspected of Shepherd's murder, hated by the people at large, and forced to flee from San Cristobal by the machinations of others. He has become a cypher, living without purpose. Marcia exists only in her love for Mark, whose silence and withdrawal in this strange world soon drive her insane and so lead to her death in the fire which consumes the madhouse. Penelope is as self-absorbed as Mark; like him, she communicates her real feelings to the reader only through the extracts we glimpse in her diary. She is attracted and stimulated at first by San Cristobal, and is responsive to the imaginative vigour of the boys, but she becomes obsessed with the Lesbian protectiveness she gradually develops towards Marcia. Whilst visiting her, she also dies in the fire. Bill is warm but emotionally impulsive, easily excited and offended, veering between admiration for Shepherd and a resolve to kill him when he wrongly suspects him of having caused the fire, whose origins are in fact purely accidental. Like Mark, Bill eventually becomes an irrelevance and has to be shipped off from an island which cannot tolerate his tentative liberal improvisations and sudden bursts of irrational activity. With more justification, he too is suspected and tried for Shepherd's murder.

But these four are not alone in their confusion. Two relatively simple islanders are also buffetted and almost destroyed by the forces that are sweeping San Cristobal. Thief, the three-fingered ruffian who suddenly discovers a capacity for devotion as the trusted servant of Penelope and Bill, has been pre-figured in Mark's old project of writing a novel about a notorious three-fingered pirate of the seventeenth century. His friend Rockey, a fisherman, becomes involved in Thief's fate through simple affection. When Rockey's boat is spattered with the blood of Crabbe and has to be burnt to destroy the evidence, he feels utterly cast adrift, separated from his only familiar self and activity. He wanders through the tense streets of the city under the eyes of the newly-arrived British soldiers, muttering to himself, 'San Cristobal get hit hard, we get hit hard with the times.' And Thief, who has decided that his old profession now promises a rich harvest, and whose love for the Butterfields has already foundered, can only reply, 'Tomorrow is tomorrow'.

The extreme violence of Lamming's plot, which leads to the deaths of five of his principal characters and capital charges against four others, all within the space of a few months, is like a mask through which he shows us what is latent in the Caribbean situation, what is ever ready to break forth if time and circumstance conspire. The book was published in 1958, the year before Castro came to power in Cuba. Three years later racial riots had broken out in British Guiana, finally shattering the national unity achieved in the 1953 election. Subsequently came the barely disguised efforts of Britain and America to overthrow Jagan and to delay independence until this had been achieved. The year 1966 saw the efforts of the 'Bay Street Boys' in Nassau to retain power through fraud and intimidation. *Of Age and Innocence* is not a documentary novel, but nothing that happens there is improbable. Even the incident of Lee mangling the dead body of Crabbe in a spasm of hatred falls into perspective when we remember that, in the words of Sidney King, 'The Caribbean tradition is, taken as a whole, a revolutionary tradition. It is the stage on which acted Cudjoe and Cuffy, Accrabah and Accra, Toussaint, Quamina, Damon, Adoe and Araby.'[1]

Unlike Lamming's earlier work, this is primarily a political novel. It is also a tragedy, for it ends (again like the events of the 'fifties in British Guiana) with a united national leadership broken, with the masses sullen, angry, and full of racial phobias, and with imperialism resurgent in the dress of martial law. Even the boys, whose society seemed a solitary focus of hope, are left in disarray. One of them is dead, two others daily expect their fathers' executions on false charges, their relationship with Ma Shepherd is ruined through another of those misunderstandings that haunt this book, and the court refuses to hear their account of the fire, though they are the only living witnesses of its beginning. In their dismay, they hold on to the only thing that hasn't failed them, the unifying myth of the Tribe Boys, and the novel leaves them beside Rowley's grave,

---

1 'A Birth of Freedom', *New World Quarterly* (Guyana Independence Issue), 1966, p. 22.

in the dark curfew-ridden town, preparing themselves for the joint suicide that seems the only expression left them if Singh and Lee senior are hanged on the morrow.

> The darkness made fearful strides towards them, and they noticed how the candles wasted away, and the flames collapsed and died. But the earth grew light where they stood. Their gifts still made a quivering fire over Rowley's grave, and they felt that it was he who kept their candles alive, that they would burn for ever in a legend which told San Cristobal and the world why they had followed their wish to climb that steep and pitiless cliff which carried the Tribe Boys to their death.
> 'Tomorrow is the trial,' said Bob.
> 'Tomorrow an' maybe till a next tomorrow it last,'
> Singh said.
> 'But hardly more,' said Bob, 'tomorrow an' a next tomorrow.'
> Lee did not speak.
> The curfew rang, ordering every street to be empty. But they would not stir. They sat in silence beside the grave. And the sound reached them again, irrelevant as the noise of the sea, an ordinary part of the night, like the howl of a dog shut out. The Law could not now enter their feeling.[1]

With this grave and beautiful compassion Lamming ends his book. The quality of the boys' grief makes the only gleam in the growing darkness. The return of that planeload has not after all been an irrelevance, but a precipitant. For it was Shepherd who conjured up the false dawn in which he and many others have perished. It was Rowley who taught the boys the meaning of sacrifice. Lamming does not encourage us to speculate about 'what happened next'. For that was to be the subject of his novel of independence, *Season of Adventure*. As the novel of a dying colonialism and the struggle for a new vision of life in the Caribbean, *Of Age and Innocence* stands complete.

Stylistically as well as structurally, it marks a big advance in Lamming's resources as a novelist. He retains the flowing, rhythmic prose he developed in his earlier books, a prose capable of great richness and density of effect. But the range of character and social milieu offered here calls forth dialogue of amazing variety and assurance. The apologetic gropings of Flagstead towards a *real-politik*, Bill's eager blurtings, the hymn-

---

1 *Of Age and Innocence*, pp. 412–13.

like invocations of Shepherd, the fresh intentness of the boys' discoveries, the rambling eloquence of Ma Shepherd and the broken exclamations of Thief and Rockey; these and other scenes offer the whole range of human encounter and language use in San Cristobal. If the theme of return to the islands presents the strongest challenge to the confidence and awareness of the Caribbean writer, it has met its response in these pages.

Part Two

The Continent

Chapter 4
Coastland

'We're reborn into the oldest native, and into our oldest nature.'

Wilson Harris

The literature of Guyana has from its very beginnings displayed its difference from that of the West Indian islands. Whereas the burden of complaint in the latter is a sense of restriction, the former counter-points the theme of restriction by its response to the challenge of a vast and empty interior, blending imperceptibly into the whole landmass of the South American continent.

Although the Guyanese are ethnically, linguistically and culturally akin to the West Indians, with a similar historical experience of slavery, plantation agriculture and prolonged colonial rule, the facts of geography are already beginning to shape a different consciousness. This is as clear in the work of Guyanese painters like Denis and Aubrey Williams and Ronald Savory as it is in that of the writers. The Guyanese who remain in Georgetown or the coastal flatlands, penned in between the seawall and the forest, may suffer from a constriction as narrow as that of the islander. But increasingly Guyana's artists and writers are looking to their own interior for the heroic challenge that the coast seems to refuse. To this extent, the interior provides an imaginative alternative to escape overseas, though it remains sadly true that eventually Guyana's established artists tend to make their imaginative voyages up-country from the interior of a London studio.

Guyana, with an area equalling Great Britain's and the most devious of communications, contains only three-quarters of a million people. In such an environment it is hardly surprising if nature sometimes appears to determine man. For the Caribbean islander only the ocean displays genuine magnitude and grandeur; to climb the highest of one's mountains is but to behold the ocean on all sides instead of one. But to the Guyanese everything in his familiar landscape enjoys a certain magnificence of scale, from the slow brown rivers and wide savannahs of the coastland to the forests and waterfalls of the middle reaches and, beyond these, the high cold plateaux and rough mountains of the remote interior. So the poet Slade Hopkinson reads lessons of unity and magnanimity in the great Essequibo River, whose waters link every race and corner of a divided land:

> Men of my time and country stand rebuked by
> The self-fulfilment of big rivers. . . .
>
> Your main and tributary waters branched
> But homogeneous, like all human blood,
> My Essequibo!
>
> Blood will be paid in full for blood, when finally
> Holy imagination dies, and intellect
> Collapses, impaled on its splintered crutches.
> Let me not think of that.
>
>   Look! Where the river
> Stacks its alluvial beach, the boys are managing
> The rainbow resurrections of their kites
> In the blue estuary of the Trades.[1]

Where the literature of the islands presents various segments of a cycle that always begins outwards, with a movement towards the world beyond the seas, the Guyanese writer turns his back upon the ocean and begins the daunting conquest of the great brooding land before him.

But first he must learn to know the shape and feel of the coastland, where Guyana's immigrant races first settled and where most of them still live. Thus Edgar Mittelholzer's first novel *Corentyne Thunder* (1941), which is also the first serious work of Guyanese literature, opens out before us the canefields and ricelands, the dykes and polders of the Corentyne Coast. The basic rhythm of this novel is the creak and rumble of a donkey-

---

1 Private MS.

cart, moving endlessly along a dusty road to the horizon. Here there is all the time in the world, because there is all the space; man in such a landscape can afford to be prodigal of both:

> He saw the cows, a group of moving spots, headed for their pen and getting smaller as they went. He could smell their dung mingled with the iodine in the air. He could see the tiny mud-house with its dry palm-leaf roof, where he and Beena and Kattree lived. It stood far off, a mere speck. Kattree must be boiling rice and salt-fish. In his mind he could see her squatting before the mud furnace, quiet and engrossed in her task.[1]

But even twenty years later, when the literature of Guyana stood poised to begin its exploration of the heartland, the journey must still begin at the coast, in the areas of settlement and population. It is from his house 'high and alone in the flat brooding countryside' that Donne, in Wilson Harris's *Palace of the Peacock* (1960), begins his amazing voyage towards the sources of being upriver. And Jan Carew's hero 'Shark', in *Black Midas* (1958), grows to manhood within sight and murmur of the sea, though it is the diamond-hunting interior that breaks and makes him in the end.

The key works in the literary discovery of Guyana are the first four novels of Wilson Harris, known as the Guiana Quartet. Each book selects a different landscape for the enactment of its rite. *Palace of the Peacock*, which challenges the ultimate mysteries of the land and the folk, is essentially a novel of the interior and belongs to the following chapter. The second book, *The Far Journey of Oudin* (1961), is a novel of the ricelands, so jealously guarded by their frail dykes, and of the East Indian farmers who work them. *The Whole Armour* (1962) moves to the very margin of land and sea, the seawall where Abram builds his hut; and to the answering margin of the wide Pomeroon River, where Magda sets her house. In this novel it is water, the element of rebirth, which dominates throughout, whereas in *The Far Journey* it was land, with its stubborn ancient aura of struggle, death and inheritance. Finally, in *The Secret Ladder* (1963), Harris places the perpetual contest between land and water at the very centre of his plot.

This novel may serve as an example of the way in which the

---

1 *Corentyne Thunder* (London, Secker & Warburg, 1941), p. 2.

personality of one of Harris's characters can be transformed and given new knowledge of itself by the force of a strange landscape, which releases upon him the charge of all its ancient dreams and sufferings.

Russell Fenwick, the hydrographic surveyor, represents the new scientific control of water, which threatens to drown with its lakes and dams the land held along the Canje river by the ancient Poseidon and his followers. Poseidon, descendant or living exemplar of the runaway black slaves who settled long ago on the banks of the river, reminds us by his name that the Greek deity was not just the god of ocean, he was god also of the immemorial equilibrium between water and land. This equilibrium is expressed in Poseidon's joint occupations of fisherman and farmer. His figure as fisherman is portrayed with elemental power when Fenwick encounters him. Here Poseidon *is* the Canje in drought, as well as all those who depend on it for life:

> He appeared somehow a more shrunken figure than Fenwick had realized when he first saw him. He was as dry as a gnarled stump which had lost its ruling submersion and element in the drought of the river. His ancient feet—webbed with grass and muck—were bare . . . and his hands were wreathed in a fisherman's writhing net of cord (all twined veins and knuckles with which he moved his fingers in a constant wrestling movement) . . . the living cords seemed to grow along his arms and body until they turned matted as thick hairy straw upon his chest— and on the black nipple over his heart—where his shirt was half-open from throat to waist.[1]

Harris has pitched his novel at the point where savannah and forest meet, 'perhaps thirty miles from the coast as the crow flies', and at the point also where everything is determined by the rise and fall of the river, dictated by the whims of a distant, hidden climate in the higher reaches. It is this movement of waters that Fenwick, with his liberal humanism and scientific training, is trying to measure. Poseidon will prevent him if he can, for magic and myth have no meeting-point with scientific benevolence. The river itself is the secret ladder, leading every man towards self-knowledge:

He liked to think of all the rivers of Guiana as the curious rungs

---

1 *The Secret Ladder* (London, Faber, 1963), pp. 48–9.

in a ladder on which one sets one's musing foot again and again, to climb into the past and the future of the continent of mystery . . .

The Canje was one of the lowest rungs in the ladder of ascending purgatorial rivers, the blackest river one could imagine.[1]

The old equilibrium, expressed by Poseidon, was not static; it was a constant shifting struggle between the elements, in the midst of which man established his perilous existence. But it was a struggle rich in meaning, since man in his own nature partook of and reflected it. The static control of environment represented by Fenwick will offer no significance to man except the dangerous spectacle of his own mastery. The strange feelings of terror and moral confusion which assail Fenwick during this expedition are a kind of last sortie by the forces of myth and mystery before they are driven further into the interior. Quoting Boris Pasternak, Wilson Harris shows us man as

> Eternity's hostage,
> Captive to time

The old environment, dynamic and complex, was continually leading man towards the recognition of his dual role in time and eternity. His true stature derives from this recognition; arrogance about his mastery of the here and now can only destroy him.

Yet Cristo in *The Whole Armour* expresses with a passion equal to Poseidon's the anger of the young at the sight of their precious soil washing out to sea with the untamed rivers. The old order contains elements of resignation as well as struggle, but there can be no resignation in the fight against the sea which is a condition of life in coastal Guyana. Not only does the sea continually gnaw at the defences of the low-lying fields, but it receives gigantic tribute from the interior in the silt which discolours it to the horizon. Cristo speaks for all those who are maddened by the fatalism of the immigrant, who has not yet grasped the relationship between himself and what sustains him:

> our *black* parents and capitalists (sometimes they're as white as snow) don't know the instability of their own earth and soil, I tell you, which *we* are now beginning to sense and find out. . . .

---

1 *Ibid.*, pp. 19–20.

What do you think they say when it happens, when the crops run away? They shrug and say they're expendable crops. They can't begin to see that it's *us*, our blood, running away all the time, in the river and in the sea, everywhere, staining the bush . . .[1]

And it is pre-eminently in the figure of Cristo that an eternally returning mythic power coexists with a modern concern and awareness. If Cristo partakes of the nature of Christ, of death and its jaguar-mask, of the sacrificed and sacrificing Son, he is also a modern Guyanese with the vocabulary of education and awareness at his command.

This same Janus quality distinguishes the entire plot of *The Whole Armour*, Harris's third novel. It may stand as our example of his coastland novels and of his ability to interweave mythic and modern themes into a single texture. Before looking in detail at the structure and meaning of this novel it will be useful to look at the theory of the fulfilment of character which Harris has put forward in a recent paper:

> The consolidation of character is, to a major extent, the pre-occupation of most novelists who work in the twentieth century within the framework of the nineteenth century novel . . . the rise of the novel in its conventional and historical mould coincides in Europe with states of society which were involved in consolidating their class and other vested interests. As a result 'character' in the novel rests more or less on the self-sufficient individual—on elements of 'persuasion' . . . rather than 'dialogue' or 'dialectic' in the profound and unpredictable sense of person which Martin Buber, for example, evokes. The novel of persuasion rests on grounds of apparent common sense: a certain 'selection' is made by the writer, the selection of items, manners, uniform conversation, historical situations, etc, all lending themselves to build an individual span of life which yields self-conscious and fashionable judgements, self-conscious and fashionable moralities. . . .[2]

Against this conventional conception of character in the novel, Harris advances his 'vision of consciousness', his effort to reach, by fulfilment rather than by consolidation of character, a personality defined by West Indian experience. Rejecting the

---

1 *The Whole Armour* (London, Faber, 1962), p. 110.
2 'Tradition and the West Indian Novel', in *Tradition, the Writer and Society* London, (New Beacon Publications, 1967), pp. 28–9.

belief that the West Indian has no distinct existence apart from the crowd, he writes:

> What in my view is remarkable about the West Indian in depth is a sense of subtle links, the series of subtle and nebulous links which are latent within him, the latent ground of old and new personalities. This is a very difficult view to hold, I grant, because it is not a view which consolidates, which invests in any way in the consolidation of popular character. Rather it seeks to visualize a *fulfilment* of character.[1]

This view of West Indian personality as uniquely if elusively shaped by landscape and historical experience, by 'broken conceptions as well as misconceptions of the residue and meaning of conquest',[2] clearly marks Harris off from a number of other observers. Both M. G. Smith, the Jamaican anthropologist, and V. S. Naipaul appear to believe that the West Indies possess no genuine inner cohesion whatever and no internal source of power. Having no common interests to cement them, the inhabitants of the area can be held together only by external force. Professor Elsa Goveia reaches an opposite but equally depressing conclusion. She argues that the West Indies have had one integrating factor historically, and this has been 'the acceptance of the inferiority of Negroes to whites'.[3] Although she goes on to say that the writers have advanced through their work the idea of a more democratized society, she clearly does not see the image of this integrated West Indian personality as something already inherent in the present. What Harris is saying here is thus of the utmost importance, for whereas the formal innovations he makes in the novel may prove to be widely applicable, the purpose for which he has made them stems directly from the environment of which he writes.

An understanding of his concept of character in the novel as fulfilled rather than consolidated should also assist the reader in his encounter with the books, since one of the main difficulties felt in many of them is the lack of any hard edge around individual character, as well as the lack of any definite location in space and time. Harris deliberately sets us adrift in a stream of experience which mingles fragments of past, present and future in a number of interwoven, mutually reflective lives. The

---

1 *Ibid.*, p. 28.   2 *Ibid.*, p. 31.
3 'The Caribbean: Socio-Cultural Framework', Caribbean Artists Movement, Newsletter 4, 1967, p. 4.

constant fusion, involution and separation of effect may leave the reader standing on very slippery ground indeed; like the coastland of Guyana, he may feel himself penned between an advancing sea and an advancing forest.[1] Yet it is Harris's remarkable sense of Guyana that helps to organize his writing and give it original form. He was for many years a government surveyor in the remote districts and every line of his writing reveals his intimate, loving knowledge of a country which very few Guyanese really know.

If we now turn to *The Whole Armour* we shall see that it begins with an ancient demiurge called Abram who has withdrawn from mankind to live alone on the margin of the sea. In the opening pages Abram dreams of his own imminent death, experiencing the sensation of it and the dismemberment of his body by swooping crows. He resolves to pay one of his rare visits to the village and to the body of Magda, his immemorial lover. But when he arrives he finds Magda obsessed with saving her son Cristo, who is pursued for the alleged murder of a woman. Magda insists that Abram carry Cristo back to the lonely hut and hide him. Already we glimpse a feature common and peculiar to Harris's novels, the way in which all his characters seem to be incestuously related, the way they frequently reflect, inhabit and even become one another. Not only does their free movement in time (deriving from the eternal element within them) make them prototypes and descendants of their living selves, but it lends them a kind of spatial freedom also. Thus when Magda insists that Cristo is Abram's son, and he replies that this cannot be so because he has only recently become her lover, both statements enjoy a portion of truth, for 'Abram could not help recalling the dying and newborn generations of the Pomeroon in his mind's eternal eye.'

The quality of spatial freedom is exemplified a few pages later, when Cristo begins to groan against his restriction in the hut at Jigsaw Bay:

> The derelict premises Abram ruled had no true geographical location Cristo felt, a region of absurd displacement and primitive boredom, the ground of dreams, long-dead ghosts and still-

---

1 The forest is literally advancing, since the early Dutch plantations were all upriver, and these were gradually abandoned in favour of the coastal strip when drainage made this accessible to settlement.

living sailors, ancient masters and mariners and new slaves,
approaching the poor uncharted Guiana coast . . .[1]

The reader, duly warned by such passages, must try to carry
many hints in the mind at once, without seizing upon any one
of them in the hope of eliminating the others. Cristo both is and
is not Abram's son. Likewise, he both is and is not Abram's
murderer when the old man, in the heat of an argument,
suddenly pitches forward stone dead. Cristo takes the canoe
and flees in panic to Magda's house but she drags him back to
the scene of the 'crime' and in a mood of elemental savagery,
forces him at gunpoint to undress the decomposing body of
Abram and exchange clothes with it. Here again, the action
itself sends out ring after ring of echoes. Cristo, finding that the
body has been taken from the hut and dragged a long way into
the savannah, argues that this must be the work of a jaguar.
Yet we learn gradually to associate Cristo himself with the
jaguar, whose hide and claws he later wears during his weeks of
hiding in the forest. It is Magda, the cruel mother-goddess, who
insists that Cristo literally put on the body of Abram's death by
exchanging clothes and identities with him. Officially, Cristo
now ceases to exist (except as the jaguar of death lurking in the
jungles), while Abram is yet again resurrected in the son who
has put on his appearance.

Magda, on the daily level of existence a prostitute, returns to
her house and persuades an obligingly lustful police sergeant to
call off the search for Cristo since he is dead and his murderer,
Abram, fled into the forest. Later she holds a nine-days wake[2]
for Cristo in her house above the black river. In the course of the
wake we learn to see Magda and Abram not only as the parents
of Cristo, but of all Guyana's lost and restless children:

> It meant the rallying of all their forces into an incestuous *persona*
> and image and alliance—the very antithesis of their dark truth
> and history, written in the violent mixture of races that had bred
> them as though their true mother was a wanton on the face of
> the earth and their true father a vagrant and a rogue from
> every continent.[3]

---

1 *Ibid.*, pp. 16–17.
2 A wake held nine days after death. Forty-day wakes are also common in
the Caribbean area. Both customs appear to be an adaptation of West
African 'second burial' ceremonies.
3 *Ibid.*, p. 43.

Now Sharon appears, daughter of a huge knotted man called Peet. Sharon is Cristo's sweetheart, and the crime for which he was pursued now defines itself not as 'woman-murder' but as the killing of Sharon's first lover. Sharon has now acquired yet another fiancé, a young trader called Mattias Gomez. We glimpse that Sharon is, in one dimension and perhaps despite her will, the cruel virgin priestess whose lovers are condemned to slay and replace one another in an endless delusion of possessing her. In the course of the wake Mattias too is killed, struck down by Peet and the drunken crowd in a frenzy of accusation that the young man has committed the rape of Sharon that is forever beyond him. Sharon remains inviolate: leaving her lover to endure his ritual death below, she climbs to the upper floor where Magda has remained aloof throughout the night. Magda's dark flesh is secretly desired by all, men and women alike, for the chosen champion who enjoys it will complete them all by the act. Earlier in the evening Peet, fired and fuddled with rum, had climbed the stair in the hope of fulfilling that role. Magda had smashed his head with his own boot, opening in the wound a frightful vision where Peet feels himself ravished and possessed by the rotten body of Abram. Magda's nails tearing his shirt are the claws of death's jaguar ripping his flesh. And Cristo, springing newborn from the wound in his head, turns to strip the clothing from the stinking carcase Peet has become. So Peet becomes almost a substitute for the body at Jigsaw Bay and we understand that Abram's rotting body on the strand, clad in Cristo's clothes, is the tomb from which the newborn spirit rises and, after forty days in the wilderness, will at length return to the world. Peet has merely been used by a part of that process. Now the presence of Cristo, striped and fanged like death itself, hovers about the dark fringes of the wake, filling it with fears and rumours.

Sharon too, like all Magda's spiritual children, feels the magnetic attraction of her body. Tremulous as a bride, she ascends the stairs to confront:

> Cristo's mother, feline, devouring, incestuous, implacable, the inordinate lust of the hermaphrodite of the species . . .[1]

Magda, consumed with jealousy of Sharon's youth and soft

---

1 *Ibid.*, p. 74.

beauty, nevertheless shows her a love-letter from Cristo. The letter tells her that he is alive and is soon coming to take her. For a moment Sharon flirts with the idea of betraying him to Mattias, so that the police may seize him. At last, however, she is ready to reject her role of virgin cruelty and be possessed. In anticipation of Cristo's love, it is the powerful, tawny presence of Magda which embraces her. And her cry of ecstasy at the penetration of that presence mingles with the death-cry of Mattias rising at the same instant from the floor below.

From here we jump instantly to the scene in which Cristo actually possesses Sharon in the depths of the forest. It is three weeks later, the very night when Cristo's forty-day wake should be celebrated, when Sharon wakes to a mysterious summons and, leaving her spent old father sleeping in the house, steals out into the darkness to meet her lover. Once again at the very moment of possession, she glimpses the hiding mother in the son; once again she senses that Magda, the 'compulsive fantastic whore', is the complement of her own stubborn virginity. But we are now ready to encounter Sharon as a modern Guyanese girl, convent-bred in Port of Spain, rather than a virgin priestess reeking of cruelty and blood. The drugging weight of mythic function and association seems to be sliding away from the lovers as they make their way back to the farmhouse in the light of dawn and sit upon the verandah drinking coffee. As they talk, we learn that Peet has hanged himself during the night and is lying dead in the inner room. Magda too, according to Cristo's account, is diminished and become like a child again. Force and vigour appear to be passing to the young, and their love for each other extinguishes any incestuous link with their parents. But Cristo has decided to give himself up. It is of a piece with the new sense of responsibility that also makes him say:

> we're *hundreds of years* older than they dream to be. . . . Because we have begun to see ourselves in the earliest grass-roots, in the first tiny seed of spring—the ancestral tide and spring of Jigsaw Bay. . . . We're reborn into the oldest native and into our oldest nature, while they're still Guiana's first aliens and arrivals.[1]

It is of a piece with the sense of national history that made him

---

1 *Ibid.*, p. 108.

dream a whole carnival of Guyana's Amerindian past while he was wandering in the jungle. His spirit is now tending towards freedom, a freedom of which death is only the simulacrum. It is this which gives meaning to his decision to submit himself to legal vengeance. As he lies dreaming with his head in Sharon's lap he hears his child, to be born a year hence, crowing within her to announce the hour of his father's execution. Yet when the distraught Magda, bursting in upon the lovers, implores him to flee before the police close in, he is listless, and she can only exclaim with piercing truth 'you' face look really dead'. For Cristo has at last understood the meaning of death as a temporary refuge, but one which cannot be avoided, one which finally prepares us for freedom:

> *Death can never be a perfect fortress.* Just a trick he wanted to cry, an eternal dumb trick whereby one could gain a little time to fight the appearance of hell. Gain time, yes, but not eternity. One's spirit had to meet the sun in the long run, absolutely free. Make its declaration to all the other spirits of light.[1]

So there is no despair when the armed men close in upon the house, for the young have prepared their sacrifice and the old have already dwindled to a shell. Cristo is ready to put on the whole armour of God.

Among the shifting qualities of Harris's plots, one anchoring factor is the great force of personality which drives through his characters, despite their tendency, along the plane of eternal being, to merge and mingle with one another. This force is often expressed in the earthy vigour of their speech, which contrasts violently with the author's complex discriminations on their behalf. For instance, after the weird encounter between Peet and Magda at the wake, when Peet is still sickened and bewildered by his vivid sensation of having become one with Abram's rotting carcase, Magda briskly says to him:

> 'Don't shame if you feel bad. Remember not a soul downstairs see what happen. If they *hear* you fall they believe me and you been having fun. Fool them and satisfy them. I don't care two dam' '[2]

---

1 *Ibid.*, p. 105.   2 *The Whole Armour*, p. 54.

Now fun is scarcely what we associate with Peet's recent experience, but the salty tone of the speech does restore a sort of sanity to the encounter.

Too often, however, Harris's desire to make every statement complex or ambivalent leads to writing which the mind cannot comprehend. Harris started as a poet and his poetry, despite the startling beauty of many lines, exhibits the same tendency to overwork language. In his prose he does not merely offer metaphors, but bunches of deliberately conflicting verbs or objects which sometimes refuse to illuminate or assist each other. An example will suffice:

> The trunk of triumphant prosperity became—in this context—a recurring fate and epitaph rather than the ascension of everlasting thanksgiving.[1]

No conceivable reading of 'trunk' prepares us for either 'fate' or 'epitaph', still less for 'ascension'. Here the reader is left outside Harris's meaning, unable to enter.

Another novelist of the coastland, Jan Carew, is as different from Wilson Harris as it is possible to be. Carew is a storyteller who always keeps his narrative moving briskly and by uncomplicated paths to a clear and simple conclusion. For Harris the stages of any Guyana journey, the river voyages, portages and treks, are also metaphors for man's spiritual journey towards self-knowledge and freedom. For Carew they have reverberation enough in themselves, for he is genuinely excited by the life and landscape of this elusive Eldorado. His first novel, *Black Midas*, is weakened by melodramatic twists of plot and an over-insistent moral shaping of the tale. But *The Wild Coast*, which is simply the story of a boyhood spent in a lonely part of the Corentyne, conveys a sense of place which is real and haunting. For Carew, as for Harris, the land of Guyana still groans for the deeds of conquest, enslavement, blood and violence which have unrolled upon it. Something of that ancient violence has sunk into the soil and lies there brooding, ever ready to spring forth and dominate the present. The killings and burnings which disfigured the early 1960's are not hard to reconcile with such a belief, which Mittelholzer, a son of New Amsterdam, seems also to have shared. A night scene in *The*

---

1 *Ibid.*, p. 93.

Wild Coast will convey something of this quality in Carew. Tarlogie is a settlement of scattered reefs and ridges set among undrained swamps where alligators still abound:

> It was moonlight in Tarlogie. The surf was quiet and the wind barely ruffled the surface of clear patches of water in the swamp. A moonstruck dog was howling in one of Chinaman's kennels and Caya was knocking up a one-three rhythm on his shango drum, preparing for the wind-dance. Most of the villagers were sitting on their rickety doorsteps gaffing in broken cadences. Cartmen on their way to the Port Mourant market shouted greetings as they rumbled by on the public road . . . Palm fronds wet with dew gleamed and rustled in cold spasms. A piper owl, the sweetest of all singing birds, fluted its song high up in a po-boy tree.
>
> Hector sat on the front porch recapturing the feel of the village after his stay in Georgetown. Sister sat close by him in her rocking chair and she said:
>
> 'The piper owl's an old higue bird.'
>
> 'How can an old higue bird sing so sweetly, Sister?'
>
> 'The voices of the damned always does sound sweet, boy. Why you think that old bird does always sing sad songs? I will tell you why, it's because the souls of dead planters does live inside them.'
>
> 'Was my grandpa a planter, Sister?'
>
> 'When I say planter, I mean them old, bad Dutch planters. Those that used to bury their gold in old sea chests, and then kill a slave so that his spirit could stand watch over the gold. Them old planters was greedy men, men with stony hearts where pity never had a place to lay its head. On nights like this when the wind is high you can hear the slaves crying out over the swamp and the piper owl does sing songs over them to mock them.[1]

The physical geography of the coastland, with its ubiquitous canals, dykes and khokers, its vast green canefields and ruined sugar-mills, breathes inescapable reminders of the eighteenth century slave plantations of the old Dutch colonies. Only in the far interior can such reminders be avoided. For there the continental theme sounds more strongly, and the surviving pockets of Amerindians speak rather of an ancient Siberian pilgrimage than of the chains and slave-ships of the distant coast.

---

1 *The Wild Coast* (London, Secker & Warburg, 1958), pp. 130–1.

Chapter 5
Heartland

*Time is the harbour that men must build in each moment
that this village flows from death to life:*

Wilson Harris

Under the high canopy of the equatorial forest there are no
seasons. In an atmosphere always moist, still and separate from
the outer world, life follows a perpetual unbroken cycle of
growth, fulfilment and decay. But one step out of the forest
into the savannah brings us into a world where seasons are as
dramatically manifest as in the temperate zones. At the height
of the dry season all is tawny and dusty gold, where it is not
blackened by the passage of fire. Even the trees may be bare of
leaves, while grasses and small plants stand gaunt and empty of
sap or lie exhausted on the cracked earth. But at the first
shower of the long rains pale delicate shoots appear everywhere; soon wild flowers appear among the springing grasses,
while the trees lose their weary look and fill their branches with
leaves and birds. Here seasonal death and rebirth are expressed
as dramatically as in the winter and spring of the North, and
life awaits the rain as breathlessly as elsewhere it expects the
thaw.

Wilson Harris's long sojourn in the Guyanese interior has
made him an equal participant in the worlds of forest and
savannah, the first expressing eternity and the perpetual flux
of life, while the second speaks of season and the limited
mortality of individual plant or tree. His poetry shows how
long he has brooded upon the power of this contrast, which
embraces the dual fate of man, who must die in season and seek
freedom in eternity. The great uniting river of time flows
through all things, stemming from eternal sources and seeking
an oceanic repose, it rolls the bodies of the dead over and over

till they are rounded like pebbles. This is the imaginative geography of Harris's *Palace of the Peacock*, as it is of Africa. Indeed, the African parallels to much of Harris's thought and imagery are remarkable. The River Congo plays in the poetry of Tchicaya U Tam'si the very role allotted to the Mazaruni or the Canje in the work of this Guyanese novelist whose veins mingle the blood of many races. Gazing into the waters of the Congo, U Tam'si sees there all the dead of his race rolled impartially towards oblivion. Struck by the sun, they have already died their second death and are ready to enter the great reservoir of the sea to which all energy must return. In the last lines the poet searches for the evidence of their rebirth, expressed in their 'absence' from the perishing body:

> twice they died
> shameful because the sun was a demon
> > against them
> they are dead
> the river gives them justice and mixes with salt
> their bodies their souls
> I see in the deep, red within black,
> the shapes of their mummies stinking the putrid water
> . . .
> I think only
> that my head is rounded
> from rolling only
> on your body
> on your body
> on your body
> at the whim of my torments
> oh sea!
> not feeling the graze of any tree's bark
> on these dirty sores at my temples
> they are dead
> by what signs shall I know when their
> > destiny dawns
> the free river which will carry their absence
> > to the sea?[1]

To understand just how striking are the similarities here to the system of ideas which Harris employs in *Palace of the Peacock*, it will be necessary to look in some detail at the way he relates

---

1 *Epitomé* (Tunis, Pierre Jean Oswald, 1962), pp. 28–9. Author's translation.

them to the successive stages of his river-journey towards the spiritual Eldorado of the interior. Harris begins his great novel with the figure of the horseman Donne, whose hard, bright energy is so expressive of self-will that we scarcely need the superscription from Yeats, 'Horseman, pass by!', to reinforce it. In these opening pages Harris writes with a brilliant clarity matching the nature of Donne, quite different from the wavering, dissolving style he employs soon afterwards when the voyage upriver begins. Donne expresses all that side of the narrator's personality which strives to dominate others and to drive a sharp distinctive self through the world.

Donne observes that he has almost forgotten the existence of his 'brother and twin'. Intent upon the domination of others, he has long lived alone in his 'high hanging house' above the savannahs. The narrator says of him, 'he was myself standing outside of me, while I stood inside of him.'[1] He is associated with the sun, whose light is blinding and terrible but not true:

> 'I've learnt,' he waved his hands at the savannahs, 'to rule *this*. This is the ultimate, this is everlasting. One doesn't have to see deeper than that, does one?' He stared at me hard as death. 'Rule the land,' he said, 'while you still have a ghost of a chance. And you rule the world. Look at the sun.' His dead eye blinded mine. 'Look at the sun,' he cried in a stamping terrible voice.[2]

On the novel's first page Donne has been shot dead by his illtreated mistress Mariella, but this is only his first death, the opportunity to begin a journey of self-discovery before his second, final death can gather him into eternity. The narrator admits that Donne's 'dead seeing material eye' still dominates his own 'living closed spiritual eye' and has become 'the only remaining window on the world for me.' For the time being he is content to ignore his inner vision and to follow the forceful, material, wilful part of himself whose physical death he has just witnessed. For death does not in itself confer freedom, but the possibility of freedom. The first death only enables us to begin the search for that abandonment of self, that second death, in which freedom will be realized. Harris had already expressed

---

1 *Palace of the Peacock* (London, Faber, 1960), p. 29.
2 *Ibid.*, p. 19.

his vision of death as the threshold to unity of being in a poem published six years earlier:

> So he must die to be free.
> Solid or uprooted in pain, his bright limbs
> must yield their glorious intentions to the secret
> root of the heart. And musing waters dart
> like arrows of memory over him, a visionary . . .[1]

The twin personality of Donne-narrator now begins a mysterious river journey. Its ostensible purpose is to enable Donne to extend his rule over the elusive people of the interior, the 'folk.' The boat is crewed by other linked personalities whose racial intermixture and incestuous connections suggest that they represent the human family of Guyana, perhaps of all mankind. All have died their first death, drowned in the great falls below Sorrow Hill on an earlier expedition. The immediate goal of the present journey is Mariella, which has now ceased to be a person and become a place, a remote Amerindian mission where the falls and rapids begin. Yet when they reach the mission the people have fled and they must pursue them further, for they are in pursuit of the folk, of Guyana's hidden collective self. The search must take them beyond finite time, into a landscape peopled only by themselves and their visions. It is this aspect of their journey that Derek Walcott has so brilliantly captured in his poem 'The Voyage Up River':

> Stillborn in death, their memory is not ours,
> In whom the spasm of birth
>
> Gendered oblivion. To chart empty savannahs,
> Rivers, even with a guide, conceives an earth
>
> Without us, without gods:[2]

As the journey progresses above Mariella it becomes a re-exploration of all time and experience, a reliving of the seven days of creation, a return to the very source of that river which flows 'from death to life'. At this stage the second deaths begin, thinning the ranks of the boatmen day by day as each linked personality eliminates his twin-self or becomes one with it. Thus on the first day the negro Carroll falls overboard and is drowned. Carroll is the son of the old man Schomburgh (per-

---

1 'Troy', *Eternity to Season* (British Guiana, 1954), p. 7.
2 'The Voyage Up River', *The Castaway*, p. 50.

haps incestuously begotten) and the half-brother of Vigilance, the Amerindian bowman. Schomburgh, released from the tension of his relationship with Carroll, now dies in his sleep and is buried below a waterfall. Jennings, the engineman, makes a vicious attack upon the man called Cameron, to whom he is linked in some indefinable fashion. On the second day Wishrop, a murderer in his earlier existence, is accidentally dragged from the boat and instantly picked clean by the darting perai, the savage carnivorous fish of these waters. The boat itself is now wrecked 'in the stream of rock' but mysteriously continues its voyage as a kind of geological skeleton within it. On the third day da Silva stabs and kills Cameron, who has been taunting and goading him. Da Silva is a part-Portuguese crewman whose twin-self has become a wavering and fitful presence among them since they left Mariella. This twin seems to be merely an image or reflection of da Silva's own fear of death; his presence or absence in the boat mirrors da Silva's own state of mind:

> His reflection was the frailest shadow of a former self. His bones were splinters and points . . . and his flesh was newspaper, drab, wet until the lines and markings had run fantastically together. His hair stood flat on his brow like ink. He nodded precariously and one marvelled how he preserved his appearance without disintegrating into soggy lumps and patches when the wind blew and rocked the pins of his bones a little . . . da Silva stared at the apparition his brother presented as a man would stare at a reporter who had returned from the grave with no news whatsoever of a living return.[1]

Also on the third day, Vigilance becomes more and more involved and intermingled with the old Arawak woman who has appeared amongst them since leaving Mariella. This involvement causes him to have a sensation of being high up above the river, clinging to the wall of rock and looking down upon the vessel in which he and the others are sailing. He is both within and outside himself as he moves towards the fulfilment of his second death.

The old woman appears to embody the immemorial Guyanese folk they are pursuing. Her body merges with the rocks and spray of the river about them; she becomes

---

1 *Palace of the Peacock*, p. 123.

mysteriously young and alluring, gathering them all into a symbolic rape of herself which confirms them as her children and her lovers:

> Tiny embroideries resembling the handwork on the Arawak woman's kerchief and the wrinkles on her brow turned to incredible and fast soundless breakers of foam. Her crumpled bosom and river grew agitated with desire, bottling and shaking every fear and inhibition and outcry. The ruffles in the water were her dress rolling and rising to embrace the crew . . .[1]

In her arms Vigilence learns to follow 'the muse of love' to the very top of the sky, where he awaits the fulfilment of the others. Now he sees that what looked to da Silva like the eye of a parrot and to Cameron like that of a vulture (thus occasioning their fatal quarrel) is in reality the eye of God. Imprisoned in the stream of rock, his old companions see only delusions or reminders of the past, but Vigilance sees:

> the blue ring of pentecostal fire in God's eye as it wheeled around him above the dreaming memory and prison of life . . .[2]

Meanwhile the fourth day has brought no more deaths, but Donne has to fight with increasing desperation to keep his dwindling crew together. Vigilance, the Arawak woman and the da Silva twin have now finally vanished from the craft. On the fifth day the boat reaches the foot of a huge waterfall. The crew abandon her and, consisting now only of Donne, Jennings and da Silva, begin to climb up the crazy ladders which are pinned to the sheer face of the rock. Donne peers through a window in the rock and sees the gentle luminous figure of the young carpenter, Christ. Through a higher window he glimpses the mother with a manger for her infant's crib. But Donne and his companions are shut out; damned by their obstinate self-will, by their acts of violence and oppression, they flatten their noses against the rock in their efforts to peer into the room. Jennings, whose wrist was injured in the fight with Cameron, is the first to fall. Soon afterwards Donne knows that he is 'truly blind at last'. His turbulent, masterful, material self is ready for its second death:

> The burning pain he felt suddenly in his eye extended down his face and along the column of his neck until it branched into

---

1 *Ibid.*, p. 73.   2 *Ibid.*, p. 116.

nerves and limbs. . . . He trembled as he saw himself inwardly melting into nothingness and into the body of his death. . . . A singular thought always secured him to the scaffolding. It was the unflinching clarity with which he looked into himself and saw that all his life he had loved no-one but himself . . .[1]

After their long climb Donne and da Silva hammer in vain upon the rock. For them there is no admittance and they fall. Now it is the face of earth itself on which Donne finds himself lying and hammering. And it is da Silva who opens for him. It is the dawn of the sixth day:

> da Silva stood within the door in the half-shadow. He looked old and finished and beaten to death after his great fall. . . . His mouth gaped in a smile and his teeth protruded half-broken and smashed. The high bones still stood in his face as when he had signalled their downfall. . . . da Silva was shivering and shaking cold as death. Indeed he had never been so bitterly cold.[2]

As the seventh day breaks we find outselves at 'the top of the sky' with Vigilance and the narrator. The latter has apparently been absent from the story ever since he surendered his will to Donne during the voyage. Now, like Vigilance, he sees that the wall of rock is in reality a palace, and that the windows of the palace are crowded with faces. There he sees again Carroll and Schomburgh, the vanished da Silva twin who has escaped his brother's fate and the slain Cameron, and Wishrop, whose skeleton was last seen wheeling and dancing in the foam of the river. Carroll is whistling, a strange creating music which flows over everything. The narrator now understands that 'this was the palace of the universe and the windows of the soul looked out and in'. He understands that 'Carroll whistled to all who had lost love in the world. This was his humorous whimsical sadness.' Perhaps he whistled for those who fell and vanished through the door of earth. For those now within the palace there is only the sensation of infinite lightness and freedom. Where there was opposition of selves there is now fulfilment. Their journey is over, and they have no more need of the masks they have abandoned:

> Each of us now held at last in his arms what he had been forever seeking and what he had eternally possessed.[3]

---

1 *Ibid.*, p. 140.   2 *Ibid.*, p. 142.   3 *Ibid.*, p. 146.

In the years since it appeared Harris's novel has gradually made its way to a commanding place in the sensibility of the modern Caribbean. Artists, poets, historians and novelists have alike been haunted by its imagery. Despite obscurities of language that are occasionally impenetrable, despite the over-working of words like 'musing' and 'dreaming' in the interests of casting the reader adrift, *Palace of the Peacock* abounds in those insights and unifying flashes of illumination which Wilson Harris uniquely offers to the persevering reader. Every fresh reading of the book is a pilgrimage in which we relive Harris's vision of Guyana's history, his intimate interpretation of landscape and his longing to liberate man from the dialectics of hatred imposed on him by time and circumstance. Savannah and forest, mountain and waterfall, have interacted with a profoundly reflective temperament and a passion for spiritual truth to produce a masterpiece.

Part Three
The City

Chapter 6
Outcasts

Castries' Conway and Brixton in London,
Port of Spain's jungle
and Kingston's dry Dungle
Chicago Smethwick and Tiger Bay

Edward Brathwaite

The city setting of Edgar Mittelholzer's novel *A Morning at the Office*, discussed in Chapter One, is implicit only, since the action of the book itself is confined entirely to the office and we see the behaviour of its characters only as this manifests itself within the office. The first writer to plunge us into the stream of West Indian city life was the Jamaican artist and novelist Roger Mais, who died in 1955. Mais is pre-eminently the novelist of Kingston, the largest city of the former British West Indies and one of the largest in the entire Caribbean area. Indeed, Kingston is the only West Indian city which has yet produced a distinctive literature of its own. To taste the unique quality of Port of Spain we must turn to the calypso rather than the novel. Trinidadian literature has been on the whole surprisingly rural in quality, considering the overwhelmingly urban impression which that island makes upon the visitor arriving from other areas of the West Indies. Apart from Naipaul's *Miguel Street* and a few plays, it is difficult to think of any Trinidadian works which are entirely urban in setting. The self-enclosed Hindu world from which both Selvon's Tiger and Naipaul's Mr. Biswas eventually make their individual escape has its greatest strength in the villages and country towns of the island. It is no accident that the rickety house which the indefatigable Biswas finally secures and in which, covered with debt, he dies, is situated in Port of Spain and is tied up with his new occupation as a journalist writing in English.

Mais is distinguished among the more important West Indian novelists in having spent the greater part of his adult life within the area. He was intimately involved in the whole upsurge of feeling, far more than merely political, which swept from island to island during the late 1930's and made inevitable the acceleration of self-rule during the following decade. He himself went to prison in 1944 for denouncing in the local press Winston Churchill's grim warning that Britain's war for freedom had nothing to do with the liberation of the colonial subjects who were also fighting in it. Like V. S. Reid, therefore, Mais is able to write of West Indian life out of an adult experience and participation; he is not confined to memories of childhood and youth, terminating in a more or less final departure for the world beyond. His own years of wandering lay fairly late in his life, as did his important activity as a writer. Mais, who was born in 1905, published his first novel in 1953 and followed it with two others before his death two years later.

His world is the streets and 'yards' of West Kingston, the turbulent slumland which is in permanent, sullen rebellion against the flashy bourgeois society whose wealth and leisure are displayed along its very fringes. It is a world in which violence seems not arbitrary but endemic, one of the few accessible means of hitting back at the system which confines one to a life without hope. Love exists in this world, even tenderness, but their existence is even more precarious than outside. Imprisonment, violent death and infidelity all take their toll, spreading their attentions impartially over the loved and the unloved. The 'yard', a patch of earth with a standpipe and perhaps a log to sit on, is the stage upon which these cramped, defeated lives emerge to play out their daily dramas of flirtation, ribaldry, defiance and hate. It is a pool into which every emotion and activity is poured without distinction, for there is scarcely room in the narrow rented rooms that surround it to eat, to make love or to die.

Mais was a poor dramatist, but the dramatic elements in his first novel, *The Hills Were Joyful Together* (1953) do not consist only in the stage-like use of its yard setting, with glimpses of a more 'private' life through the doors and windows opening upon it, but also in the long exchanges of dialogue between a constantly varied selection of its inhabitants. Mais even begins his book with a cast-list and follows this with a description of the yard which amounts to a stage direction. The choice of a cast which embraces whores, card-sharpers, thieves, layabouts and drunkards is not without its twin dangers of patronage and sentimentality. Errol John's play *Moon on a Rainbow Shawl*, which confines itself to a similar cast and setting, certainly does not avoid the latter danger, perhaps because its characters are all too quintessential of the West Indian situation. This almost robs them of the possibility of surprising us by opening the hidden corners of their lives; we know at once what they are and largely how they will behave. With Mais's characters, however, we have said nothing when we have said 'whore' or 'card-sharper'. In this sense they are the very opposite of stagey. And because they all retain the capacity to surprise, because they retain through all their suffering and degradation something of their autonomy as human beings, Mais manages to remain completely inside his story. A setting of this kind may be chosen by writers in search of folk-authenticity or of a sanction for their political radicalism. In such cases they can hardly avoid calling attention to their astonishing knowledge of low life, or wagging an invisible finger at their comfortable readers. Because the characters in Mais are so abundantly alive he avoids these perils also.

The inhabitants of the yard in *The Hills Were Joyful Together* may be divided into those who accept their lot with a certain amount of philosophy and those who seek to escape it through drink, sex, evangelical religion or crime. Prominent among the first group is Ras, the angular, bearded Rastafarian barrow-pusher who is the yard's only peacemaker. The others either seek or avoid trouble, but seldom attempt to quell it. Ras makes his presence and his values felt gradually as the plot advances, as acts of folly or violence involve more and more of the yard-dwellers in tragedy. The group of active escapists is dominated by Surjue, a man whose sense of right and wrong may not accord with that of the law but who possesses nonetheless a particular kind of personal integrity and valour. Surjue and his woman Rema are deeply in love, but he is restless and looking for a break. His gambling crony Flitters finally induces him to go on a 'job' and, when the police catch them on the roof, runs off leaving Surjue to take the rap. Angry though Surjue is with Flitters, he refuses to tell the police the names of any of his accomplices. To do so would be to violate his own curious sense of honour, but he has no qualms about arranging for Flitters to be hunted down and murdered by his underworld acquaintances. The same unyielding defiance attracts terrible treatment upon Surjue after his conviction, making him the favourite victim of the more sadistic warders. Hearing that Rema is going mad in her loneliness, Surjue resolves to escape and see her. Again he is unlucky; just as he is about to haul himself to the top of the wall he is shot and killed by the guards:

> He hung suspended another instant, and then he seemed just to let go all he had won so desperately . . . fell back with a thud on the ground below.
> He fell spread-eagled on his back and lay still.
> A scudding, shapeless mass of flimsy clouds drew over the face of the moon. The stars put out again.
> A dog howled in the darkness outside the wall.
> He lay on his back, his arms flung wide, staring up at the silent unequivocal stars.[1]

Surjue's death ends a novel whose small cast has already been ravaged by similar tragedies, many of them resulting from heedlessness or from the violence which continually wells up in their random relationships. Surjue never knows that Rema has died before him, burned helplessly in a fire she herself has started in a crazy effort to drive off her delusions. Surjue's own escape plan had involved the deliberate starting of a fire to panic the warders and set them running in the wrong direction. Despite this sardonic coincidence, Mais does not appear to invoke a Hardyesque fate to account for such things. They simply happen, especially to those who court disaster like Surjue by trying to make their own rules.

He is often at his best in such sequences of rapid action as that leading up to Surjue's death, or to the murder of Flitters in a dark alleyway, ending all his frantic efforts at escape:

> He slumped to one side, and pitched like that across the open garbage box, reeking with its three-days sour garbage smell.
> The lower part of his body kicked and bucked, spasmodically. He was still conscious. With the third strike Crawfish sent the six-inch blade through his back up to the hilt.
> Baju came round in front and split the skull open with his blackjack. It gaped, and the grey matter, streaked with blood, spilled out.
> They left him there and walked, unhurried, down the dark lane.[2]

---

1 *The Hills Were Joyful Together* in *Three Novels of Roger Mais*, p. 288.
2 *Ibid.*, p. 234.

King Street, Kingston, and the Blue Mountains, Jamaica

In a Jamaican village

Arrival at Victoria Station, London

'The high canopy of the equatorial forest'

An Ibo forest village

The beach at Jamestown, Accra, Ghana

Acoli grasslands in Northern Uganda

The fusillades of dialogue that fly around the standpipe and the chopping-block also show Mais full of controlled energy and a fine instinct for the motions of these lives that refuse to be as cramped as their surroundings. Here two boys are talking outside the yard. Manny has so far manifested himself as nothing but a cruel bully. He is still that, yet is as far in love as his bruised nature will permit. For a brief while the lout is in subjection to the lover:

'Manny, you know somep'n, you got your hands full.'

'I know it man, I know it.'

'She wouldn't even look your way.'

'I know that too, but it don't make no difference. It's not a thing you can control, ever—your feelin's about a woman, I guess.'

'You know, you got the same force-ripeness in you still? Only different now. A bit worse, I should say.'

'Yeah? Well, if it be so it just happened, an' that's all.'

'I don't get it. I don't get it at all. The last bloody thing I'd figure for you.'

'I didn't figure it either, it just happened, I tell you.'

'Don't look, there she is now, just comin' in through the gate.'

'She wouldn't even look my way.'

'She got troubles plenty, I guess.'

'Anybody got troubles like that you'd think could use a friend.'

'You know somep'n boy, she'd piss you up. That baby she's tough. She'd make you piss.'

'She piss me up . . . anything . . . just so long she let me be her friend, I wouldn't care.'[1]

This strength is not generally matched in the impressionistic attempts at verbal scene-painting which Mais interposes here and there through the book. These appear too mannered for the harsh realism that surrounds them, and add nothing to the compassion with which he reports it. They stem from that side of Mais's complex and turbulent personality that made him sometimes, despite his fine talents, a bad artist. The striving for effect in a passage such as the following exposes this weakness:

Who are they that passed along the weary beachheads and sang their songs before us? . . . they have hung their harps on the willows and gone their way . . . this curvature of rock was limned

---

1 *Ibid.*, pp. 149–50.

into being out of reluctant granite . . . these sterile grains of sand have told their tales before . . . and the wind writes its tireless songs along the stricken hollows . . . and the sea is a weary old man babbling his dreams.[1]

In *Brother Man* (1954), his second novel of Kingston slum life, Mais narrows his canvas considerably and concentrates his attention upon four characters only. These are Girlie and her lover Papacito, who fight like cats every time they make love; and Minette and her strange, other-worldly guardian, Brother Man. The last is a full-scale version of Ras in the earlier book, a man of gentleness and peace, yet without the compassion to calm the fever in Minette's young flesh until she is humiliated into virtually begging him to do so. Meanwhile the insatiable Papacito is lurking in the background, only too willing to oblige; yet Brother Man remains oblivious of this danger also. Thus there is a self-absorbed quality about his goodness which renders him curiously blind to what those around him are feeling and suffering, though it is not quite certain that Mais intends this as critically as the reader receives it.

Minette is a teenage prostitute when Brother Man takes her under his protection. At first she expects love-making as part of a perfectly acceptable bargain, since he is housing, feeding and educating her. Brother Man, however, persists in treating her as an adopted daughter. Since she is still a child in age, this also is for a while acceptable. But as she approaches full womanhood without her companion ever manifesting the slightest awareness of the fact, as her love of him deepens and intensifies, so her need for a fuller emotional relationship begins to drive her to despair. What is disturbing about Brother Man is that he seems fascinated by the spectacle of his own sanctity. He has less human understanding than many a less kind, gentle, and self-disciplined man.

Similarly, when a notorious rape and murder case at Gunboat Beach is popularly blamed on the Rastafarians, Brother Man believes that his own reputation and goodwill will protect him against mobs who are seeking hungrily for any poor and bearded wretch they can find. He does not see sadism as a profound human instinct, or the mob as an organism with a

---

1 *Ibid.*, p. 63. The passage is quoted *verbatim*, without omissions.

very small collective conscience, or violence as one of the few ways these urban outcasts have of hitting back at established order. The popular hysteria against 'Rastas' is a hell-sent opportunity for expressing all these things under a vague halo of righteous indignation. Once again, Brother Man remains unaware of things many less intelligent men have perceived. Consequently he is an easy victim both of deliberate malice and of spontaneous savagery. Papacito, to protect himself and get easier access to Minette, frames him on a counterfeit charge. When Brother Man is arrested and released on bail, he is shocked to find that the charge is generally believed in the lane; he forgets that people judge more easily by their own weakness than by others' strength. This prepares the way for the final scenes of the book where Brother Man, after foolishly allowing a kind of vanity to take him walking alone late at night, is set upon, stoned, beaten and fouled by the mob. As in *The Hills Were Joyful Together*, Mais brings various related sub-plots to a climax at the same time. Papacito, who has left Girlie and is planning his final assault on Minette, is stabbed to death by his fierce inexorable mistress. Cordelia, a soft-headed recluse who has been used in the plot against Brother Man, kills her baby and hangs herself. Her sister Jesmina, hungry for sex, goes to bed with the first available man, seeking tenderness where there is only pain and awful choking desire.

In switching the reader rapidly from one to another of these sub-plots, Mais uses a technique that is strongly reminiscent of film-cutting. Indeed, his work as a photographer may well be relevant to the analysis of his narrative method. In *The Hills Were Joyful Together* Mais generally allows an entire scene between a group of his characters to play to a finish before switching to another. Examples of this would be the fight between Euphemia and Manny, or Bedosa's death at the level-crossing, or the night when all the inhabitants sing, drink and dance together in the yard before splitting into various amorous combinations, some of them secret and new. Only towards the end of the book does he quicken the tempo of these changes, as he cross-cuts rapidly between Surjue's developing escape plot and Rema's incendiary madness. In *Brother Man*, however, he maintains this technique of rapid cross-cutting between fragments of action right through the novel. He also employs a new device: a sort of dramatic chorus composed of the typical, unassigned voices of the lane who comment upon the main action as it unfolds:

> All same, Papacito better watch him step, no mind dem live or don' live, Minette is fo' Bra' Man gal, me say.
> —Gal, hush you' broad-talkin', yaw. Anybody hear you t'ink say you know somep'n.
> —Know somep'n, no know somep'n, is what oonu sayin' any at all?
> —Sayin' say Minette is Bra' Man gal, anyt'ing wrong in dat?
> —Bra' Man is a man of God.
> —True wud, sisters, true wud.
> —Praise de Lawd!
> —T'ank God![1]

In the quality of its portrayal of the spawning, boisterious life of Orange Lane, *Brother Man* is quite the equal of Mais's earlier novel; Girlie and Papacito might almost have stepped from it. Any uneasiness felt in the contrast stems from the suspicion that Mais himself is obsessed by the theme of passive suffering. Brother Man's nature partakes more of the gentle Jesus of the Sunday School than the passionate iconoclast who sweeps through the Gospels. The dignity and aloofness of the Rastafarians make a bewitching spectacle, but their songs adjure them to 'Burn down Babylon'. To ignore the nature and pervasiveness of evil, the imperious demands of passion, as Brother Man does, may not be the most effective way of living the good life. Above all, we suspect that he seeks refuge in general benevolence because he is afraid of becoming deeply involved with particular people. There are hints on the last page of the novel that he has learnt all this at last, but they are not fully realized and there is still a disturbing suggestion of the sacred object about the battered hero as Minette guides him back to bed after gazing with him upon the sunset:

> 'You see it, out there, too?'
> She looked up above the rooftops where the great light glowed across the sky.
> She said; 'Yes, John, I have seen it.'
> 'Good,' he said, and again, 'Good.'
> He moved away from the window, back into the cool dimness of the room beyond. And she went before him, carrying herself proudly, shielding the little flame of the candle with her hand.[2]

---

1 *Brother Man*, p. 139.   2 *Ibid.*, p. 191.

Two Jamaican writers of a younger generation than Roger Mais show some traces of his influence in their work. John Hearne, who was Mais's companion in his European wanderings, has developed a much more 'international' style of fiction, however. Only his handling of the bar-owner and her Rastafarian peasant father in *Land of the Living* (1961) show some awareness of Mais's achievement in revealing the quality and tempo of life among the Jamaican masses. But whereas Mais enters completely into his world, Hearne always remains frankly a middle-class 'campus' novelist of a type familiar in America. Indeed, modern American fiction and short-story writing in the *New Yorker* or *Atlantic Monthly* tradition are the dominant influences in Hearne's narrative style, plot-making and dialogue. He also displays an American relish for the material impedimenta of middle-class living; cars, long drinks and cigarette lighters gleam and sparkle from his pages. The setting is not so much urban as suburban; for few prosperous Jamaicans, and Hearne's main characters are always prosperous, choose to live in central Kingston. Even in *Land of the Living* his Central European refugee hero, a professor at the University, is consciously making a sortie into another world in his affair with the black bar-keeper, Bernice. It is almost with a sigh of relief that he abandons this secret liaison and turns to a public, socially-accepted involvement with the drunken Joan Culpepper, who at least has the merit of being a member of his own set. Thus in Hearne's work the values and social habits of the professional middle class and the masses coexist in the same island but are held consciously apart; any fuller contact between them is conducted deliberately, is never free from tension, and can be broken off at any time as a release from this tension. Normally their relations are formalised, either domestically or officially, like those of Miss Eleanor and Sonny in the following passage from the opening of *The Autumn Equinox*:

> 'Miss Eleanor,' Sonny said suddenly, 'Miss Eleanor, we not gwine home now, eh?' I hated it when his voice took on that half-threatening, half-pleading whine. I pressed down hard on the accelerator and gave a little swerve to the wheel as we went past our turning, just to show him.
>
> 'Lawd God, Miss Eleanor, you not gwine to see dat old crazy man again? Cho, Miss Eleanor, we don't eat breakfast yet, you know?'

'Shut up, you big ape,' I told him. I felt quite savage . . .

'But him crazy, Miss Eleanor. What you want boder wid an old crazy man like dat for? Jus' an old crazy black man an' you treat him like him was your daddy.'[1]

The impulse towards democratization which Elsa Goveia has detected in West Indian literature[2] appears to be absent from Hearne's carefully-shaped novels. Rather, he is intent on reporting West Indian experience, from a certain viewpoint, to an international English-speaking bourgeois readership. For such a readership his books hold no difficulties of form or style such as Lamming, Mais or Harris may present; they are essentially familiar, and their generally favourable critical reception in the West belongs with this quality. Whereas many exiled West Indian writers create out of their memories of folk experience, Hearne, who lives mainly in Jamaica, reports with more immediacy in time and place but from an angle which somewhat detaches him from the mainstream of popular life.

Orlando Patterson, on the other hand, has sought an ideological position as a refuge from one based on class, colour or money. His first novel, *The Children of Sisyphus* (1964), plunges the reader straight into the life of a Kingston slum, in a manner superficially reminiscent of Mais. We soon sense, however, that Patterson's people are fated in a manner never suggested by the earlier novelist. The yards and lanes of Mais's novels form a more or less enclosed world. Few people escape from it to a kinder one; the main exits lead only to madness, ecstatic religion, imprisonment or violent death. But there is no suggestion that some inscrutable power has ruled it so. The difficulty of escape is merely a consequence of certain specific conditions: there are, for example, no school children in his books. Patterson, however, states it as an article of faith in the 'Dungle', the swampy shanty town where his novel is set, that no-one ever escapes from it. His heroine strives to do so by marriage and emigration with a self-made evangelist, while another group of characters have their eyes set upon an African deliverance. The dénouement brings all of them, in disappointment or in death, to the Dungle whence they began. Despite the strength of much of the descriptive writing, this mechanical doom lends a

---

1 *The Autumn Equinox* (London, Faber, 1959), pp. 15–16.
2 *vide* p. 67.

puppet-like quality to the action of the novel. Patterson's insistence upon the inevitability of return to the Dungle may be well-founded in sociological fact, but as a philosophical proposition it has the effect of robbing his characters of their autonomy as human beings. Mais's people are never dwarfed by their fate; through everything, they remain tragic, unpredictable men and women.

Papacito or Surjue are as far removed as anyone could be from representing West Indian 'characters', such as those exhibited by V. S. Naipaul in *Miguel Street*. Naipaul's affectionate satire upon the eccentricities of his neighbours is not a falsification of street life in Port of Spain, but by concentrating upon all its more exuberant and extreme manifestations it does reinforce the common conviction, perhaps shared by Naipaul himself, that West Indians are essentially comic people. Not quite life-size, dwelling on the periphery of the serious world, they make a calypso of their poverty and exclusion. The laughter, warmth and human variety stressed by Naipaul do indeed temper the harshness of existence and make it bearable. But only in *A House for Mr Biswas* (1961) does Naipaul temper his own irony with the compassion that is demanded of a major novelist. In *Miguel Street* the very way in which he opens a story shows his determination to keep the reader's attention rivetted upon the coruscating surface of anecdote as he parades his characters one by one:

> A stranger could drive through Miguel Street and just say 'Slum!' because he could see no more. But we, who lived there, saw our street as a world, where everybody was quite different from everybody else. Man-man was mad; George was stupid; Big-Foot was a bully; Hat was an adventurer; Popo was a philosopher; and Morgan was our comedian.[1]

But this is essentially a world selected and created in reminiscence. In the city-world of Mais a slum remains a slum, whatever eccentricities it may breed. Hunger and humiliation hurt as bitterly here as anywhere else, though the sun may be warmer. To the insecurity and drift inseparable from urban poverty are added the legacy of slavery, with its unstable relationships and ragged armies of fatherless children. Humour does miraculously streak this world with light, love does fuse with its charge

---

1 *Miguel Street*, p. 79.

the passionate clutches its inhabitants make at one another. Both are of the same stature as the pain, the horror and the fear which also inhabit these dark hovels and narrow, stinking lanes.

The slum dwellers of the Caribbean are its real outcasts, for they live at a double remove from the Africa or India of their forbears. The restless energy and invention of ska or calypso is their music, rather than the relative formality of folksong. The West Indian countryside has established its own norms, its own codes of socially-acceptable conduct, its own deliberate rhythm. A Jamaican mountain village or an Indian settlement among the canefields of Trinidad is often almost a scenic recreation of rural life in the mother continents. Most of the crops and vegetation are the same; goats and chickens scrabble about the compounds; children crawl in the dust; the very styles of speaking, gesturing and moving are the same. But the city soon imposes upon the inhabitant its swiftier, jerkier tempos, its depersonalized environment, its apparatus of exclusion. Here there is nothing to remind him of what or who he is. To discover this he will probably need to move beyond the islands altogether.

Chapter 7
Exiles

What the arse happening, Lord? What all us doing, coasting lime? ...
Every year he vowing to go back to Trinidad, but after the winter gone and
the birds sing and all the trees begin to put on leaves again, and the flowers come
and now and then the old sun shining, is as if life start all over again, as if
it still have time, as if it still have another chance. I will wait until after the
summer, the summer does really be hearts.

Samuel Selvon

The city of exile is the great solvent which produces a black
race out of the mingled elements coming to it from America,
Africa, the Caribbean, and even Asia. In a social context
where all 'blacks' are treated alike, they will to some extent
begin to feel alike. This kind of solidarity in adversity, this
discovery of a common temperament and a common plight,
are evident even in the work of a pioneer writer like Claude
McKay, who preceded the mass exodus of West Indians to the
cities of 'Babylon' by some forty years. His novel *Banjo* cele-
brates the shiftlessness of the black Americans, Africans, West
Indians, Arabs and others who hung around the Marseilles
waterfront during the post-war decade. Some of these had
jumped ship, others were between ships or between jobs, others
again had been demobilized but had never gone home. All
lived from hand to mouth, begging tips or food from visiting
steamers, picking up a few francs for touting or playing in the
seamen's nightclubs, united in their horror of those who took
steady jobs, settled down in one place, or otherwise compro-
mised with the white world. The only morally justifiable
relationship to that world was a parasitic or predatory one,
since the black man had played no part in framing the moral
codes or laws by which he was expected to live. Banjo, one of
the heroes of the book, expresses his philosophy in justifying
himself for jumping ship after signing on and collecting a
month's pay:

'I know youse thinking it ain't right. But we kain't afford to choose, because we ain't born and growed up like the choosing people.'[1]

McKay intrudes himself in the story as Ray, the writer who remembers both Jamaica and Harlem with nostalgia but who must keep perpetually on the move. Contemplating the 'rude anarchy' of these lives and the negative values which unite them, Ray nevertheless perceives important differences between the Africans on one side and the 'Aframericans' on the other, with the West Indians lying somewhere in between, divided spiritually as well as geographically between America and Africa. These differences, which were to grow in importance with the onset of national independence in Africa and the growth of American hegemony in the Caribbean, also lay concealed at the heart of the *négritude* movement, which was developing during these same years among black student circles in Paris. What is not clearly stated in the poetry of *négritude*, whose writers were naturally anxious to stress what united rather than what divided them, is enunciated by Ray at the end of *Banjo*:

> The Africans gave him a positive feeling of wholesome contact with racial roots. They made him feel that he was not merely an unfortunate accident of birth, but that he belonged definitely to a race weighed, tested and poised in the universal scheme. They inspired him with confidence in them. . . . Even though they stood bewildered by the imposing bigness of white things, apparently unaware of the invaluable worth of their own, they were naturally defended by the richness of their fundamental racial values.
>
> He did not feel that confidence about Aframericans who, long deracinated, were still rootless among phantoms and pale shadows and enfeebled by self-effacement before condescending patronage, social negativism, and miscegenation. At college in America and among the Negro intelligentsia he had never experienced any of the simple, natural warmth of a people believing in themselves, such as he had felt among the rugged poor and socially backward blacks of his island home. The colored intelligentsia lived its life 'to have the white neighbours think well of us', so that it could move more peaceably into nice 'white' streets.
>
> [Only in the country did he find] Boys and girls were proud

---

1 *Banjo* (New York, Harper, 1929), p. 319.

of their brown, sealskin brown, teasing brown, tantalizing brown, high-brown, low-brown, velvet brown, chocolate brown.[1]

McKay's schematization here is, of course, overstated. There is injustice in comparing the Jamaican peasant with the Afro-American bourgeois. And he could not foresee the emergence of an African bourgeoisie whose attitudes might in many ways parallel those of their class elsewhere. But he does dramatise some of the issues that still lie at the root of the debate between integrationists and Black Warriors in the major cities of the West. It is the fear of losing that 'natural warmth' in return for social acceptance that still dominates the minds of many black exiles. Full integration and intermarriage in the United States, for example, would lead to the virtual disappearance of the negro as a social or cultural entity without even substantially darkening the pigmentation of the surrounding population. The black man, then, has come to demand acceptance for what he is, and not as a reward for becoming something else.

In McKay's day, however, the question of what the negro is tended to be answered in terms of the image projected upon him by the white world; Genet-like, the negro often insisted upon performing the role of laughing, spontaneous and irresponsible child of nature in which the white world had cast him. In poetry, music and song he rejoiced in his difference from the sober, grey responsibility which he in turn projected upon the West. Many passages of *Banjo*, like much of the contemporary Afro-Cuban and Haitian poetry of 'negro affirmation', read today like a parody of everything the black man is popularly supposed to be. The time was soon to come when he would seek to escape from this role in favour of something more purposeful, deliberate and violent; but for the historical moment of the 1920's he was often content to play it. And the West, whose confidence and self-sufficiency were already dented by the senseless slaughter of 1914–18, and whose taste for the exotic or the primitive was consequently sharpened, was happy to form an enthusiastic audience. Here is McKay's account of a dance in a crowded waterfront bar:

> Black youth close to the bush and the roots of jungle trees, trying to live the precarious life of the poisonous orchids of civilization. Shake that Thing! . . .

---

1 *Ibid.*, pp. 320–1.

The slim, slate-colored Martiniquan dances with a gold-brown Arab girl in a purely sensual way. His dog's mouth shows a tiny, protruding bit of tongue. Oh, he jazzes like a lizard with his girl. A dark-brown lizard and a golden-brown lizard . . .

Black skin itching, black flesh warm with the wine of life, the music of life, the love and deep meaning of life. Strong smell of healthy black bodies in a close atmosphere, generating sweat and waves of heat. Oh, shake that thing![1]

McKay's novel is innocent of plot. Ray, Banjo and their acquaintances drift between the dockside, the bars and the brothel-quarter for three hundred pages, eating or hungering, dancing or fighting, as fortune may dictate. Occasionally someone is shot or stabbed, another seaman joins the group, or one of them disappears for a few months to 'work' the ships and tourists of another port. The book ends because even McKay's enthusiasm for his subjects has begun to wane; most of them take ship to America, while Ray and Banjo prepare to move on to another waterfront. It remains as a classic expression of that image of the negro which prevailed in the literature of the 1920's, whether among the writers of the 'Harlem Renaissance', the rumba-rhyming poets of Cuba or those of infant *négritude* in Haiti and Paris. It is interesting that this image is essentially an urban one; it emerges into literature, not directly, but *via* the avenues of Harlem, Havana and Montparnasse. The negro who moves in these pages is exiled not only from Africa but from himself. Only the Cuban poet Nicolás Guillén began at this time to utter a more sombre music, a music which articulated the spasms of political rather than bodily revolutions. And the characteristic landscape of Guillén's early poetry is the canefield rather than the street, the café or the nightclub. He was the first to satirize the carefree, dancing negro so beloved of other writers of the era, for he perceived that the steps of the dance might slide with perilous ease into those of a hired clown.

No echo of this radical formulation finds its way into the English literature of the Caribbean for another twenty-five years. The bitter, lost, divided figures who scatter through the later pages of *The Emigrants*, George Lamming's novel recording the second exile of the black West Indian, express a range

---

1 *Ibid.*, pp. 49–50.

of feeling and experience that the unfree image of the 1920's did not permit. If there is an excess in Lamming's pages of the gloomy and the bizarre, this in itself may be an indication that all his characters are embraced by a tragic vision of life. The black ones do not set themselves apart by breaking into a song-and-dance routine at the slightest opportunity. The odour of the jungle is less apparent in a Brixton cellar than the odour of urban poverty.

This is not to subscribe to the old liberal fallacy that all people are the same. They are, and are entitled to be, very different. But the differences are largely conditioned rather than genetic; the effects of climate, tradition, social organiza-tion, economic activity, cultural expectation. To meet a coloured person born and brought up in the old East End, before the emergence of the semi-ghettoes of recent years, is to meet a Cockney rather than a West Indian, a Somali or a Lascar. What Lamming shows in *The Emigrants* is the initial impact of English experience upon a group of newcomers readily identifiable by their colour, who have grown up and been conditioned elsewhere, partly by false notions of what modern England is like. The effect of this impact upon most of them, as discussed in Chapter Two of the present work, is a severance from their former selves which makes many things, including complete moral corruption, possible. At the end of the book only the Strange Man remains as an unwelcome reminder of what they once were.

Only two years later appeared the lyrical, sad and wrily funny novel *The Lonely Londoners* (1956), Samuel Selvon's record of an entirely different mood and phase of West Indian exile experience. By the middle 'fifties the unrestricted flow of immigrants had begun to cause resentment not only among many Britons but among those earlier arrivals who felt that it would make things more difficult for them. There is a sense in which the very difficulties of adjustment encourage exiles to band together into little communities within the community, thereby causing for themselves much harder and more pro-longed difficulties than the individual would ever meet with. For such a community, feeding upon every incident or slight encountered by any of its members, soon builds up its own mythology. Every newcomer must now be inducted and told exactly what to look for and what to expect; for any experience differing from that recorded by the group will be resented, as casting doubt upon its validity.[1] To quote one example, the coloured singer Lena Horne has described how she kept reciting at the white man whose only wish was to marry her a favourite phrase of black folk mythology, 'They'll lay you but they won't marry you.' Whereas an individual, like many pre-war coloured residents in Britain, may make his adjustment to a new society in a matter of years, the same process for a group thus organized may take anything from a generation to centuries. Where there are differences of language and religion distinguishing the group from its neighbours, these will tend to perpetuate themselves for the very reason that their disappearance will threaten its cohesion. But even differences of colour, temperament and social habit will be enough to encompass its existence and, given plenty of new blood, ensure its survival.

Such a group is depicted by Selvon in the friends of Moses Alloeta who gather every Sunday morning in his little bedsitter to pool the experiences of the week. Like McKay's Marseilles community of thirty years earlier, this is not a purely West Indian group. London brings them together and defines their common character as 'spades', which would certainly not suffice to unite them in Lagos, Kingston or Port of Spain. But this is altogether a more earthbound group than that which washed along the Marseilles waterfront. Whether from differences of epoch, climate, social environment or the vision of the writer, Selvon's people have an altogether harder attitude towards work and towards the sheer business of daily living in a vast, indifferent city, be it shillings for the gas-meter or yams for the next good meal. Any job is preferable to an existence based on 'hustling' or 'panhandling' a few shillings from the more fortunate. If the café-bar formed the dominant landscape of *Banjo*, that of *The Lonely Londoners* is the narrow furnished room, with everyone huddled in overcoats around a guttering gas-fire. Selvon fills in the background grimly enough:

> The place where Tolroy and the family living was off the Harrow Road, and the people in that area call the Working Class. Wherever in London that it have Working Class, there you will find

---

1 There are even similarities here with the indoctrination practised by white colonial communities upon new arrivals from Europe.

a lot of spades. This is the real world, where men know what it is to hustle a pound to pay the rent when Friday come.

The houses around here old and grey and weather beaten, the walls cracking like the last days of Pompeii, it ain't have no hot water, and in the whole street that Tolroy and them living in, none of the houses have bath . . . All the houses in a row in the street, on both sides, they build like one long house with walls, separating them in parts, so your house jam-up between two neighbours: is so most of the houses is in London. . . .

It have people living in London who don't know what happening in the room next to them, far more the street, or how other people living. London is a place like that. It divide up in little worlds, and you stay in the world you belong to and you don't know anything about what happening in the other ones except what you read in the papers.[1]

It will be noticed that Selvon spends relatively little time on physical description. For him, a landscape exists only in terms of the people who inhabit it. The drabness of the narrow back-to-backs of Harrow Road seems to be an expression of the drab lives they contain. A slum yard 'back home' might be technically more squalid, but at least it would have a collective life of its own. Its poverty need not be augmented by loneliness or by a pinched unawareness of others. But to make matters worse, most poor immigrants come from peasant families in the countryside. To them such a way of life is not merely strange, but inconceivable. The rejection of it is one of the most powerful factors making for new immigrant groupings within British cities, who see themselves as distinct and wish to remain so.

The contacts of Selvon's characters with individual whites, as distinct from their intimate contact with the realities of life in London, are decidedly casual and are always reported back to 'group headquarters', like the observations of a patrol. They are an affair of picking up 'a sharp thing' by Marble Arch or having an altercation with 'a white fellar' at the corner. Occasionally some deeper involvement will occur, but this is likely to be a subject of regret to the 'boys', and often to the principal himself. Thus in Selvon's story 'Waiting for Aunty to Cough'[2] the hero is afflicted by the fear that his fellows are 'coasting a line someplace' while he is escorting his English girl

1 *The Lonely Londoners* (London, MacGibbon and Kee, 1956), pp. 56–7.
2 In *West Indian Stories*, edited by Andrew Salkey (London, Faber, 1960).

to her home 'behind God back'. Even the comic episode which gives the story its title is reported through the group and is immortalized by them; it is almost a warning of what befalls those who plunge too deeply into the surrounding society.

By contrast, the relationship with London itself is complex and profound. By writing throughout in a carefully-composed Trinidad dialect, Selvon is able to impose a distinctive rhythm upon the life of the city as experienced by his characters. We see its moods and seasons through the alien but affectionate eyes of those for whom it remains through everything an exciting place to be. The feeling begins with the sheer sensation of being there, in London, 'centre of the world,' the goal of many years scrimping, saving and dreaming. It means beginning a letter home with a phrase like, 'Last night in Trafalgar Square ...'. Gradually it accumulates detail, colour and particularity. The most memorable passage in *The Lonely Londoners* is Selvon's long anthem to the coming of summer, that moment which always postpones his departure for another and another year:

> Oh what a time it is when summer come to the city and all them girls throw away heavy winter coat and wearing light summer frocks so you could see the legs and shapes that was hiding away from the cold blasts ... you bound to meet the boys coasting lime in the park and you could go walking through the gardens and see all them pretty pieces of skin taking suntan and how the old geezers like the sun they would sit on the benches and smile everywhere you turn the English people smiling isn't it a lovely day as if the sun burn away all the tightness and strain that was in their faces for the winter and on a nice day every manjack and his brother going to the park with his girl and laying down on the green grass and making love in the winter you would never think that the grass would ever come green again ... and this time so the sun in the sky like a forceripe orange and it giving no heat at all and atmosphere like a sullen twilight hanging over the big city but it different too bad when is summer for then the sun shine for true and the sky blue and a warm wind blowing ...[1]

So Selvon gives a twist to the wheel and sets the seasons spinning, though it comes to rest on summer again and again. The 'nice

---

1 *The Lonely Londoners*, pp. 115–16.

pieces of skin' whom the boys boast of encountering may often prove the degraded tarts of Hyde Park, the adventures summer brings may include all the varieties of exploitation by impotent men or perverted women that Lamming has already exposed, but the lyricism which enfolds and sustains the whole passage is not ironical. Summer does genuinely gild the scene and render even such human failures less sad.

To find a West Indian hero genuinely alone in London, making his own terms with the city and not concerning himself with membership of any discernible group, we have to look as late as Andrew Salkey's *Escape to an Autumn Pavement* (1960). Whereas Selvon's immigrants huddle together for emotional warmth and Lamming's regret their failure to 'stick together' as the Strange Man advised, Salkey's hero Johnnie Sobert has a great desire to be left alone. It is the struggle within him between this desire and the more common ones for women and company that dominates the action of the novel.

This is a fast-moving tale told with a slightly self-conscious toughness, the word 'crap' being used with obsessive frequency. Sobert lives in a rooming-house where he happens to be the only black resident, though there is an Indian girl whom he satirizes with pitiless intensity. He also works in a nightclub run by two English girls, and catering mainly for American servicemen. With all these people Johnnie has to achieve a more or less direct, individual relationship, since there is no warm, uncritical group into which he can retire whenever he gets hurt or confused. At first he moves through the days with a certain jazzy but cool insouciance, but soon he gets drawn into an affair with the insatiable Fiona, the wife of his landlord, who lives on the floor below. For a while he is flattered and sensually delighted by this involvement, but gradually Fiona begins to appear in the guise of a succubus, not merely available but inevitable and demanding. Johnnie has already felt himself attracted to Dick, a white chauffeur and fellow-tenant whose apparent detachment makes him seem like an escape from the morass of female sexuality into which he feels himself sinking. The suspicion that Dick is a homosexual is one that Johnnie does not allow to rise very far in his mind; when Dick proposes that they move out and share a flat he eagerly falls in with the arrangement, telling himself that it implies just that and no more. He breaks with Fiona and luxuriates for a while in the sense of relief this brings him. Resolutely averting his attention from the mounting strain in their relationship, he continues to treat Dick as a friend, confidant and flatmate, while Dick patiently waits for a sign which never comes. For Dick believes that Johnnie is an unavowed homosexual who needs time to come to terms with himself and must not be hurried. His very agreement to share the flat was, in Dick's eyes, an admission of his real nature. But when Johnnie takes up with Fiona again and begins making assignations with her, Dick's patience finally snaps. He quits the flat and leaves a note telling Johnnie that he must now take a decision between them. The reader is left with the suspicion that neither Fiona nor Dick is really as important to Johnnie as they suppose, and that he will probably choose neither. He ends the book, as he began it, alone.

Johnnie Sobert is in flight from Jamaican middle class values, which he feels to be not only shoddy in themselves but not in any way validated by the social realities of the island's life. His escape to England seems to have been in part a search for real social values, but a rooming-house is hardly the place to look for these. He is spiky, alert, afraid of being judged by the standard of his fellow immigrants and therefore anxious to avoid involvement with them. His quest for his own real nature is conducted without intimate witnesses; his mother, to whom he writes frequently, seems closer to him than anyone around him. He has the supreme merit of being prepared to launch out into the alien life of London, perhaps hurting and disturbing others in the process, but at least not withdrawing impregnably into himself. Those who try to categorize him will be discouraged by his wary wit:

'Why are you so angry, Mr. Sobert?' the dragon on her damp throne asks me.

'I dislike the Third Programme and I adore the idea of C.D. & W. That's why.'

'But surely, Mr. Sobert, you're different from the others I've seen working on the Underground?'

'And on the dust-carts,' I offer, assisting her Old English benignity.

'Yes. And those on the dust-carts, as you say. Surely, they have some sort of child-like right to be angry. Not you.'

'Mrs. Blount.'

'Yes!'

'Do you feel the same about the Covent Garden porter?'

'An English porter, you mean?' Cunning hesitation. Inclination of neck. Flick of finger-tip and wrist. 'Yes. Yes, Mr. Sobert. I most certainly do.'

'A child-like right to be angry, eh?'

'Mr. Sobert, you're making quite an issue of this, aren't you?'

'My chip on the shoulder, Mrs. Blount. A small one from my well-preserved forest.'[1]

Salkey writes in a fairly non-specialized modern urban style which makes his book the greatest possible contrast with such London writing as Selvon's. The passages of dialect are confined to the few occasions when Johnnie's path crosses that of a fellow West Indian. The weakness of the book is that the first person narration gives one no rest from Johnnie's personality and one tires of his wisecracking energy and lack of real feeling for others. He is adequate as a character but not as a window on the world, unless the limitations of his vision were exploited more deliberately by the author.

What is liberating about Johnnie Sobert is his relative self-sufficiency as a West Indian in London. He neither depends upon membership of an immigrant group which experiences and reacts to London collectively, nor does he play unduly the part of a professional black man. The last is a particular hazard for those with genuine personality and bounce, since the audience is always waiting and will soon clarify the limits within which the role is licensed to be played. Johnnie's sexual ambiguity and stillborn rebelliousness are problems he must encounter as a man, an individual alone in a big city, but not specifically as a black immigrant. Too much dwelling upon the last can bring out something disturbingly like a Christ-complex, or a self-congratulatory mystique of negro potency. This 'no-nonsense' quality in Salkey's novel is perfectly defined by comparing it with an African novel of exile like Mbella Sonne Dipoko's *A Few Nights and Days*, (1965). Dipoko's Camerounian hero Doumbe is also to some extent making his own separate way through the stream of Parisian student life. The only compatriot with whom he is directly involved in the course of the book is the black girl Ndombe, who serves as one of his numerous mistresses. But we suspect that

---

1 *Escape to an Autumn Pavement*, (London, Hutchinson, 1960), pp. 11–12.

Doumbe has only cast himself adrift to this extent the better to play his part as black-man-in-exile. It is as such that he expects the predominantly white circle in which he moves to react to him, and he reaps his fill of the sexual harvest it brings. He participates in this student life, but continually makes judgements upon it from the point of view of his independent African values and beliefs. Thus he is able to indulge in the ambiguous exercise of despising the white world for its promiscuity while taking the fullest advantage of it. This same ambiguity makes him a success with Madame Vaele, the mother of his French fiancée Thérèse, but a dismal failure with her husband, whose opposition to the match is really more pragmatic and less discriminatory than it appears. M. Vaele correctly assesses Doumbe as someone who likes the idea of being engaged to a French girl—especially one who might not sleep with him otherwise—much more than he will like the reality of marrying her and taking her back to Africa with him. Though Doumbe's real attitudes are partly hidden even from himself, M. Vaele is really observing them, as well as his own prejudices, in persuading him to return to Africa alone, with the promise of sending for Thérèse at some indefinite date in the future. Unfortunately, M. Vaele understands his own daughter less clearly than he does Doumbe and the tragedy of her suicide, occasioned as much by her realization that Doumbe does not now mean to marry her as by her father's opposition, takes him completely by surprise.

The transition within Doumbe's mind from the idea of marriage to its reality is dramatized by the receipt of a letter from his father. The old man wants his son back quickly, since he feels the approach of death and wishes to see the care of farm and family in younger hands without delay. Doumbe's instant acceptance of his father's wishes, far transcending Thérèse's in importance, is partly a measure of the two relationships and partly a reminder of the depth and enduring strength of his links with Africa. If Doumbe is to fall in with his father's wishes he must either marry Thérèse at once or abandon her, since he never seriously contemplates sending for her once he is back in Africa. Here M. Vaele's opposition to the match assumes its true significance, for Thérèse is only nineteen and cannot marry without her parent's consent. He is not prepared to bear the obloquy of publicly opposing the marriage, and the plan he proposes to Doumbe over a private dinner enables him to shelter behind the urgency of Doumbe's departure as a reason for postponing the match. Doumbe's readiness to fall in with this scheme, which can only lead to the destruction of Thérèse's happiness and, in the event, her life, is a sign that he is grasping at straws in order to extricate himself. If he were determined to marry Thérèse he would certainly not be ready to accept the apparent blame for not doing so. The finale finds him dumb, but not especially remorseful; already he is preoccupied by another problem, the pregnancy of Thérèse's friend, Bibi, with whom he has also been sleeping.

Dipoko records the life of café, night-club and student bedsitter in a style which seems alternately naïve and laconic. The mechanical recording of detail in brief, almost breathless, sentences gives a wide-eyed impression of one describing this extraordinary Parisian world to those back home:

> He smoked for about a minute. The restaurant wasn't crowded. There were a number of couples, eating. Others had finished eating. They talked, in almost inaudible voices. . . . Some talked over coffee. Others talked over table cloths that carried nothing besides ashtrays. A man ate by himself a few tables away from ours. It was rare to see a woman eating alone in those plush restaurants.[1]

The flatness and caution of such descriptive writing is often irritating, but Dipoko does grind out from these small wheels a dry wit of his own. He is especially good in clipped exchanges, where the situation behind the fragments of conversation charges them with force and significance beyond themselves. The whole complex of resentment, curiosity, hostility and plain sexual jealousy which Ndombe feels towards Doumbe's white girls, especially Thérèse, is conveyed in the scene where Thérèse finds the two Africans together. Dipoko is the first novelist to register the sudden acute loneliness and insecurity of the European among Africans when they begin speaking in the vernacular. An expression of generalized goodwill can only deepen his absurdity in this situation:

> 'Look at her neck!' Ndombe mocked, not looking at Thérèse.

---

1 *A Few Nights and Days* (London, Longmans, 1966), p. 107.

'It's a crane's neck,' I laughed. 'A swan's neck.'

'Would you marry her?'

'*Na*! You haven't any other thing in that big head of yours but marriage?'

Her head wasn't big.

Thérèse looked first at Ndombe, then at me. Then she asked: 'What are you two saying?'

'It's our language,' Ndombe said in French, wickedly. '*C'est notre langue*. If you don't understand it, that's your business. It isn't our fault. *Je regrette.*' This silenced Thérèse. In order to cheer her up I began to talk of the Centre where, according to the invitation, the Ivory Coast Ambassador was going to speak that evening on *The Industrialization of Africa.* . . . Ndombe licked her fingers.

'I am eating with my fingers,' she said, in Duala. 'Kill yourself, white woman, if you want. That's how my grandmother ate. She lived to be eighty.'

Ndombe got up.

'What's there to drink?' she asked.

'Everything, from champagne to rainwater,' I said.

She opened the sideboard. She looked from one corner to the other.

'I can see only a little whisky and a little water, that is mineral water.' She straightened up. 'You haven't any wine?'

'No'.

'How can one eat without a little wine?'

'Ndombe, your grandmother didn't eat with wine. She lived to be eighty' . . .

'Are you angry?'

'Yes. I've never been so angry before.'

'Knock your head against that wall to prove that you are angry. . . . If I don't eat now, when will I eat again? Soon your white wife will block the doors like Ekwe's. *Aye*, that one!'

'I like your language,' said Thérèse, innocently.

'How stupid!' Ndombe said in Duala. 'You are being abused in that language and yet you like it all the same.[1]

Often the terseness of Dipoko's narrative conveys the essential detachment of his hero from the life of Paris that surrounds him. His least demanding mistress is Bibi, the Swedish *au pair* who is a foreigner like himself. The intensity and seriousness of Thérèse appeals to him in a way that is partly sentimental, but

---

1 *Ibid.*, pp. 69–70.

it also presages the disaster that attends their relationship. Through everything, Doumbe never has more than one foot in Paris. His commitments are all qualified by the possibility, and later by the imminence, of departure. If one may hazard any general distinction between West Indian and African attitudes towards the Western city of exile, it is this very detachment which frequently seems to express their difference. The African holds no conviction that exile or wandering are part of his destiny; they are usually no more than incidental accompaniments of his education. Africa is always there, waiting to receive him again, and has seldom been rejected as the West Indian so often rejects his island and its society. And ultimately, as with Doumbe's *affaires*, it is Africa which remains the measure of everything. It is this detachment which makes possible the relaxed irony of a poem like Wole Soyinka's *Telephone Conversation*, where the poet can afford a compassion for his reluctant landlady which is so much more telling than angry indignation:

> 'Facially, I am brunette, but madam, you should see
> the rest of me. Palm of my hand, soles of my feet
> Are a peroxide blonde. Friction, caused—
> Foolishly madam—by sitting down, has turned
> My bottom raven black—One moment madam!'—sensing
> Her receiver rearing on the thunderclap
> About my ears—'Madam,' I pleaded, 'wouldn't you rather
> See for yourself?'[1]

In the lonely poetry of another Nigerian, Gabriel Okara, it is Africa which gives life and meaning to the cold imagery offered him by the North American winter:

> Then I awoke. I awoke
> to the silently falling snow
> and bent-backed elms bowing and
> swaying to the winter-wind like
> white-robed Moslems salaaming at evening
> prayer, and the earth lying inscrutable
> like the face of a god in a shrine.[2]

---

1 'Telephone Conversation', in *Modern Poetry from Africa* (Penguin, 1963), p. 112.
2 'The Snowflakes Sail Gently Down', *ibid.*, p. 93.

Even the shrill anger of J. P. Clark's *America, Their America* (1966), so different apparently from these reactions, is another indication of the profoundly alien impact which the great Western cities make upon most African visitors. By comparison, even the most ideologically hostile West Indian has been shaped to some extent by the immense cultural and material pressures which America projects across the islands. He knows what to expect, because of the Americans in his midst, because of the accumulated lore of a hundred years of West Indian movement in and out of the Americas; and the holiday for which he is saving is more likely to be spent in Caracas, New York or Montreal than in visiting another island. He may even feel, like Salkey's hero Johnnie Sobert, that in the West he is at last handling the social archetypes which the middle classes of the Caribbean have been imitating for three hundred years.

Such a reaction is found at its most naïve in Jiffy Jacket, the hero of O. R. Dathorne's early novel *Dumplings in My Soup*. This is another novel-of-exile basing its social world in the tight little immigrant group, here the random occupants of a dilapidated rooming-house. Watching the dancers at an international club, the newly-arrived Jiffy reflects that he is seeing life at last:

> He thought to himself that coming here to England was an education in itself. You really came to grips with naked reality. In the West Indies everyone was play-acting at being real. Here the reality was so real that it frightened you with the immensity of it.[1]

The crudity of the expression here, characteristic of this high-spirited but immature and overwritten novel, should not obscure the fact that there is an element of Jiffy's reaction in many West Indian breasts when they first inhale the damp fogs of Brixton or Paddington. The arrival in England is something much more than the climax of educational ambition; it is more like the fulfilment of a quest, though many attain it only to find the sacred cistern dry. Nostalgia for the islands will not prevent the development of the loving, intimate awareness of the city displayed by Samuel Selvon, for there is a

---

1 *Dumplings in My Soup* (London, Cassell, 1963), p. 30.

sense in which London is simply the largest city in the West Indies.

The West Indian relationship to America is also a complex one. If the ethnic links are often with Africa or Asia, and the historical and cultural links often with Western Europe, there is no denying the geographical proximity of the American land-mass. The relative ease and cheapness of modern travel is making this proximity more and more evident. Thus Derek Walcott looking out over the New England forests, asks himself 'Mine, or another history there?'[1] Sitting in his little room in Greenwich Village, cold and hungry through the long winter, he feels his desire crawl across snow 'like smoke, for its lost fire.'[2] But, remembering the dead American friend who fed and cheered him during those months, he produces imagery that shows an extraordinary sympathy for the American myth and its ideal landscape:

> Going away, through Queen's we pass
> a cemetery of miniature skyscrapers. The verge
> blazes its rust, its taxi-yellow leaves. It's fall.
> I stare through glass,
> my own reflection there, at
> empty avenues, lawns, spires, quiet
> stones, where the curbs rim
> wheels westward, westward, where thy bones. . . .
>
> Montana, Minnesota, your real
> America, lost in tall grass, serene idyll.[3]

The common experience of exile, of segregation and discrimination in urban ghettoes, of calling a spade a spade, may, as we have seen, obscure these differences and produce an apparently homogeneous mass of unassimilated black resentment. It is chiefly when West Indian and African can encounter one another directly, without the interposition of white society, that they have a real opportunity to measure their distance from one another and assess its importance. This more direct encounter is likely to occur in the African continent itself.

---

1 'Lines in New England', *The Castaway*, p. 49.
2 'A Village Life', p. 18.
3 *Ibid.*, p. 18.

Part Four

Guinea

Chapter 8
The Revenants

*'We goin' home, we goin' home! Israel is redeem'! King Rasta a come fo'
'im pickney them!'*

Orlando Patterson

The black West Indian approaches Africa with the same heightened expectation as he approaches England, but the expectation is of a different quality, for failure in this encounter will be more disturbing than any failure to adjust to the reality of English life. England may be the origin of much that he has been exposed to at second hand, but Africa is the racial fount itself, the land in which, but for the abhorred slave trade, he might still be living. The more precise his expectations, the more likely they are to be dashed. The happy voyager is he who does not view this as a return home so much as the opportunity to see a strange, exciting continent where blackness is a normal condition, and white colonialism an episode rather than the formative influence of a whole society.

Ever since the Reverend Hope Waddell landed at Calabar in 1846 with his little party of Jamaican missionaries, or since, very shortly afterwards, Edward Wilmot Blyden arrived in Monrovia from St. Thomas, West Indians have been making this pilgrimage to the ancestral shore. In those early days they sometimes passed upon the very ocean the Spanish or Portuguese slavers who continued the trade for another forty years. In more recent times many writers and intellectuals have followed in the footsteps of Blyden and George Padmore and have come to live or work for considerable periods in the newly independent nations of Africa. They include Neville Dawes, George Lamming, Denis Williams, Garth St. Omer, Edward Brathwaite and O. R. Dathorne. Lamming's experience at Accra airport in the moment of arrival sums up the dual nature of modern Africa's impact upon the revenant: first, the familiarity of the colonial charade embodied in the Scout Parade; then the shock of realizing that this is only the thinnest of uniforms to cover cultures still exuberantly different in their languages and ways of feeling:

> What were they quarrelling about? Or what were they rejoicing about? For it was difficult to distinguish which noise was war and which was peace. I turned to ask my West Indian friend what it was all about. He smiled; and suddenly I realized the meaning of that smile and the fact about that invading noise. Neither of us could understand a word of what those boys were saying. Nor could the English scoutmaster. It was at this point that the difference between my childhood and theirs broke wide open. They owed Prospero no debt of vocabulary. English was a way of thinking which they would achieve when the situation required it. But their passions were poured through another rhythm of speed.[1]

Beyond this, the very presence of the West Indian writer in these surroundings is a further mark of the difference which Lamming is beginning to register. For to the common restlessness bred by slavery, poverty, over-crowding and islanded remoteness, the writer adds his passion to escape from the philistinism and self-doubt of Caribbean society. The mere desire to live as an artist seems to dictate, sooner or later, his escape from the islands to an environment where he can at least compete on his merits. In Africa almost the opposite is true, for the vast majority of African artists feel that only by working in their own countries, whatever the difficulties, can they give life and relevance to their activities. Writers like Achebe, Tutuola, Okigbo and Soyinka, along with the painters, sculptors and musicians among their contemporaries, have produced all their major work in an African environment. The same years saw the creation of a West Indian literature and art (one thinks of sculptors like Ronald Moody, painters like Frank Bowling and Denis and Aubrey Williams) by a group of people largely based in London. Consequently there is an extensive West Indian literature recording the experience of Africa, but very little record of the reverse process. Only the South African writer Peter Abrahams, himself an exile

---

1 *The Pleasures of Exile* (London, Michael Joseph, 1960), p. 162.

for thirty years, has been able to offer an African impression of the West Indies in his novel of Jamaican public life, *This Island Now*.

What is often lamented as the rootlessness and uncertain identity of the West Indian can easily be viewed as his greatest asset, the foundation of his peculiar freedom and modernity. While others obscure their humanity within a variety of tribal, linguistic, racial or national categories, the West Indian carries all the world's blood in his veins, speaks by birthright a major international language, enjoys special historical or geographical links with all the major continents, and inhabits an environment which naturally carries his eyes outward to the horizon. This characteristic helps to explain the distinctive relationship which West Indians quickly develop with apparently distant and alien cities like New York, Amsterdam, Paris and London. Lamming has drawn attention to it in *The Pleasures of Exile*:

> We in the West Indies can meet the twentieth century without fear; for we begin with colossal advantages. The West Indian, though provincial, is perhaps the most cosmopolitan man in the world.[1]

But in his encounter with Africa this particular kind of freedom is unlikely to help him, unless he has the personal confidence to rejoice in it. The reproach hurled at Lionel Lobo Froad, the hero of Denis Williams's *Other Leopards*, by the Southern Sudanese journalist Mojo Kua, is one that he will have to learn to expect and to turn aside:

> 'I am the true original thing, pure African. I've never been sold, never been a slave. I've got a name, Mr. Lionel Froad, and a tribe. Now tell me who you are!'[2]

Froad is peculiarly unable to deal with this sort of attack, because he is always making it upon himself anyway. He would be incapable of telling Kua that it is his misfortune to have a tribe. Froad is obsessed by a sense of guilt which belongs properly, if anywhere, to the descendants of those who enslaved and exiled his ancestors. Freedom can sometimes be lonely and Froad is incapable of realizing his situation as one of freedom; he sees it only as exclusion or as lack of any tangible

---

1 *Ibid.*, p. 37.
2 *Other Leopards* (London, New Authors, 1963), p. 74.

existence at all. He only exists for himself at the end of the novel when he has regressed through every stage of infantilism to a state of naked and entreed savagery, thus severing his connection with everything that condemns him as a man.

Denis Williams's choice of the Sudan (here called Jokhara) as the setting of his novel seems at first to present his hero with a task of peculiar and perhaps unfair difficulty; for how can the most accommodating negro fit in to a country where even the indigenous negroes are facing a war of assimilation or extermination waged upon them by the Arab north? But fuller reflection shows us that the returning negro cannot legitimately select his bit of Africa in such a way as to exclude all its areas of real conflict. Or rather, if he does so he is making a purely individual adjustment with no significance beyond himself. Modern Africa is not just the negro heartland within the tropics; it is also the Arab and Moorish North, the Somali and Ethiopian North-East and the white-ruled South. To dwell on one of the frontiers of black Africa, as Froad does, is to confront the continental reality of Africa in a painful but perhaps necessary manner; a manner akin to that of the little band of Rastafarian leaders who actually reached Ethiopia, only to be told by the acquiline Emperor that he experienced no shortage of poor, uneducated and unskilled inhabitants.

Early in the novel Froad attends a press conference given by a visiting black Prime Minister. The usual Pan-African clichés are sprayed over his largely Arab audience, who smother in polite applause their conviction that all negroes are by nature their slaves. Someone asks a question about race prejudice and is firmly told that this is a concomitant of colonialism and must automatically disappear with colonialism. Froad goes off into the evening reflecting:

And the question not answered. It will destroy Africa like a creeping plague, Arab and African, but no-one dared to face it.[1]

Froad's own mixed ancestry is dramatized in his two first names of Lionel and Lobo, which he sees as two distinct personalities warring within him for mastery (the name Lobo actually suggests Portugal rather than black Africa, but this was not apparently Williams' purpose in selecting it).

---

1 *Ibid.*, p. 75.

The Lobo in him rejects absolutely the values thrust upon him by his white boss Hughie, values obsessed with time and with constant demonstrations of evidence, competence and superiority. This rejection reaches a climax in the scene where Froad, becoming hysterical under Hughie's incessant prodding and exhortation, exclaims:

> 'Me, I'm like none of yours—get that? So take your beak from out my clothes, and your heart from off my beak.'

Lobo also rejects the love of Catherine, Hughie's Welsh secretary whose cool, solicitous beauty haunts him like the unattainable. Stepping back to take her into view he adds:

> 'Take your clothes from off my heart!...
> You anyone-but-you Sunday-teacher!
> Chapel-hound...!'[1]

Then, in front of both of them, he is sick in the middle of the carpet.

But Lionel Froad loves and respects Hughie, who once saved his life when their expedition ran out of water. Hughie is an archaeologist and Lionel is his immaculate draughtsman, lending himself to Hughie's scheme of finding at Meroë the clue to the non-development of this indigenous ironworking civilization on the Upper Nile. Lionel also loves Catherine and longs to marry her, to lose himself in the grey, misty lakes he sees in her eyes. The struggle between Lionel and Lobo in the breast of Froad is not expressed in this crudely diagrammatical way, but an understanding of it is necessary to explain his erratic behaviour, his sudden explosions of violence and collapses into impotence.

Apart from his involvement with Hughie and Catherine, Froad is also tormented by another group of people who project their expectations upon him with equal insistence. The Chief is a West Indian missionary who has come to Africa over thirty years before Froad, bringing with him no expectations of resolving any personal dilemma, but buoyed up by a robust and unquestioning faith in his spiritual task. The Chief has thrown himself fully into the task of estranging the black South from the Arab and Moslem North, yielding to no son of Islam in fanaticism. Thus an already chronic problem is

---

1 *Ibid.*, p. 108.

further exacerbated, for the British administration, who first cast themselves in the role of paternal protectors of the South, have already departed and the Christian missionaries will shortly be forced to follow them. Several million Africans will thus be left with nothing to stand between them and the vengeance of Khartoum. The Chief expects Froad to assist him in stiffening Southern resistance, but he is also approached by the Arabs who hope that he, as an emancipated 'Western' negro, will persuade the Southerners that their real interests lie in peaceful assimilation to an Arabic and Moslem identity. Perversely, perhaps partly to torment Catherine and disappoint the Chief at one blow, Froad accepts money from the Arab politicians and begins a series of apologist articles in the press designed to justify their Southern policy.

The measure of the Chief's fanaticism is that he has cast off his daughter Eve for marrying an Arab army officer; not to do so, he claims, would be to fail 'his people'. But Eve, who is certainly no intellectual, is in fact the only one who has made some adjustment to the realities of Sudanese life. Although a West Indian by birth, she really feels herself to be an African and moves with relative ease in both Coptic and Moslem circles. But she has run away from her husband and is living alone with her baby. Her very Africanness is what makes her irresistibly attractive to Lobo Froad:

> her smell, like humus on a forest floor, will come up from inside the bosom, for surely there it grows. . . . She'll sprout with meanings and break the earth in green spaces and heave, oh, and heave! And you will plunge from your tree-top into the warm depths of creek-water, forgetting . . .[1]

Yet despite all this self-excitation, Froad always resorts to violence before making love to Eve. And when Catherine offers herself to him damp and naked from the Nile he is unable to take her. Instead, he treats her to a lurid account of his relations with Eve. But Catherine is unimpressed; she urinates visibly in a corner and begins calmly to get dressed. Only then, as she begins to resume her usual cool, inviolable appearance, does he force her to the ground and take her by violence.

---

1 *Ibid.*, p. 67.

Froad's impotence at such moments, springing from his self-divided introversion, prepares the way for the steady regress towards infantilism which now overwhelms him. Catherine never recovers from the scene by the river and goes miserably home to Wales, Eve having told her in the meantime, quite untruly, that she is carrying Froad's baby. Eve tells the same lie to her father in an attempt to force Froad to marry her. Instead, he beats her until she confesses the truth. His relationships with Catherine, Eve and the Chief now lie in ruins, but some communication with Hughie is still possible. Almost despite himself, Froad carries to Meroë some flickering hope of finding in the pyramid of Queen Amanishakete some expression of immemorial Africa with which he can communicate. He sees only a figure of majestic and terrifying cruelty, a flogger and killer of slaves, a figuration in stone of the desert around and within her:

> She was queen and destroyer. She knew hate and law. No trace of love and care . . .
>
> She was all but the skin and sweat of Eve, myself, the Chief; we were one in her, vessels dipping into time to be filled and emptied, filled and emptied; passive. . . .
>
> This was humiliating, this attitude—which was no attitude— to the Queen of Time, to my own past, to the past of my people. The vague guilt I'd all along been feeling began now to burn and throb inside like liquor . . . At the heart of the mirage there was no water.[1]

Now Froad's link with Hughie, the hated and desired father who goads him onward, also snaps. We learn in retrospect of an extraordinary adventure that befalls him on his return from Meroë. He has resigned his job and lost Catherine; now he goes to find Eve at night in a Moslem village, where she has gone to take part in a *zaar*, a secret ceremony of purification. Approaching the house from behind, under cover of the night-soil scavengers, he enters it through a lavatory and is discovered there by a voiding female. Only Eve saves him from being torn to pieces by the enraged women of the segregated household. Here is undisguised imagery of anal re-entry to the womb of infancy which, added to the imagery of sexual withdrawal, vomit and urination that has preceded it, marks

---

1 *Ibid.*, p. 155.

the completion of Froad's retreat from maturity. On a last trip with Hughie, goaded beyond endurance by his increasingly withering contempt, Froad stabs him through the neck with a screwdriver and, grabbing nothing but a jerrican of water, runs off into the darkness of the bush.

In a series of broken, confused scenes we learn of his uncertainty whether Hughie is now dead or, like a hound of heaven, searching him out. And, if searching, will it be in vengeance or in love? The whole nightmare seems to mingle with recollections of their endurance of thirst and delirium together on that other trip long ago. Above all, Froad is determined to 'act outside the limits of Hughie's intelligence'. He retreats further and further from the road, takes off and buries his vomit-covered clothes and washes himself. Then, horrified by the odour of his sweat, which is the last secretion left him, he mixes his remaining drinking-water with clay and begins to encase his whole body in it, beginning characteristically with his privates. Finally, he climbs up a tree, fulfilling a retreat to the embryo, not only of the individual, but of the human race. 'I am a savage, shadowless,' he reflects. Only by this last extremity of withdrawal has he escaped from his divided state and the guilt that is born of division.

Other Leopards may appear to suffer from this plunge into fantasy at the end of what began as a realistic novel, but it is the detail with which the fantasy is elaborated, the care with which it is developed out of realistic episode, that make this a harsh and necessary book. Less and less is Froad able to disguise his dilemma in the trappings of daily action and expected behaviour. The gradual onset of his crisis of withdrawal corresponds with the movement of the book itself into the phantasmagoria of an isolated and afflicted imagination. Not only are the two parts of the book related, but the second is a resolution, however drastic, of the conflict displayed in the behaviour of the first. Denis Williams has pegged out the markers which enclose a great area of the West Indian experience of Africa. The essential hollowness of a character like the Chief is an exposure of the insufficiency of his particular kind of loud positiveness. Himself a product of colonialism, he is unable to confront the reality of independent Africa, and his work is at an end. Catherine too feels 'useless and defeated' after her experience of the Africa she came to with such hopes. Even Hughie's trim self-sufficiency must eventually run itself into the sand. Only Eve, who lives by instinct, can flow naturally back into the stream of African existence. *Other Leopards* is the record of a personal failure, but it is a failure of the kind necessary to understanding.

Froad sees the Sahara Desert as profoundly expressive of the West Indian condition. Contemplating his own barrenness, his lack of love and pity, he exclaims:

> Between Europe and Africa there is this desert. How fitting! Between the white and the black this mulatto divide. You cannot cross it, whoever you are, and remain the same. You change. You become, in a way, yourself mulatto—looking both ways.[1]

And later, as his self-annihilation proceeds in the darkness and silence of the desert itself:

> I am a man hunting and running; neither infra nor supra, not Equatorial black, not Mediterranean white.[2]

Edward Brathwaite also begins his poem of the African migration, *Rights of Passage*, in the Sahara. But the meaning of his choice may be different, for to him the desert passage seems to symbolize what was carried from Ancient Egypt and Libya to acquire new life, new forms, in the black South. To Williams it is an uncreating divide, an embodiment of spiritual drouth, a field where nothing flourishes but the hatred and destruction still marking the eroded countenance of Amanishakete. Brathwaite shows us a desert in which nothing can live, but out of which come the forces which will build a new African civilization in the grasslands of the Western Sudan. In the desert's pitiless expanse:

> Camels wrecked
> in their own
> shit
> resurrect butter-
> flies that
> dance in the noon
> without hope
> without hope
> of a morning.[3]

---

1 *Ibid.*, pp. 208–9.   2 *Ibid.*, p. 221.   3 *Rights of Passage*, p. 3.

But soon the humped stones of dry riverbeds appear, guarding little pools of moisture in their shadows. Here, perhaps too near the desert fringes, the first settlements arise:

Build now
the new
villages, you
must mix spittle
with dirt, dung
to saliva and
sweat: round
mud walls will rise
in the dawn
walled cities
arise
from savanna and
rock river bed:[1]

Now the poem moves swiftly through the failure of the first settlements, ruined by plague and drought, to the building of the great cities of the high savannah, and southwards again to the forest empires of Ashanti and Dahomey, where this long surge encounters the first probing columns of the slave-raiders. So the movement of the poem is never arrested, but flows unbroken into a new migration across the ocean into the continent of bondage and exile. The hurrying movement of the verse itself, with its breathless lines and densely-packed assonances, perfectly contains the urgent quality, driven but aimless, which Brathwaite imparts to the journey that has carried negroes to every corner of the world to labour in the enterprises of other men. There is no sense here in which the desert represents the condition of a divided people and a divided culture; it is merely the first of many vicissitudes endured by the negro race in the unending process of 'moving on'. For Williams, it expresses a static, intermediate condition from which there is no apparent escape; for Brathwaite, it projects his people upon a pilgrimage without fulfilment and without rest, in which hope obstinately survives.

But *Rights of Passage* is only the first part of a poetic trilogy, that part in which Brathwaite traces the process whereby millions of negroes became disfranchised of language, culture

---

1 *Ibid.*, p. 4.

and home; of everything which distinguishes one man from another except the colour of his skin. In the second part, *Masks*, he recreates his own personal pilgrimage to the forest empire of Ashanti, a pilgrimage made across time as well as across water, and does so with such intensity as to make of it a representative West Indian experience of homecoming. *Masks* opens and closes with rhythms and phrases based upon the Akan drum language, the language with which the drummer prepares and sanctifies his wood, his skin, his sticks and the special destiny of his drum. When the drum is made it is ready to speak to Odomankoma, God of the Sky:

> Odomankoma 'Kyerema says
> Odomankoma 'Kyerema says
> The Great Drummer of Odomankoma says
> The Great Drummer of Odomankoma says
>
> that he has from come sleep
> that he has come from sleep
> and is arising
> and is arising
>
> like *akoko* the cock
> like *akoko* the cock who clucks
> who crows in the morning
> who crows in the morning
>
> we are addressing you
> *ye re kyere wo*
> we are addressing you
> *ye re kyere wo*
>
> listen
> let us succeed
>
> listen
> may we succeed . . .[1]

Thus Brathwaite announces in the very opening of his poem that its rhythms will now be based, not on the regretful wail of the blues or the restless energy of jazz, but on the heavy, confident beat of the *Atumpan*, the talking drums of Ghana. Within this bold framework the poem conducts a twofold movement. First, in the sections called 'Path-finders' and

---

1 *Masks* (London, Oxford University Press, 1968), pp. 11–12.

'Limits', i[retraces the ancient migration from North-eastern Africa (Axum, Agades, Wagadugu) which mythically brought the Akan people to the banks of the Volta River. The claims of modern Ghana upon Axum are perhaps even more tenuous than its connections with the historical Ghana of Kumba Saleh, but the West Indies have perpetuated the classical identification of 'Ethiopia' with Black Africa and it may serve as a poetic token for whatever cultural or ethnic tides may have flowed over the Nile-Chad watershed during three millennia. Certainly Ashanti, like Oyo, had strong roots in the savannah before it moved southwards to develop a forest empire based on indirect trade with the coast. And Brathwaite brilliantly evokes the change of character and tempo which this transition to the high forest must have demanded of a people accustomed to ranging movement and unshadowed sun:

1
Like walls the forest stops us.
Over the ford at Yeji it was waiting:
tangled squat mahogany out-
riders and then the dense, the
dark green tops, bright
shining standing trunks:
wawa, dahoma, esa and
odum; the doom
of the thick stretching green.
Leaves gathered darkness; no
pathway showed the way . . .

2
But the lips remember
temples, gods and pharaohs,

gold, silver ware, imagination
rose on wide unfolded wings.

But here in the dark,
we rest:

time to forget
the kings;

time to forget
the gods . . .[1]

---

1 *Ibid.*, pp. 25–6.

128

'Limits' ends with the arrival at the coast and the ships, images of slavery, degeneration and exile. So the way is prepared for the second major movement of the poem, the movement of 'Return', 'Crossing the River' and 'Arrival'. Now it is the modern, western-educated, individual West Indian who returns to the very shore from which his ancestors were taken. He moves through the streets of Takoradi, sensing colour, warmth and welcome, but finding nothing which stirs ancestral memory:

> I travelled to a distant town
> I could not find my mother
> I could not find my father
> I could not hear the drum[1]

Yet something draws him onward, 'eating time like a mudfish', and slowly he mounts towards the River Pra, ancient frontier dividing the hybrid Fanti kingdoms from the powerful, long inviolable Ashanti Federation. And again he is journeying in time. If his face is no longer recognizable, let it become a mask, let it remain empty and resigned to separation until the encounter which he still expects, towards which he is still urging:

> So for my hacked
> face, hollowed eyes,
> undrumming heart,
>
> make me a black
> mask that dreams
> silence,
>
> reflects no light,
> smiles no pretence,
> hears not my brother's
>
> language.
> Let me without
> my mother's
>
> blood, my father's
> holy *kra*,[2] traverse
> paths where yet

---

1 *Ibid.*, p. 38.   2 soul or portion of god.

the new dead
cannot know that
time was evil,

but where dew's
ears prepare
for my coming . . .[1]

As the poet mounts towards the place where at last he feels a
sense of arrival, a parallel movement takes place in the opposite
direction; perhaps the movement of his own ancestor who
carries, locked up in his chained body, the secret of why that
ancient strength and splendour finally failed in its encounter
with the West. On the banks of the Pra, approaching Kumasi,
he finally sees him:

You there on the other
bank, walking away
down the slope,
can you hear,
can you hear me?[2]

So he comes at last to Nana Tano, sacred river and symbol of
primal creative force, while the drums which opened the poem
return with the Akan funeral chant of condolence, *damirifa dūe*.
He does not find the secret of that ancient failure, he does not
find the burial place of his birth-cord, he finds only the certainty
of death and the certainty that he must soon depart again, for
even the Prodigal Son forgiven does not linger in his father's
household. Night comes as he walks to the shrine of Nana Tano,
but it is on a note of dawn and awakening that he finally turns
his back upon the land of his forefathers to tread again 'the
dark path' of exile. And it is now especially that he needs help
and blessing from Asase Yaa, goddess of that earth which gave
him a momentary sense of homecoming but refused him the
ultimate secrets of origin:

Asase Yaa, Earth,
if I am going away now,

You must help me.
Divine Drummer,

---

1 *Ibid.*, p. 45.   2 *Ibid.*, p. 51.

'*Kyerema,*
if time sends me

walking that dark
path again, you
must help me . . .[1]

Now Brathwaite closes the poem with the drum refrain that
must be beaten for every new Akan drum which is learning its
task of praising, lamenting and rejoicing:

I will rise
and stand on my feet.

Like *akoko* the cock
Like *akoko* the cock

who cries
in the early dawn . . .

I am learning
let me succeed.[2]

I am learning
let me succeed.

Masks stands as the most impressive and complete work yet
produced in this literature of the black revenant who finds in
Africa something less than a real homecoming, but something
infinitely more than failure or disappointment. Here Brathwaite
finds something with which he can connect, something from
which both his life and his art can feed and grow. But ultimately he must abandon it and return to the islands which
are his own real and now sufficient world. The third, as yet
unpublished, part of his trilogy promises to be the story of that
return.

---

1 *Ibid.*, p. 73.
2 *Ibid.*, pp. 73–4.

Chapter 9
The Claims of the Past

A touch at that rounded moment of the night
And the dead return to life
Dum-belly woman, plantain-breasted
Mother! What human husband folds
His arms, and blesses randy ghosts?
Keep away now, leave, leave the dead
Some room to dance.

Wole Soyinka

Lionel Lobo Froad failed in his attempt to find an African past with which he could communicate; for him the past was dead because it had never consisted of living people. Seeking to discover the quality of ancient life through the study of its monuments, he was repelled by the discovery that these celebrate nothing but the lust of rulers, to perpetuate their own deeds of slaughter and oppression. Yet the same is true of most political art, and much of the surviving art of the ancient world is essentially political in character. Even today the streets of London, capital of a repentant imperialism, are lumbered with the immense equestrian statues of obscure commanders.

In spite of occasional gestures in the direction of Egypt, African writers have in the main sought to release the energies of the past by methods more humdrum, direct and humane. They have not sought an artefact they could thrill to, so much as a grandfather they could recognize, a living and suffering man who knew what it was to make moral choices and to endure their consequences. It is literally true that most tropical African communities have thought of themselves as inhabiting a society which holds the dead, the living and the unborn in a single embrace. But simple assertions of this belief are hardly found outside the realm of lyric poetry; dramatists and novelists have found it necessary to systematize the relationship of living and dead in some way which makes it actively significant, and in doing so they have often borrowed concepts from other ancient societies as well as their own. Greece, Sumer and

Japan have all contributed to the vocabulary of forms through which it has been transformed from a pious belief into a dramatically functional idea.

Since the dead are concerned with the living, the initiative for communication comes as often from them as from their descendants. This is no inert débris of vanished cultures such as Froad scrutinized in vain, but a dynamic source of energy seeking for release and which, failing to find it through creative communion, may spend itself in thunderbolts and convulsions of nature. In trying to express this creative communion through literature, the good writer will discover ancestors who are not demi-gods, not larger than life, but exactly life-size. The task has been made more difficult by the demonology of the past promoted by missionary and colonial vindicators of European rule. Faced with the proposition that one's great-grandfather was a benighted savage in desperate need of salvation, the temptation is either to agree or to seize the open end of the dialectic and maintain that he was a paragon of all the virtues. Insofar as this argument was a political and cultural one conducted by publicists, it would have seemed intolerably flat to show only that one's great-grandfather was a man like other men; it is the artist who will appreciate that this demonstration is the most relevant and difficult of all.

The Nigerian dramatist Wole Soyinka deliberately challenges the sanctification of the past at the very opening of his first major play, *A Dance of the Forests* (1960). A Prologue informs us that we are about to witness the return of two ancestors who have been sent from 'the understreams' in response to a call from the living. They are to lend glory to the Gathering of the Tribes (the play was written for Nigerian Independence) and Adenebi, the Council Orator, soon tells us the sort of thing they had in mind:

> The accumulated heritage—that is what we are celebrating. Mali, Chaka. Songhai. Glory. Empires. . . .[1]

But when the empty stage breaks open to admit the visitors they emerge as a mouldy and obscure couple who have returned to the world simply to vent the grievances they have been nursing for centuries. No-one wants to speak to 'these

---

1 *Op. cit.* in *Five Plays*, (London & Ibadan, OUP, 1963), p. 8.

obscenities', yet it proves that their selection was not random after all. The deaths which they resent so bitterly were inflicted upon them at the ancient court of Mata Kharibu by the forebears and historical prototypes of those who have now sent for them. Forest Father, the divine *régisseur* of the whole dramatic action, is leading their living exemplars into the depths of the forest, there to confront them with their earlier and essential selves, with their repetitive patterns of folly and crime. By so doing he can open for them the possibility of escape from the endless cycle, but it is up to them to effect that escape by taking just one choice which is not already written in their natures. The only one to choose with this sort of freedom is Demoke, descendant of the Court Poet and committer of jealous murders in both existences, whose attempt to snatch the 'Half-Child' of the Dead Woman from its doomed cycle of stillbirths cannot save the child but may redeem himself. As Forest Father himself comments:

> I must do this alone, and no more, since to intervene is to be guilty of contradiction, and yet to remain altogether unfelt is to make my long-rumoured ineffectuality complete; hoping that when I have tortured awareness from their souls, that perhaps, only perhaps, in new beginnings. . . .[1]

Then, turning to his servant-spirit, the lame Aroni, he asks whether Demoke knows the meaning of his act. Aroni then speaks his warning:

> Demoke, you hold a doomed thing in your hand.
> It is no light matter to reverse the deed
> that was begun many lives ago.[2]

Thus the dead not only claim a hearing from the living, they are the innate selves or tendencies of the living. Their return is precipitated by 'a touch' at the full of the night, and it takes the form of a compulsion upon their descendants to conform to the ancient pattern, which only a huge individual effort of self-knowledge and self-transcendence can break.

The system of ideas which is expressed in *A Dance of the Forests* has in part been teased out of the Yoruba symbol of eternal repetition, an abstract figure of the snake eating its own tail.

---

1 *Ibid.*, p. 82.   2 *Ibid.*, p. 82.

It has already been pointed out in Chapter 5 that the tropical forest does not evoke symbolism of a seasonal death

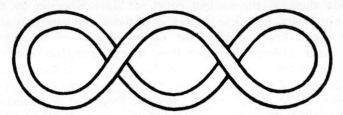

followed after some interval by a seasonal resurrection, but rather of a continuous, unbroken process of decay and renewal. Thus the snake's ever-devouring mouth expresses life drawing its sustenance from decay and death, even as the young shoots of the forest do. Linked to this is the concept of the vital energy of the dead transmitting itself to unborn generations, a concept apparently universal in tropical Africa:

> If a father has begotten a child—
> however long it may take
> the child may yet beget the father[1]

But the specific use of dramatic ritual to show the cycle as one of doomed repetition from which both dead and living (the Dead Man and Woman of the play and Demoke) strive to escape, might also owe something to the Buddhist belief in the 'Wheel of Life and Death,' which underlies the Nō plays of Japan. The only escape from this Wheel is through *satori* or 'Enlightenment', which is the realization that material phenomena are only thoughts, not external facts, and are thus under the control of the will. The Zen Buddhists add that this truth cannot be transmitted by speech or writing, but lies hidden in the heart and can be discovered only by Zen or contemplative meditation.[2] Forest Father appears to operate in some such way by presenting to the living the re-enactment of the crimes and follies of their past selves, but making no comment upon them. In the Nō, also, the dead appear to the living and dance again the obsessional situations from which they seek to escape and from which only the living can release

---

1 from an *Odu* (oracle poem) of the Ifa cult, Western Nigeria.
2 See *The Nō-Plays of Japan*, Arthur Waley (London, Allen & Unwin, 1921), p. 58.

them. Much of the play's meaning, however, could also be drawn from the widespread Nigerian belief in *Abiku*, 'spirit-children', who are doomed to a series of reincarnations and infant deaths from which their families strive, by certain rituals, to save them. The Half-Child of the play has much in common with such an *Abiku*, emphasized by his own tragic song:

> I who yet await a mother
> Feel this dread,
> Feel this dread,
> I who flee from womb
> To branded womb, cry it now
> I'll be born dead
> I'll be born dead.[1]

Soyinka's lyrical poetry often contains clues to the meaning of his plays and his poem on *Abiku* is no exception. It offers little hope that human rituals can ever release the child from the cycle in which it is closed and which locks it away utterly from ordinary love or concern:

> In vain your bangles cast
> Charmed circles at my feet
> I am Abiku, calling for the first
> And the repeated time.[2]

If there is indeed a glimpse of Zen Buddhism in the handling of the play-within-the-play, the mythological world of *A Dance of the Forests* is otherwise completely Yoruba, the nation-tribe of Western Nigeria to which Soyinka belongs. Underlying Forest Father's attempt to liberate Demoke's soul there is a struggle between two slightly less powerful gods to control it. Ogun, the god of carvers and artists, as well as iron, hunting and war, seeks to protect Demoke from the consequences of his acts. As the *oriki* (praise-songs) of Ogun avow:

> The lion never allows anybody to play with his cub;
> Ogun will never allow his child to be punished.

But the god Eshuoro is determined to frustrate him, and even seeks to thwart Demoke in his attempt to snatch the Half-Child from its destiny. Demoke has compounded the murder

---

1 *Five Plays*, p. 74.
2 *Modern Poetry from Africa*, ed. Moore and Beier (Penguin, 1963), p. 118.

of his assistant by cutting the top off the *araba* (silk-cotton) tree which was too high for him to climb. Eshuoro embodies the spirit of this tree (Oro) and the god of mischief, fate and the unpredictable (Eshu) in a combination that bodes ill for Demoke. Forest Father, however, leads Demoke to confess his crime to him in the dreaming, suspended world of the deep forest. This confession, we gather, helps to save Demoke from the worst consequences of Eshuoro's wrath and to prepare the way for his later gesture of 'Enlightenment'.

The poetry of George Awoonor-Williams, which draws much of its imagery from the traditional life of the Ewe people of the Ghana-Togo border, also shows us a world where the dead exist through their expectations of the living, expectations which are nowadays seldom fulfilled. His poetry abounds in laments for the neglected shrines and forgotten gods, ignored by a society now intent upon individual status and materialism:

> On the sacred stone with the neglected embers
> the cock offering has fluttered and gone
> the palm oil on the stone gods has turned green
> and the gods look on concerned and forgotten[1]

Here the sickness and instability which the poet sees in the life around him is directly related to its failure to maintain organic continuity with the past. Far from being useless or outmoded as guides through the bewildering maze of contemporary existence, the forefathers alone can give man a sure sense of his own identity, his own life-style. They will enable him to make the right choices, choices which he can defend with good conscience when he revisits their shrines or moves among their more faithful and conservative descendants. This profession of faith in the old gods can be taken literally, but more probably it is a symbolic language offering a vocabulary of peculiar richness to the poet concerned with continuity and with the quality of modern life. To ensure that the new culture of Ghana will bear some distinction of its own, it must be related coherently to those values which man has developed in his historical existence on the Guinea coast; a complete divorce from those values can lead only to sterility and imitation. So,

---

[1] George Awoonor-Williams 'The Years Behind', *Rediscovery* (Ibadan, Mbari, 1964), p. 24.

using the words of a traditional Ewe song, Awoonor-Williams calls upon the fathers to make a garment of their wisdom which will protect and guide him in the coming times:

> Sew the old days for me, my fathers
> sew them that I may wear them
> for the feast that is coming
> the feast of the new season that is coming[1]

In another poem he complains of sickness in his 'god of songs'. Consulting the oracle, he is told in his own tongue, (Ewe, not English) to carry him to his 'father's gods'. Thus the poet's gift of song is seen as a wooden image which he carries upon his head, for the head is the seat of inner being and transmitted wisdom. So he carries his god of songs towards the shrine of his father's gods:

> But before they opened the hut
> My god burst into songs, new strong songs
> That I am still singing with him.[2]

The strength of Awoonor-Williams' poetry at its best derives in part from his knowledge and understanding of traditional Ewe songs. The writing of English poetry for publication is not merely a new occupation in itself, but in Africa it has often involved the separation of words from the music, dance and singing voice which have always been an integral part of their social expression. In Europe the isolation of poetry from its concomitants began centuries ago. Not only did the isolated reading of poetry in the study emerge as a species of literary enjoyment, but its composition largely disappeared into the study also. With the qualified exception of opera, the setting of poetry to music became a retrospective activity entrusted to another profession, and then considered appropriate only to certain *genres*. The recent vogue for poetry readings, often against unrelated jazz accompaniment, is a partial attempt to restore the public situation of poetry, but does not always affect the conditions of its composition as an isolated art form. More hopeful was the dramatic function of songs composed and set as a joint operation by Brecht with Kurt Weil or Hans Eisler or Paul Dessau. Much of the emotion, meaning and

---

1 *Ibid.*, p. 24.
2 'My God of Songs Was Ill', *ibid.*, p. 31.

dramatic continuity of *Mother Courage* or *The Caucasian Chalk Circle* were conveyed through song and musically-controlled mime or movement. This is closely comparable to the functions of song, masquerade and dance in Soyinka's plays and is in marked contrast to the role of songs in Shakespeare and other Elizabethan dramatists, where they have already become little more than pleasing interludes. But even the giant influence of Brecht has not succeeded in moving European drama significantly closer to 'total theatre', the expression of many arts through one, which has endured so long in the classical drama of the Orient and seems to have excellent prospects of stabilizing itself in Africa as a central dramatic tradition.

Awoonor-Williams' predecessors, the traditional poets of Guinea, often composed their works spontaneously in performance, through the constant re-working, extension or elaboration of tunes and phrases transmitted from the past. Thus a song might retain the same music and pattern of repeated chorus or refrain for generations, but could in the hands of a good poet-singer-musician acquire an entirely new set of verses. These in turn, if his influence were strong enough, might be transmitted to his contemporaries and descendants. The emergence of a completely new tune was probably a comparatively rare event, though new tunes were constantly acquired through diffusion of influence and the arrival of new instruments with special demands and possibilities.

What does such traditional but ever-changing vernacular poetry offer to the young educated poet working in English? Awoonor-Williams does not connect himself to the past merely through his choice of themes, but also through certain technical devices. Several of his images and refrains are taken straight from Ewe poetry, but some of his poems go beyond this to a reproduction of the kind of methods by which a traditional song conveys its message. Much traditional poetry translates naturally into a species of free verse (none, in any case, makes use of rhyme in its vernacular form), in which each line contains a complete image or attribute, corresponding to a musical phrase. Sometimes one line will be somewhat gnomic and the next a direct attachment of its meaning to the purpose of the poem, be this praise, abuse, mourning or rejoicing. Here is an example from Yoruba:

Only the finger that fits the nose should be used to
clean the nose.
The king cuts off a man's head—because it befits him to do so[1]

In other instances, however, a poem may avoid any direct
statement of its meaning, offering instead a series of images
which move parallel to it and appeal to some recognized
truth in other spheres of existence. Again, the Yoruba language
offers a good example of this technique, which is especially
favoured in oracular poetry, demanding interpretation by the
priest who quotes it. In the following Odu of the Ifa priests
there appears to be advice to the questioner that he should
worship Obatala, the god of material creation. The great God
who rules in the sky (Olorun) once advised Obatala that the
sky grows no grass; that is a matter for earthbound creativity.
In the last couplet Obatala himself appears to be speaking, but
he is also providing an image of what the new worshipper
himself must do:

The sky is immense; but grows no grass.
This is what the Oracle said to Obatala,
to whom the great God gave the reins of the world.
God of the Igbo, I stretch out my hands.
Give the reins of the world to me.[2]

Awoonor-Williams makes use of both these techniques in his
English poetry. In the course of a war song, the poet turns
aside from his menaces to ask:

Where has it been heard before
That a snake has bitten a child
in front of its own mother?[3]

The question suggests indirectly that the enemy is now
threatening their very huts and must be driven off. It is left to
make its own meaning clear in the context. But in another
poem Awoonor-Williams uses imagery of the weaver bird and
its notorious colonizing habits, which often kill the chosen
tree, to unfold a vision of the whole colonial period in Ghana.
The transition from tolerated missionary and trading activity

---

1 'Eye', from *Yoruba Poetry*, translated by Beier and Gbadamosi (Ibadan,
Black Orpheus, 1962), p. 40.
2 *Ibid.*, p. 26.
3 'Song of War', *Modern Poetry from Africa*, p. 80.

to outright annexation is conveyed in the opening lines. But the poem goes on to confess that even the new horizons of independence are still bounded by what the weaver bird taught, though the enfranchized African has no will to join the rituals the bird prescribed:

> The weaver bird built in our house
> And laid its eggs on our only tree
> We did not want to send it away
> We watched the building of the nest
> And supervized the egg-laying.
> And the weaver returned in the guise of the owner
> Preaching salvation to us that owned the house
> Its sermon is the divination of ourselves
> And our new horizons limit at its nest
> But we cannot join the prayers and answers of the communicants.

Only then does the poem turn to call for a rebirth of vision and creativity, distilling its arrested bitterness into the single word 'excrement'. The poem's allegorical detail is retained throughout, for such shrines do indeed often stand under the homestead trees and are so defiled by the irrepressible weaver bird:

> We look for new homes every day,
> For new altars we strive to rebuild
> The old shrines defiled by the weaver's excrement.[1]

Poetry of this kind, strongly concerned with relating itself to a vernacular tradition and using a locally-recognizable vocabulary of images, more or less dictates a free-verse style and an avoidance of surrealistic clustering or coagulation of metaphor into tight, many-faceted bundles. Imagery in a traditional poem may be cryptic but it is always separable; so one may get a string of images designed to emphasize, by analogy, a single characteristic of the subject. Evoking the anger of Eshu, the Yoruba god of mischief, his praise-song observes:

> When he is angry he hits a stone until it bleeds.
> When he is angry he sits on the skin of an ant.
> When he is angry he weeps tears of blood.[2]

Here the images add to but do not displace each other. The

---

1 *Rediscovery*, p. 16.   2 *Yoruba Poetry*, p. 15.

poem works by an accumulation of attributes and much of Awoonor-Williams' poetry works in the same way. His 'Songs of Sorrow', for example, achieve their effect of desolation and abandonment by listing the evidence that the dead have failed to safeguard their descendants and the patrimony they bequeathed them. The dying Agosu is told to carry a message of reproach to the spirit world; here the images of disintegration draw their force from the very things most valued in traditional society:

Agosu if you go tell them,
Tell Nyidevu, Kpeti, and Kove
That they have done us evil.
Tell them their house is falling
And the trees in the fence
Have been eaten by termites;
That the martels curse them.
Ask them why they idle there
While we suffer, and eat sand . . .[1]

Those who seek a more radical approach to English prosody may decide to ignore the devices of African traditional poetry, intended for singing or reciting on public occasions, and make use of metrical, stanzaic and rhyming devices offered by the new language. Thus the late Christopher Okigbo uses the type of broken melody perfected by T. S. Eliot to evoke the reproachful sadness of abandoned shrines and rotting images, symbols which quite naturally carry the whole weight of an African tradition which has always concentrated the expression of its values upon them. These fractured and haunting lines mark a formal break with African poetic tradition, but they exploit the resources of English in a manner which matches exactly the shattered, undying gods they celebrate:

And the gods lie in state
And the gods lie in state
     without the long-drum.

And the gods lie unsung
And the gods lie
     veiled only with mould,
Behind the shrinehouse.

---

1 *Modern Poetry from Africa*, p. 79.

> Gods grow out,
>   abandoned;
> And so do they . . .[1]

The sombre beat of these lines marks the nadir of destruction and loss, recorded in 'Fragments out of the Deluge' the second part of *Limits*. The twin gods, male and female, who represent the harmonious balance of the old religion with its concern for social unity, have perhaps been broken and divided by the predatory eagles of colonial and missionary interference, splitting the whole social organism into warring factions of converted and unconverted, Catholic and Protestant, young and old. But at this low moment of the poem the Sunbird, who was killed by the conquerors, sings again outside the window. His long beard of mould grew while he slept, awaiting resurrection; it did not betoken his death. Here the Sunbird is both the poet and the resurgent energy of the old culture which sings in his throat. He looks upon that culture not with ignorance but with knowledge, and finds it still worthy of life:

>   BUT at the window
> Outside
>   at the window,
> A shadow—
> Listen. Listen again under the shadow . . .
> Give me a spooknif and shave my long beard . . .
>   The Sunbird sings again
> From the LIMITS of the dream,
>   The Sunbird sings again
> Where the caress does not reach,
>   of Guernica,
> On whose canvas of blood,
> The newsprint-slits of his tongue
>   cling to glue . . .
> *and the cancelling out is complete.*[2]

The last six lines have become the most disputed in the criticism of Okigbo's poetry. What looks like a smooth movement towards the resolution of the conflict that runs right through 'Fragments out of the Deluge' is apparently disrupted by the

---

1 'Limits IX', *Limits* (Ibadan, Mbari, 1964).
2 'Limits X', *op. cit.*

sudden intrusion of Picasso's Guernica and its images of agony. The key surely lies in the line:

Where the caress does not reach

which, despite its gentle cadence, proves to be ironic when we learn the nature of the 'caress' which does not reach the resurrected Sunbird singing upon its spray. Okigbo concentrates into the one word 'Guernica', as Picasso did into his canvas, the whole force of an outraged humanity. That exaltation of will and national purpose into a great Moloch upon whose reeking altar everything must be sacrificed has stretched its purposes to Africa also; but the Sunbird sings despite and beyond its 'canvas of blood'. The 'cancelling out' is the completion of the process of adjustment and recovery which makes possible the resurrection of the Sunbird. It is the penultimate line which still presents difficulties, for assuming that 'his' refers to the Sunbird—and it is difficult to accept any other attribution—its presence apparently *within* the canvas contradicts the whole sense of the poem elsewhere. The horse at the centre of Picasso's canvas expresses in his straddled and fragmented limbs all the torment of uncomprehending rage and anguish: he is rendered in a texture which suggests newsprint and is built up, like the rest of the composition, with a knot of intersecting strips and planes which suggest the clamant tongues of a mankind not yet beaten into silence. Is there, perhaps, some lightning transference here from bird to horse as the centre of the poem's sympathy? However we interpret the lines, there is no doubt that Okigbo has weakened one of his finest poems by suddenly obscuring the resolution which seemed already achieved a few lines earlier. Here as elsewhere, his obscurities do not spring from wordiness or over-elaboration, but from the extreme simplicity and economy of expression given to complex ideas and esoteric references. An example of such references occurs in the very first poem of 'Fragments', which begins with the lines:

Upon an empty sarcophagus
    out of solid alabastar,
A branch of giant fennel,
    on an empty sarcophagus.

The image here conveys its meaning spontaneously, for the

145

fennel inevitably suggests that which obstinately keeps growing even in the charnel house, while the empty sarcophagus speaks both of ancient death and burial and of the resurrection which defeats and denies death. But the lines also refer to an actual excavation in Egypt where such a discovery was made, and the presence of ancient Egypt behind the lines introduces another dimension of meaning, for the resurgent culture of Africa might be seen as the fennel still springing on the empty sarcophagus of Egyptian Civilization.

It is this last association that is followed up a few lines later:

> You might as well see the new branch
> in ENKI;
> And that is no new thing either. . . .

Here Okigbo traces the 'new' branch beyond Egypt to Sumer, then abandons the enterprise with a hint that we can never name a source for what is self-renewing. Enki or Ea was one of the divine Triad of ancient Sumer. Known as 'the Lord of the watery deep', he dwelt in the subterranean ocean which supported the world (analogous to Soyinka's 'understreams') and was the bearer of divine wisdom to mankind. It was Enki who taught man the arts of cultivation and architecture, who introduced writing and geometry, and who fertilized the earth-goddess Ninhursag to bring forth vegetation and the animal world.[1] These qualities of the primeval demiurge and teacher lend additional depth to his presence in the closing lines of the poem, though they will be evident only to the learned or the assiduous. Others, as some critics have already done, will take Enki to be part of a mysterious sign-language which the poet charges entirely with meanings of his own.

Wole Soyinka has recently urged that the African writer must now free himself from his fascination with the past. He goes on to argue, 'the past exists, but it is vitally dependent upon the sensibility that evokes it.'[2] The poems of Awoonor-Williams and Okigbo which we have examined, as well as Soyinka's own dramatic evocations of the past, would all seem to accept this conditional view of its nature. The implication of

---

1 See *The Ancient Gods*, by E. O. James (London, Weidenfeld and Nicolson, 1960), p. 74 *et seq.*
2 'The Writer and the Modern African State', Kampala, *Transition* No. 31, p. 13.

this view is that the past does bear upon the present, but not decisively. The burden of decision and of choice rests with the living, and it is they who determine what new chapters shall be added to the story. A knowledge of the past may guide them in this responsibility but cannot relieve them of it.

The only African writer who seems to offer us a deterministic view of the past, a concept Greek in its inexorability, is J. P. Clark, a poet and dramatist from the Delta region of Nigeria. His first two plays, *Song of a Goat* (1961) and *The Masquerade* (1963), are linked tragedies which follow the working out of a hereditary curse upon a group of Delta fisherfolk. At the opening of the first play we learn that the fisherman Zifa has lost his potency and is unable to impregnate his young wife Ebiere. When he consults a traditional masseur he touches upon a piece of family history that is to rise from the grave and blast him:

ZIFA.
     My father who they dared
Not spit at when he lived is dead
And lying in the evil grove. Was that
not enough penalty?

MASSEUR.
     ... You did what every
Dutiful son would do when you brought
Him back home among his people.
It may have been a little bit early
For one who died of the white taint.[1]

The 'white taint' is leprosy and we are to learn that the casting of his father's body into the evil grove (reserved for those deemed unfit for burial in the village) was not, indeed, 'enough penalty'. A further ominous note is struck in the last speech of the scene when the Masseur, left alone, prays:

     Oh you dead
And gone, take your fat and flesh
But leave us our skin and bones.[2]

Earlier, he had advised Ebiere to get herself made over as a

---

1 In *Three Plays*, J. P. Clark (London & Ibadan, OUP, 1964), pp. 9–10.
2 *Ibid.*, p. 13.

wife to Zifa's young and lusty brother Tonye. Ebiere indig-
nantly flouts the suggestion, but soon afterwards makes a
totally unsanctified grab at Tonye when her husband is away
at sea. They spend the night together and Zifa, guessing the
situation on his return, terrorizes Tonye by a macabre ritual
of making him force a goat's head, horns and all, into a narrow
pot. Tonye, fleeing from his brother's murderous wrath,
hangs himself inside the house, and Zifa comments bitterly:

> I sought to kill
> You but in that office you have again
> Performed my part.[1]

Leaving the sorrowing relatives around the house, Zifa walks
off and casts himself into the sea, his end being recounted to the
audience in a Messenger's Speech which, like much else in the
play's structure and philosophy, is familiar to us from Greek
tragedy.

In *The Masquerade*, too, the whole plot hinges upon a secret
hereditary contamination which, revealing itself, destroys
everyone in touch with it. Tufa, the fruit of Tonye's and
Ebiere's incestuous union, has grown up in ignorance of his
fateful origins and has wandered to another Delta town in
courtship of the young girl Titi. On the eve of their wedding
the secret of Tufa's accursed history is revealed. Titi refuses to
renounce her lover, taking the 'modern' view that Tufa is not
responsible for these buried crimes, and her enraged father
shoots her down like a chicken. While this deed is recounted to
us by a chorus of priests, Tufa and the girl's father enter and
fight upon the stage and Tufa is shot with the same gun which
killed his sweetheart. As he staggers off to die, he gasps that the
purging is now almost complete. So we suppose that the taint
introduced when Zifa's father was first brought into the village
for burial has at last, several deaths and two generations later,
been cleansed. One of the priests, however, adds the heavily
Greek comment:

> Who
> The gods love they visit with calamity.[2]

which suggests that the gods' purposes are inscrutable as well
as inexorable.

---

1 *Ibid.*, p. 40.   2 *Ibid.*, p. 87.

These echoes are not necessarily entirely derivative, for to unfold a ritual action between homestead, shrine and market-place comes as naturally to a tribally-reared African as it did to an ancient Greek. To both, the ceremonies of sacrifice, appeasement, expiation and social rejection are not the distant, mythical foundations of drama but the immediate and visible circumstances of daily life, whose meaning and purpose are understood by the whole community. Drama is a popular language, therefore, not simply because it transcends the boundaries of literacy but because it reunifies its audience by appealing to them at a level which they all recognize. If poetry and song can keep their connection with the theatre in Africa they can perhaps stave off that cultural polarization which inevitably accompanies the appearance of printed novels and poetry in a partly illiterate and largely non-reading population.

Clark's work, however, shows far less awareness than Soyinka's of the vigorous new dramatic life centred around the folk-operas of Duro Ladipo and Ogunmola, the popular musical-moralities of Hubert Ogunde or the racy pidgin English sketches of Theatre Express. Many of these Nigerian groups work largely in the vernacular (Ladipo's and Ogunmola's, for example) though their plays have been successfully performed in English, German and other translations. The popular idiom they exploit, however, which has greatly affected the intellectual theatre of university and city circles, is one derived from years of work in the vernacular among alert, semi-literate audiences who delight in every display of musical, choreographic and linguistic dexterity. Their work is largely based on traditional legends of gods, kings and heroes already familiar to these audiences, so that the interest centres, as in much popular Elizabethan drama, not in the novelty of the story itself but in how it is told and the glosses that are put upon it. This re-interpretation of the past, through dramatic recreation in a contemporary context, is a vivid demonstration of its continued influence and vitality.

The uneasiness induced by Clark's first two tragedies stems partly from the oddly implacable nature of the gods they present and partly from their excessively literary character. It is always hazardous to generalize about African traditional religions, but it is certainly true of most of them that they offer means by which contamination can be expiated or cleansed. These means may involve the death or expulsion of a single person, but the guilt in Clark's plays seems to bring out a positively Atrean thirst for blood on the part of the divine powers. It is true that a creation myth of the Ijaw, the tribe to which Clark belongs, recounts how every child at birth makes choice of the attributes it will bear in life from the goddess Woyengi, who explains that these choices cannot be rescinded. There is no suggestion, however, that the consequences of choice endure beyond the life-span of the person making it.

So far as Clark's verse-style is concerned, he has chosen a rather slow-moving blank verse of predominantly Elizabethan flavour. *The Masquerade* is particularly full of phrases and inversions of word ordre which are oddly Shakespearean:

> Tongue
> Cannot tell what eyes saw, what heart rejects
> But hands cannot shake off.[1]

> Let not
> A breath of these tidings get past the gates
> Else rank corruption overflows us all.[2]

> It is the time
> Of night. There is a catch in the air
> Will not hold.[3]

There are also occasional felicities, both in the choice of images and the judicious use of proverbs to lend a rooted, local quality to the speech. The Third Priest says of the dead Titi:

> Now she lies squashed
> Like a lizard in the sand.[4]

And the Masseur in *Song of a Goat* remarks:

> I am too old
> To start raising green thatch for my grey hair.[5]

Such passages remind us that Clark early found his voice as a lyric poet of distinction. He has, however, no consistent ear for what is dramatically speakable on the stage and too often lands his actors in bathos at a critical moment of the action.

---

1 *Ibid.*, p. 84.   2 *Ibid.*, p. 79.   3 *Ibid.*, p. 77.
4 *Ibid.*, p. 79.   5 *Ibid.*, p. 10.

If he can develop a dramatic language of greater range, variety of tempo and assurance, as well as a closer concern with the demands of staging, it is possible that he will prove an important dramatist. His output to date lends itself better to radio or television presentation than to the less controllable conditions of the theatre. His latest work, *Ozidi* (1966), although apparently based on a traditional Ijaw cycle, is a highly episodic dramatic poem rather than a play.

All the writers we have examined so far in this chapter have established some kind of dynamic connection with the past, whether they place their emphasis upon the expectations of the dead, upon those of the living, or on both equally. Among certain novelists, however, it is possible to find an imaginative interest in the past which does not seek to relate it dynamically to the present, but simply to recreate it as a credible world inhabited by living men and women. This act of restitution is necessary both as a piece of social history and as offering a ground for some degree of cultural continuity. It does not demand the demonstration of some sort of spiritual inter-dependence between past and present, because even a purely naturalistic rendering of human situations fifty or a hundred years ago will establish its resemblance in countless ways to the living world we know. To reveal in the past a pattern of recognizable dilemmas, recognizable areas of motive and choice, may prove more fertilizing of the life of today than any rhythmic invocation of the ancestors.

It was the distinctive contribution of Chinua Achebe to the African novel that, though a certain natural piety might have drawn him to attempt the life of the past, his performance when he got there was always that of a realist. This is not to discount the role of fantasy in the interweaving of character and experience across time, but it is useful for fantasy to have something to work on. Achebe has rescued the past of Iboland for others to work on as they may. Thus his first novel, *Things Fall Apart* (1958), has made a deeper impression upon the literary sensibility of Africa than all the valued labours of historians and archaeologists put together. For readers who possess little historical sense or curiosity may find their attention commanded by the dramatic energy of the tale, and it is through this tale that Achebe exposes for us the lineaments of a vanished society.

Once Achebe has succeeded in carrying us imaginatively into the past, which he does in his very first page, he firmly keeps us there. There are no authorial interjections to remind us of the contemporary novelist clicking the switches of his magic lantern. We will remain in that phase of buried existence, with all its complex texture of agony and joy, until the action is fully played out. The achievement of this degree of density and consistency calls for a control of language to match the imaginative control of the writer's vision. The boredom of daily routines in an isolated forest village must be felt, but not suffered, by the reader, in order that he may feel also the excitement of the festival and the thrilling fear of the un-heralded event. Achebe needed an English vocabulary of images, allusions and metaphors utterly new to the novel, yet he was able to discover these simply by fidelity to the way men and women still spoke in the quieter villages of his own childhood. A judicious mixture of translation and authentic invention produced a conversational style which walked through his pages with all the weight of formality, precedence and tradition, yet never stumbled over itself through ineptitude.

These virtues of consistency and fidelity are demonstrated on the very first page of *Arrow of God*, Achebe's third novel and to date his finest achievement. The dating of the novel's action (circa 1927) may be something we can only guess gradually from the intermediate, semi-colonial nature of the village society it depicts, but the opening paragraphs already give us the lonely strength of Ezeulu, set apart from his fellows as 'half man, half spirit', together with a certain hard arrogance which later makes him rejoice in the role of scourge rather than protector:

> This was the third nightfall since he began to look for signs of the new moon. He knew it would come today but he always began his watch three days before its time because he must not take a risk. In this season of the year his task was not too difficult; he did not have to peer and search the sky as he might do in the rainy season. . . .
>
> His *obi* was built differently from other men's huts. There was the usual long threshold in front but also a shorter one on the right as you entered. The eaves of this additional entrance were cut back so that sitting on the floor Ezeulu could watch that part of the sky where the moon had its door. . . .

Ezuelu did not like to think that his sight was no longer as good as it used to be and that someday he would have to rely on someone else's eyes as his grandfather had done when his sight failed. . . . But for the present he was as good as any young man, or better because young men were no longer what they used to be. There was one game that Ezuelu never tired of playing on them. Whenever they shook hands with him he tensed his arm and put all his power into the grip, and being unprepared for it they winced and recoiled with pain.[1]

The first lines give us the intensity of Ezuelu's vigil and the importance for some implied human community of his being the first to sight the new moon (for no-one can announce its appearance until the Chief Priest has done so). The special architecture of his *obi*, in the next paragraph, further under-lines the peculiarity of his position and the way in which it is stamped even upon his surroundings, while the third paragraph makes it clear that Ezuelu occupies a position long held by his family and which he confidently expects to keep as long as life shall last. A moment later comes the first appearance of the moon and his announcement of it by beating his iron gong; we are ready to move out from the taut, seated figure of High Priest to explore his family, his village and his era. Thus the beating of the gong announces the action of the novel, but that first isolated impression of Ezuelu remains planted in our minds throughout, helping us to understand the interaction of temperament and office which finally brings him to madness.

Later in the novel Ezuelu's son has committed abomination by killing the sacred python, a puerile demonstration of his new-found Christian 'faith'. A rival village sends a young man to Ezuelu with an insulting message about the incident. In the ensuing dialogue it is the very lack of customary respect behind the relative formality of the exchanges which generates the tension of the scene and gives us the measure of Ezeulu's rage. His reply to the message is no casual threat but one carefully proportioned to the magnitude of the insult he has been offered in his own house:

'I am sent by Ezidemili.'
'True? I trust he is well.'

---

1 *Arrow of God*, (London, Heinemann, 1964), p. 1.

'He is well,' replied the messenger. 'But at the same time he is not.'

'I do not understand you.' Ezeulu was now very alert. 'If you have a message deliver it because I have no time to listen to a boy learning to speak in riddles.'

The young man ignored the insult.

'Ezidemili wants to know what you are going to do about the abomination which has been committed in your house.'

'That what happened?' asked the Chief Priest, holding his rage firmly with two hands.

'Should I repeat what I have just said?'

'Yes'.

'All right. Ezidemili wants to know how you intend to purify your house of the abomination that your son has committed.'

'Go back and tell Ezidemili to eat shit. Do you hear me? Tell Ezidemili that Ezeulu says he should go and fill his mouth with shit. As for you, young man, you may go in peace because the world is no longer what it was. If the world had been what it was I would have given you something that should always remind you of the day you put your head into the mouth of a leopard.'[1]

In Achebe's work the lineaments are visible of so much that still exists in Africa that his books scarcely constitute historical novels. They are more akin to those many Victorian and twentieth century novels whose authors have set them one or two generations back, so that they exhibit both a certain historical completeness and a thousand points of contact with the present. Except for the institution of warrant chiefs, the elements of action in *Arrow of God* could still be found in the Nigeria of the 1950's, but with the village less isolated, the younger generation more dispersed and a new power-group of embryo politicians emerging on the twin crutches of patronage and corruption. Even the world of *Things Fall Apart* is not as remote from us as it seems, for the son of Okonkwo's tormenter could still be living in Cheltenham and many parts of Nigeria did not come under effective European administration until the 1920's. Mbonu Ojike's *My Africa*, the autobiographical memoir of an Ibo politician of the late colonial period, offers many striking parallels with the events of *Things Fall Apart* and *Arrow of God*. For instance, the church in Ojike's

---

1 *Ibid.*, p. 65.

town was burnt down by pagans in reply to some fanatical excess committed by the local Christian converts. The British District Officer intervened immediately and imprisoned all the elders of Arondizuogu until full reparation had been made. The original insult to local belief and tradition went unpunished. Later Ojike's father, a pagan and polygamist chief of the area, permitted one of his younger sons to attend the mission school, hoping that the others would follow traditional ways and be ready to take over his farms and titles and his wide compound with its lofty *obi* and many traditional structures. But, with the exception of his eldest son, the others all insisted on flocking to the mission as well. All became Christians and rejected the ways and values of their father. Ojike describes his father's plight, which was that of thousands of African elders in those years, in the most moving terms:

> From every side misfortune visited my father. He was old and no more productive. His first son, the only one who had not been Christianized, suffered a fatal heart attack in 1926. The second son, Abanogu, who was to succeed him, was an arch Christian. There was no hope of saving the family from crumbling. . . . Before my father's eyes his lofty compound began to fall in ruins. He knew that Abanogu would not care to occupy the premises when he died. He knew it early. He fought like a hero to stay the hand of fate. . . . His sun set by degrees. May his star rise again to honour his deeds.
>
> When I left home in 1927 against his tearful protests, I knew that these disappointments had shortened his days. He was a man whose cry the world had not heard.[1]

This epitaph may stand for Okonkwo and Ezeulu also. Achebe offers back to his readers, in many instances, their own fathers and grandfathers, so that their cry may be heard at last.

The past and present may also be brought into creative relationship by the juxtaposition of characters rooted in the one and the other. Much of the comic machinery of Soyinka's play *The Lion and the Jewel* (1963) depends upon such a confrontation between the modernizing schoolmaster Lakunle and the unregenate old chief Baroka, though here he loads the dice somewhat by making the latter much the stronger character.

---

1 *My Africa* (New York, John Day, 1946), p. 108.

The Ugandan poet Okot p'Bitek similarly lends fire, imagination and tragic passion to his traditionally-minded heroine Lawino, who sings of her abandonment and neglect by a husband now sunk in his own muddled versions of progress. Lawino uses the imagery of traditional Acoli funeral and dancing songs, rather as Achebe's elders use proverbs, to give her song depth within the culture and enable it to drink from the abundant springs of inherited experience. Ocol, who loved and courted her in the days when a lovely village girl was the summit of his desires, has now turned aside to pursue his painted and powdered city mistress. Donning his tight black suit, he sweats his way through cocktail and garden parties, dancing to the tune of alien expectations until, in Lawino's words, he has become:

A dog of the white man![1]

In one of the poem's most beautiful and impassioned sequences, Lawino reminds Ocol what he once was and what he once admired, when:

He had not yet become a woman,
He was still a free man,
His heart was still his chief.

My husband was still a Black man
The son of the Bull
The son of Agik . . .
Was still a man,
An Acoli.[2]

She reminds him of the tense challenge between youths and girls which is embodied in the deeply satisfying ritual of the *orak* dance, beside which the sluggish cuddling of the modern night-club is so insipid and meaningless:

When the daughter of the Bull
Enters the arena
She does not stand there
Like stale beer that does not sell,
She jumps here
She jumps there

---

1 *Song of Lawino* (Nairobi, E. A. Publishing House, 1966), p. 204.
2 *Ibid.*, p. 200.

When you touch her
She says 'Don't touch me!'

The tattoes on her chest
Are like palm fruits
The tattoos on her back
Are like stars on a black night;
Her eyes sparkle like fireflies,
Her breasts are ripe
Like the full moon.

When the age mate of her brother sees them,
When, by accident,
The eyes of her lover
Fall on her breasts
Do you think the young man sleeps?[1]

Okot's poem was first composed in Acoli, and was then translated into English by the author himself. A great deal of the energy and freshness of its language seems to derive from this uninhibiting, liberating process, for the poem is thus able to feed directly upon the imagery in which the Acoli people project their own culture in dance and song.

The roots of English in East Africa are shallower and more recent than in West Africa, leave alone the Caribbean, and no distinctive dialect of English has evolved there which can be compared to West African pidgin, Freetown Krio, or the various West Indian dialects. It may be, therefore, that English will not prove to be a major vehicle for initial literary creation in Eastern Africa, but rather a medium through which the fruits of that creativity can be made available to us, as Okot has unlocked the riches of his vernacular song.

One East African writer, working directly in English and considerably influenced by Achebe, also concerns himself with the near past and its countless connections with the dilemmas of the present. James Ngugi of Kenya has returned in all three of his novels to the events preceding the Mau Mau Rebellion of 1952–56, illuminating the deep-seated and ever-mounting tensions at the heart of Kikuyu society which conspired to bring it about.

In *The River Between* it is Chege, father of the hero Waiyaki,

---

1 *Ibid.*, pp. 34–5.

who represents all that impetus of tradition which has projected the tribe's identity through the centuries. Early in the novel he leads Waiyaki to the top of a high hill from which they can overlook all the countryside of Muranga, heartland of the Agikuyu people. Here grows the sacred Mugumo tree, a wild mountain fig under which the most precious rites of the tribe were celebrated. Standing at this height in the calm of early morning, Waiyaki seems to see a deep unity embracing all the land. The contest between the Christianized, 'progressive' ridge of Makuyu and the sternly traditional ridge of Kameno, a contest which later dominates the book's action and symbolizes the tragic division of the whole people, is for a moment stilled:

> The ridges slept on. Kameno and Makuyu were no longer antagonistic. They had merged into one area of beautiful land, which is what, perhaps, they were meant to be. Makuyu, Kameno and the other ridges lay in peace and there was no sign of life, as one stood on the hill of God.[1]

This passage already hints at a feature of Ngugi's novels which markedly distinguishes them from Achebe's, the presence of landscape as a major actor in their development. The setting of Achebe's novels of tradition is the Ibo village, with its wide market place frequently filled with communal activity, its many walled compounds and tight pattern of intersecting paths. We are aware of the surrounding forest which shuts each village off from its neighbours, and certain scenes are enacted there, but the centre of his attention is always the crowded human landscape of the village.

Ngugi's people are lonelier, as befits the inhabitants of a vaster scene, framed by the distant summits of Kerinyaga and Nyendarua. The Agikuyu live in detached homesteads and there are no natural centres of activity corresponding in scale to the thronged streets and market places of an Ibo village-cluster, shut in by the imminent walls of the forest. Consequently, landscape prevails over man; its grandeur enfolding and dwarfing his activities, lifting his eyes daily from the details of household care towards the mountain's glittering snows. So Chege and Waiyaki look down at what seems an empty land still slumbering in its primeval peace. And Ngugi begins

---

1 *The River Between* (London, Heinemann, 1965), p. 19.

his novel by evoking the presence of the ridges themselves, before introducing us to their inhabitants:

> The two ridges lay side by side. . . . Between them was a valley. It was called the valley of life. Behind Kameno and Makuyu were many more valleys and ridges, lying without any discernible plan. They were like many sleeping lions which never woke. . . .
>
> A river flowed through the valley of life. . . . The river was called Honia, which meant cure, or bring-back-to-life. Honia river never dried: it seemed to possess a strong will to live, scorning droughts and weather changes. And it went on in the same way, never hurrying, never hesitating. People saw this and were happy.
>
> Honia was the soul of Kameno and Makuyu. It joined them. And men, cattle, wild beasts and trees were all united by this life stream.
>
> When you stood in the valley, the ridges ceased to be sleeping lions united by their common source of life. They became antagonists.[1]

Before peopling his landscape Ngugi has already expressed its essential harmony and unity when seen from above, its apparent division and hostility when viewed from below. His touch as a novelist sometimes fails him when handling people, tending towards sentimentality or a certain over-explicitness. But the setting of his human drama is always firm and sure. This alone gives us the love of land and heritage, the outrageous sense of loss, the brooding tension, bitterness and fear from which the tragic rebellion grew.

Only one African novelist has carried us deep into the past, recreating deliberately a village world which could be that of the nineteenth, eighteenth or seventeenth century. Elechi Amadi's *The Concubine* (1966) also owes a clear debt to Achebe but its aims are different, for it does not show us how and why an organized pattern of life broke down under the onslaughts of change, but how it persisted and what were the limits of the existence it offered. Amadi's story of the lovely widow Ihuoma whose lovers all die horribly is arresting; he does not challenge rational scepticism because he presents the events of his story simply, as they happened and as they were seen by their contemporary witnesses. His priests and medicine men act in good

---

1 *Ibid.*, p. 1.

faith, display genuine knowledge and wisdom, but are not infallible. They are neither magicians nor charlatans, but specialists and men of austere life.

Where Amadi's skill often deserts him is in the quality of his dialogue and in his tendency to explain features of traditional Ibo culture rather than exhibit them in action. The following passage of dialogue displays an inability either to transliterate Ibo idioms or to find acceptable equivalents for them:

> 'Mark her language, mother! If she goes on I shall be compelled to deal with her.'
> 'She has not abused you yet, my son.'
> 'Are you waiting for her to abuse me outright before telling her to check her tongue?'
> 'Mother, why bother?' Ahurole said, 'we all know he fights for food.'
> 'Look here, Ahurole, don't take undue advantage of your seniority. I have had enough.'
> 'Will you slap me?'
> 'I won't but I sincerely hope your husband will give you a severe beating first thing when you get to his house.'
> 'Mother, do you hear him wishing me ill luck?'
> 'Aha, mother, you are up and doing now.'[1]

Phrases like 'compelled to deal with', 'undue advantage', 'had enough' and 'up and doing' are all rather weary colloquial English usages which give a false and stilted quality to the whole passage. More care in writing would have enabled Amadi to render for us the sense and texture of this exchange as it would unfold in Ibo.

Elsewhere he sometimes twists dialogue so as to make things explicit for the non-Ibo reader, as when the hero Ekwueme's mother counts through the four days of the Ibo week before deciding that next Nkwo day is too long to wait before consulting the diviner. The days are listed by her simply so that the reader may be familiar with the Ibo calendar. Again, the use of expressions like 'reception hall' and 'sitting-room' instead of their Ibo equivalents invests them with a slightly false aura of the familiar, but the images these words suggest to the reader unfamiliar with Iboland are utterly misleading. A novelist can describe a room and its contents without being

---

1   *The Concubine* (London, Heinemann, 1966), p. 127.

accused of exoticism, so long as his motive is to illustrate the story. Most of these faults could have been avoided merely by a more sedulous study of Achebe, who has anticipated them. But Amadi's book, which may truly be called a historical novel, does represent a considerable imaginative achievement. It establishes that the past has claims upon the writer for its own sake, as well as for what it can illuminate and what it can teach.

From Achebe onwards, African novelists have avoided nostalgia for the supposed simplicity of past societies. Only by establishing their complexities can the writer rescue them from oblivion, and a mature encounter with these can never commend itself as a mere escape from present anguish.

Chapter 10
Vision and Fulfilment

Then we must sing
Tongue-tied without name or audience,
Making harmony among the branches.

Christopher Okigbo

The visionary writer does not journey into the past but into himself, where he encounters the gleams and fragments of many pasts and many possible futures. Loneliness is essential to his journey and he must not expect to report to us more than a metaphor of what he found there. The visionary must construct a symbolic language which gives meaning to his isolation and thus connects him with those who will listen. He must sense his uniqueness but temper it so with humility that he avoids all savour of Messianism. For what is unique in him is not the capacity for visionary experience, for prolonged voyages of self-discovery, but the readiness to develop his life in this direction. By so doing he re-enters the world of myth which modern man has so often ignored as a key to the meanings of adult life. Yeats declared that every important poet needs a mythology to give cohesion to the imagery through which he explores experience. It does not matter fundamentally whether he constructs one from disparate elements significant to him, like Yeats himself and the early Eliot, or whether he accepts a traditional structure of metaphysical belief like Hopkins, Auden and the later Eliot. But if he does neither his poetry will never rise above the occasional and the fragmentary; his poems will not add to one another, forming an organic entity which feeds them with new life and significance. *Byzantium* would be a lesser poem if we had not *Sailing to Byzantium* to set beside it.

The first important writer in the Anglophone literature of tropical Africa was also its first visionary. Amos Tutuola's *The Palm-Wine Drinkard*, published in 1952, remains his most remarkable achievement and the most complete record of his lonely, withdrawn sensibility. The symbolic language chosen here is the folk-tale and the overall pattern is that of a descent into the world of death. The Drinkard is finally 'master of the two worlds' because he has learnt the meaning of both. Elsewhere[1] I have attempted to show how the phases of his journey correspond with those of the heroic monomyth as we know it from *Gilgamesh* in the third millennium B.C. to the *Kalevala* in medieval Finland. What is important here is to show how Tutuola has achieved a narrative style in a language still largely strange to him. Mr. Segun Olusola of Western Nigeria has demonstrated in live performance how intensely oral is the manner in which Tutuola unfolds his tales. To see and hear him tell the story of the debt-collector who killed himself in order to follow his debtor to the spirit-world, a story which Tutuola embeds in the texture of the Drinkard's epic, is to realize how completely the author has transposed the tempo and naïve, inexhaustible energy of vernacular story-telling into the English language. Although Tutuola must be familiar with pidgin English, the genuine and autonomous English speech of the Guinea coast, he does not use pidgin in his writing. Rather he attempts a literary English, but is quite unable to suppress his own ebullience or impede the onward rush of his narrative. And this is of particular importance because the hero, although he thinks he makes his journey to the world of death simply in order to find his palm-wine tapster, is in fact acting for mankind. Through the boon which he brings back from the underworld he renews the contract between man and the fruitful earth, just as the sacrifice which closes the book restores the harmony of Heaven and Land.

The energy of Tutuola's narration marries with the deeper significance of what he tells to produce a unique and unforgettable rhythm new to English prose. Occasional clumsiness and superfluity should deafen no alert reader to presence of this rhythm in almost every page. Consider the elegiac tone in which the Drinkard recounts the flat and tasteless days of mourning for his tapster and the lost days of convivial plenty:

When it was early in the morning of the next day, I had no

---

1 See the chapter on Tutuola in my *Seven African Writers* (London, OUP, 1962).

palm-wine to drink at all, and throughout that day I felt not so happy as before; I was seriously sat down in my parlour, but when it was the third day that I had no palm-wine at all, all my friends did not come to my house again, they left me there alone, because there was no palm-wine for them to drink.

But when I completed a week in my house without palm-wine then I went out and I saw one of them in the town, so I saluted him, he answered but he did not approach me at all, he hastily went away.[1]

Nothing happens during the course of the week, but the gradual transition from the first morning to the third day to the week's end gives us a sense of the slowly lengthening emptiness of that time, exactly as the medieval ballad-singer evokes the waiting of the forlorn mother or sweetheart:

They had not gone a week, a week
A week but barely three

Immediately after the passage describing his abandonment comes the dawning of the Drinkard's resolution and a slight quickening of tempo as he sets out on his quest:

When I saw that there was no palm-wine for me again, and nobody could tap it for me, then I thought within myself that old people were saying that the whole people who had died in this world, did not go to heaven directly, but they were living in one place somewhere in this world. So that I said that I would find out where my palm-wine tapster who had died was.

One fine morning, I took all my native juju and all my father's juju with me and I left my father's home-town to find out whereabouts was my tapster who had died.[2]

The journey is not undertaken as an escape from life, but for the renewal of life. It would be over-literal to suggest that the forest into which the Drinkard now plunges represents the indigenous tradition of Africa, but it is only there that he can encounter the truths he seeks. The emptiness he finds in the days before his journey begins may not be entirely without reference to the affluent living of the emergent African élite in these years, just as the ancient story of the 'Complete Gentleman' who was really a skull, and who led astray the headstrong

---

1 *The Palm-Wine Drinkard* (London, Faber, 1952), pp. 8–9.
2 *Ibid.*, p. 9.

girl who ignored her parents' wishes, is certainly not without reference to the Nigerian society of the 1950's. Those who compare Tutuola unfavourably with the 'realism' they discover in certain African novelists are perhaps more amiss than they realise. Tutuola leads us, not outwards into the world of social appearance, but downwards into the abiding world of imagination and memory. The Drinkard's journey is not made in vain and the symbolic language which sustains it has not lost meaning.

The Drinkard eventually marries the girl whom he saves from the 'Complete Gentleman who was reduced to a Skull' and so acquires a companion in the later part of his travels; marriage is a part of the maturity with which he returns to his town. Another visionary writer of Nigeria, the late Christopher Okigbo, remains essentially alone throughout his quest for reunification of the self. The 'watermaid' who comes to him in moments of vision is no sooner glimpsed than lost, leaving the poet abandoned upon the shore. Only at the very end of his poetic cycle does he enter the eternal instant of her embrace.

Okigbo's first long poem, *Heavensgate*, opens with the poet-prodigal leaning upon an oil-bean tree and gazing into the swift enigmatic waters of Idoto, the sacred river of his birthplace. There follow images of conjunction and expectancy. Rain and sun 'in single combat' form a rainbow which resembles the sacred boa of the earth-goddess. Solitude invites the poet to sing like a sunbird, isolated upon a spray. But instantly the sunbird has become a heron, gazing at its own reflection in the hurrying river, awaiting passage to a new phase of being:

> Rain and sun in single combat;
> on one leg standing
> in silence at the passage
>
> the young bird at the passage.[1]

Here Okigbo's imagery joins with that of Wilson Harris, who compares that instant when the inner and the outer life become one to a *vodun* dancer in trance or to 'a one-legged bird which joins itself to its sleeping reflection in a pool.'[2]

---

1 *Heavensgate* (Ibadan, Mbari, 1962), p. 8.
2 *Tradition, the Writer and Society*, p. 51.

Section three of the poem offers a sombre image of African churchgoing, the worshippers like 'long black/column of ants' filing behind the bell tower to worship. The organist, 'Anna at the knobs/of the panel oblongs,' only reminds Okigbo how much lovelier is the wind heard alone among crops and rushes. Next come the first missionaries and invaders, scrunching their boots through the sacred places and clamping their alien law upon the land

> Behind the walled gods
>   in market,
> boots over mandos
> and byelaws thereto appended
>   by Leidan,
> archtyrant of the holy sea.[1]

Okigbo was bred a Catholic and he now prepares himself symbolically for the initiation of baptism which the church offers to its new members:

> rank smell of olive oil
>   on foreheads,
> vision of the hot bath of heaven
>   among reedy spaces.[2]

These lines close the first movement of the poem, 'Passage', where the poet seems to recapitulate all the preparations for an initiation which was to prove inadequate for the attainment of true vision. The movement which follows describes a Christian initiation terrifyingly imaged as the branding of a crucifix on the right breast of the celebrant. A bridge-passage then leads the poet from 'Initiation' to the movement called 'Watermaid' in which he first glimpses the vision that will finally complete him. The poet is now *above* the sacred stream which he gazed upon at the opening of the poem. We may see him as standing astride it, with one foot in his old being and the other in his becoming; or we may see him as literally standing upon a bridge, a universal symbol (allied with both rainbow and boa) for that which joins two modes of experience:

> I am standing above the noontide
>   with my head above it,

---

1 *Op. cit.*, p. 11.   2 *Ibid.*, p. 11.

> Under my feet float the waters:
>   tide blows them under.[1]

In ritual terms he is now ready to attend his destiny as a man. The first section of 'Watermaid' finds him waiting upon the beach, gazing out over the sea, element of renewal and rebirth, in imminent expectation of the maid who now suddenly rises amid the foam:

> wearing white light about her;
>
> and the waves escort her,
> my lioness,
> crowned with moonlight.[2]

But her presence endures only an instant and soon her brilliant particles are sinking through the waters that upheld her, like the golden shower which fell upon Danae:

> So brief her presence—
> match-flare in wind's breath—
> so brief with mirrors around me.
>
> Downward . . .
> the waves distill her:
> gold crop
> sinking ungathered.
>
> Watermaid of the salt emptiness,
> grown are the ears of the secret.[3]

Okigbo, like the hero of a well-known African folk-tale, has whispered the secret of the watermaid's approach into a hole in the sand, telling it to no man. But the secret sprouts a crop of ears, imaging the human ears to which it was refused.

Now a sensation of abandonment and lassitude assails the poet. Islanded in his grief, he counts each wave as he awaits the return of that bright presence which seemed for an instant to open all paths for him:

> So I who count in my island
> the moments
> count the hour which will bring
> my lost queen
>
> with angel's ash in the wind.[4]

But the fleeting irrecoverable vision serves only to show that

---

1 *Ibid.*, p. 21.   2 *Ibid.*, p. 25.   3 *Ibid.*, p. 25.   4 *Ibid.*, p. 26.

he is in need of another cleansing. The ritual in 'Lustra', the poem's next movement, has a marked pagan flavour, in contrast to the imagery of a ruthless, triumphant Catholicism in 'Initiation'. It begins with a powerful movement of ascent:

> So would I to the hills again
> so would I[1]

which carries the poet through moonmist to the hilltop, where he presents to the goddess two symbols of sacrificial purity:

> Here is a new laid egg
> here a white hen at midterm.[2]

Where Christianity inflicted itself as an indelible wound upon the breast, the pagan imagery of Okigbo's poetry is all of offering and surrender; the poet is ready to offer himself, but cannot easily change himself. In the second section of 'Lustra' he lingers on the fringes of a pagan festival. Summoned by drums and cannons to the palm grove, he feels at once the genuine uprush of the spirit in those around him. But, unable ever to plunge himself into the midst of things, he leaves his pentagon symbol cut upon a tree and draws away.

The last section finally unites elements of Christian and pagan expectation into a mood of stillness. The virgin flower weeps for her slain and silenced Son. Here emerges that Christ-figure, analogous to the poet himself, who is to dominate much of *Limits*. The 'dumb bells' which celebrate his advent echo the condition of the poet whose tongue has not yet learnt to transfigure or to bless. And 'the argument in heaven' is surely an ironic allusion to *Paradise Lost*, where the windy rhetoric of Book III obscures the real meaning of Christ's coming by dressing it up for debate. This last section of 'Lustra' distills a marvellous quietness:

> And the flower weeps
>   unbruised,
> *Lacrimae Christi*,
>
> for him who was silenced;
>
>   whose advent
> dumb bells in the dim light celebrate
>   with wine song:

---

1 *Ibid.*, p. 30.   2 *Ibid.*, p. 30.

Messiah will come again,
After the argument in heaven;
Messiah will come again,
Lumen mundi. . . .

Fingers of penitence
bring
to a palm grove
vegetable offering
with five
fingers of chalk.[1]

The Ibo custom of presenting five chalk sticks as a symbol of penitence gives Okigbo another gesture of offering with which to close his poem. It is almost as if the fingers of the penitent outstretched in repentance where left behind, transmogrified into the fingers of chalk which remain in the receiving hand of the goddess.

Heavensgate, as published in 1962, adds a fifth movement called 'Newcomer' which seems to contribute little to the major development of Okigbo's theme. The poet comes to Christian worship estranged from the innocent self which he associates with worship. He must wear a mask:

my own mask
not ancestral—

as he makes the sign of the Cross and he implores Anna with her organ noise to protect him from:

them fuckin angels,[2]

The next two sections of 'Newcomer' are really occasional poems dedicated to the poet's friend Peter Thomas and to Georgette Okigbo, the mother of his newborn niece. Lastly, another bridge-piece prepares us rather consciously for the silence which must attend the appearance of his next poem:

The moon has now gone under the sea.
The song has now gone under the shade.[3]

lines which are painfully close to those with which Eliot closes *East Coker* II, teaching himself the necessity of humility and

---

1 *Ibid.*, p. 32.   2 *Ibid.*, p. 35.   3 *Ibid.*, p. 39.

only humility, as a refuge from the folly, fear and frenzy of old age:

> The houses are all gone under the sea.
> The dancers are all gone under the hill.

Limits, when it duly appeared in 1962,[1] proved to be a much more closely organized poem than *Heavensgate*. More precisely, it is really two poems; *Limits* I–IV being a continuation of the search for a personal revelation begun in *Heavensgate*, while *Limits* V–X, sub-titled 'Fragments out of the Deluge', is a much more objectified account of the Western invasion of traditional Africa, where the poet appears only as the murdered and resurrected sunbird.[2]

Limits I again begins with the poet-prodigal presenting himself and his life to the goddess in the 'damp half light' of the sacred grove. He tells her that he has had his cleansing, yet follows this declaration abruptly with an image of unrepentant sensuality. This he will not renounce, nor does his salvation apparently require it, since it is a symbolic union with the goddess that he seeks. *Limits* II presents the poet's growth and straining for audience in imagery of a forest sapling which finally bursts through into the sunlight and rides there unified and serene in its great head of leaves:

> A green cloud above the forest.[3]

In *Limits* III the forward movement of the poem begins, the poet is launched once more upon his quest in a soft, hushed surge towards the unknown:

> So we must go,
> Wearing evemist against the shoulders,
> Trailing sun's dust saw dust of combat,
> With brand burning out at hand-end.
> *& the mortar is not yet dry*[4]

The refrain which ends this passage is used and repeated, exactly as in much of Eliot's poetry, to suggest incompleteness, striving and the finest glimpse of fulfilment. Soon the pace

---

1 In *Transition*, No. 5.
2 'Fragments out of the Deluge' is discussed briefly in Chapter 9.
3 *Limits* (Ibadan, Mbari, 1964), II.
4 *Ibid.*, III.

quickens and the feeling of expectancy mounts to feverish urgency with the new refrain:

Hurry on down—[1]

The poet reaches the waterside which is the scene for all his visionary moments, but pulls upon the rope he finds there only to reveal a big white elephant. The 'mortar' refrain returns to teach him the basic discipline of patience, while the false moment itself evaporates like a drop of dew in the sunlight:

and the dream wakes
    and the voice fades
In the damp half light
    like a shadow
Not leaving a mark.[2]

Still the poet is urged onward, through *Limits* IV, by the image of union with his 'lioness', his 'watermaid', the cruel rose image of immaculate and inviolable femininity. The 'twilight moment' of vision has eluded him once again, but the closing lines of *Limits* IV leave him sinking into anaesthesia, drugged by the 'armpit-fragrance' of the goddess. He is ready to endure all her probing so that he may find completeness at last, for is not the poet always something of an auto-vivisectionist, rummaging in his own living entrails so that he may show us truth? Now Okigbo is ready to surrender the scalpel itself into her hands:

Distances of your
    armpit-fragrance
Turn chloroform,
    enough for my patience—

When you have finished,
and done up my stitches,
Wake me near the altar,

& this poem will be finished.[3]

The poet's lapse into unconsciousness leads directly into the opening lines of *Distances* (1964), Okigbo's most important achievement and the completion of his quest. Even the title echoes one of the closing lines of *Limits* IV, and Okigbo also quotes these as a superscription to his new poem, thereby

---

1 *Ibid.*, III.   2 *Ibid.*, III.   3 *Ibid.*, IV.

directing us to see the sequence *Heavensgate—Limits* I–IV—
Distances as the mainstream of his development. The first part
of *Distances* opens with a composite image followed by a
declaration that the poet has at last accomplished his union
with the goddess, symbolic of unification of his own alienated
and divided being:

> From flesh into phantom,
> on the horizontal stone:
>
> I was the sole witness to my homecoming . . .[1]

Here 'the horizontal stone' is at once the operating-table on
which the poet passes from waking to dreaming and the altar
on which his reunion is consummated. Having retrospectively
announced this consummation, Okigbo now begins to trace
the final process of the journey to the 'Chapel Perilous'. As in
Tutuola's vision of purgatory, *My Life in the Bush of Ghosts* (1954)
the poet plunges into an anthill in order to enter the underworld labyrinth through which he is guided by a voice:

> Miner into my solitude, incarnate voice of the
> dream, you will go, with me as your chief
> acolyte, again into the ant-hole . . .[2]

Now the poet must encounter Death, for she too waits in
ambush within the white chamber which, continuing the
composite imagery of the opening line, is also the operating-
theatre towards which he shuffles, in a line of pilgrim-patients.
As the poet lies 'pinned . . . to the marble stretcher' he catches
sight of the white-robed figure of Death herself:

> the chief celebrant,
> in a cloud of incense,
> paring her fingernails . . .
>
> At her feet roll their heads like cut fruits;
> about her fall
> their severed members, numerous as locusts.[3]

Now the poet is at the archway which alone can lead him to

---

1 *Distances* I in *Transition* 16, 1964, p. 10.
2 *Distances* I, *ibid.*, p. 10.
3 *Distances* II, *ibid.*, p. 11.

the goddess. Here he encounters two mysterious riddles. The first, shaped into a triangular lintel to the arch itself, reads:

> *the only way to go*
> *through the marble archway*
> *to the catatonic pingpong*
> *of the evanescent halo* . . .[1]

And beyond this he reads a huge crucifix built of the words:

> *after we had formed*
> *then only the forms were formed*
> *and all the forms were formed*
> *after our forming* . . .[2]

But a few lines later, in Distances V, we are past the archway, we are within the sanctuary where:

> each sigh is time's stillness[3]

And now the poet is able to read the meaning of the riddles, for:

> in the intimacy
> of the evanescent halo,
> the symbol, forsaken
> in a cloud of incense,
> delivers herself of her bandages . . .[4]

The evanescence of the halo is perhaps what the poet has glimpsed in earlier, abortive moments of vision but he has not understood its meaning as a timeless moment in the midst of time, a moment beyond season, accident or change; appearing evanescent only to those who are trapped in the stream of time. The meaning of the second riddle we can only guess: the crucifix is the form of man upon the tree, whose form is therefore primary; but it is also 'the scar of the kiss/and of the two swords,' the intersection of the timeless with time and of man with god.

Now he hears the voice of the goddess calling him clearly and boldly:

> Come into my cavern, O stranger,
> shake the mildew from your hair[5]

---

1 *Distances* IV, *ibid.*, p. 11.   2 *Distances* IV, *ibid.*, p. 12.
3 *Distances* V, *ibid.*, p. 12.   4 *Distances* VI, *ibid.*, p. 12.
5 *Distances* VI, *ibid.*, p. 13.

He is ready to receive her embrace, and he perceives that it is with the same blood, the same breath and the same voice that he comes there, 'darkening homeward', for now he is at one with her and with himself. And now the line which appeared at the beginning of the poem returns with a new meaning, transformed into the eternal present, for the poet is now alone because he and the goddess are no longer apart, no longer separable. He is alone as only completeness can be, because it seeks nothing beyond itself:

I wash my feet
in your pure head, O maid,
and walk along your feverish,
solitary shores,
seeking,
among your variegated teeth,
the tuberose of my putrescent laughter:

I have fed out of the drum
I have drunk out of the cymbal

I have entered your bridal
chamber; and lo,

I am the sole witness to my homecoming.[1]

Such, at any rate, appears to be a possible reading of poetry which is by its very nature cryptic and arcane. The 'difficulty' of Okigbo is such as to demand a real familiarity with his poetry, which handles a common body of symbols and turns continually upon a central pre-occupation. It is not such as to prevent his being the outstanding poet of English-speaking Africa. The familiarity he demands is no greater than that required by Eliot, by the later Yeats, by Rilke or Valery; required, in fact, by any modern poet whose poetry rises above the occasional or the descriptive and seeks to record a whole cycle of spiritual and historical exploration.

Just how much does he owe to Eliot as a precursor in this type of poetic quest for reality? More, I believe, than is usually owed by a poet of his original talent to a single mentor. But then Eliot himself found it necessary to quote and echo other poets to an extent unprecedented in European literature.

---

1 *Distances* VI, *ibid.*, p. 13.

What Okigbo learnt from Eliot, and thus brought into the tradition of African poetry in English, was the art of handling complex ideas in simple language, by the constant re-arrangement of a selected group of words and symbols. Okigbo re-handles such words as laughter, dream, light, presence, voice, blood, exactly as Eliot teases out all the possible meanings of beginning, middle and end in *East Coker*. Both poets use fragments of Catholic liturgy mixed with others from the classical world, paganism and magic; but where Eliot depends upon his reading of Frazer and Jessie Weston, Okigbo is able to draw upon a living knowledge of pagan ritual and symbolism, set in the familiar landscape of his forest village. It is above all the constant presence of this landscape which makes it such nonsense to dismiss Okigbo as 'non-African'. Obscurity itself has, in any case, a most respectable African ancestry in the poetry of oracle priests and diviners, whose concern lies close to Okigbo's own. Finally, nothing could be less like Eliot's dry world-weary tone than the lyrical, passionate voice of Okigbo with his rich, darting imagery and abundant youth. His apprenticeship was long, but the completion of his visionary sequence from *Heavensgate* to *Distances* in only three years (1961–4) is an achievement that African poetry will not easily surpass.

Chapter 11

The Meaning of Sacrifice

There are dangers in the Quest I know, but the Word may be found companion not to life, but Death.

Wole Soyinka

Sacrifice may be defined as the ritual shedding of blood for the sake of the living community. Its purpose may be to preserve the harmony existing between man and god, or to restore this harmony when it has been disturbed by some human act or omission. The notion of sacrifice postulates a divine greed for blood-letting, which demands both routine satisfaction and especial placation. The sacrifice, whether animal or human, dies for the community, but quits it for the divine embrace that gathers him out of it. Some communities would add that the sacrificial subject, to be fully effective, must be willing and must be properly prepared for this moment when he restores the covenant between man and god by his instant transition from mortality to spirituality. The shedding of his blood is thus symbolic of the shedding of his mortal part so that the world may be renewed. It follows that the sacrifice must be in some way set aside from his kind, distanced from the mundane processes of life, in preparation for the act itself.

This cycle of individual ritually-sanctioned death followed by communal renewal, the agon-death-resurrection of archetypal tragic action, may find only fragmentary expression in a work of modern literature. A death can be perceived by us as sacrificial only if it confers some benefit upon those who remain behind or if, at least, it leaves the prospect of such benefit in the air around it. In common parlance it has thus become distinct from a 'tragic' death, for we tend to confer this title upon deaths which appear to us wasteful, pointless and of no benefit to anyone. Modern African literature offers many examples of deaths which are 'tragic' in this sense, but relatively few of deaths which can be perceived as sacrificial. The death of Professor in Wole Soyinka's play *The Road* appears, however, to be fully sacrificial in the sense outlined above.

The benefit which Professor's death confers must be assessed in terms of his role as a teacher, guide or forerunner. Professor is studying the meaning of death and is learning to master his fear of it for, as he says, 'One must cheat fear, by foreknowledge'.[1] All the characters in the play stand at some discernible distance from the full knowledge of death which Professor is seeking, and are measured accordingly. The closest to the reality of death, when the play opens, is Murano, who has actually entered upon its processes. Murano is in what Yorubas call the *agemo* phase, the phase of physical dissolution and gradual withdrawal from the world which follows immediately upon his apparent death. For Murano has just been killed, knocked down by the lorry-driver Kotonu in the moment when he is masquerading as the god Ogun at the annual Drivers' Festival. Kotonu and his tout Samson have hidden the body in the back of their lorry and brought it back to town; but Professor, finding it, has taken Murano as his companion in order that he may learn from him the ultimate secrets of dissolution. As Professor himself ironically describes it, he found him 'Neglected in the back of a hearse.'[2] To the others Murano appears deaf and dumb, though he understands Professor well enough. In the half-light of dawn he disappears from the lorry-park where the play is set to resume his old trade of palm-wine tapper, returning always in the half-light of evening with a full gourd. Murano walks with a limp because, as Professor explains:

> When a man has one leg in each world, his legs are never the same. The big toe of Murano's foot—the left one of course—rests on the slumbering chrysalis of the Word. When that crust cracks my friends—you and I, that is the moment we await. That is the moment of our rehabilitation.[3]

---

1 *The Road* (London, OUP, 1965), p. 94.
2 *Ibid.*, p. 44.
3 *Ibid.*, p. 45.

Professor's aptest pupil is Kotonu, for his new horror of death, instilled by the accident, has made him resolve to trade in it like Professor rather than to seek it out as a driver. He consents to run the 'Aksident Store' which Professor keeps stocked by the systematic looting of wrecks and bodies. For, on the level of sardonic comedy within the play, Professor's metaphysical quest for the meaning of death expresses itself in this activity eked out by the judicious forging of licenses and an occasional deliberate wrecking to keep up the flow of material. Kotonu dimly perceives the real nature of Murano, for he finally demands of Professor whether Murano is 'the god-apparent'. And there is a double irony in the question, for Murano is not only a newly killed man but a man killed in the moment of his possession by Ogun. Professor replies eliptically that in effect:

I held a god captive, that his hands
held out the day's communion![1]

In contrast with Kotonu, Samson is the naïve blurter whose occasional unassimilated insights have not yet prepared him to recognize the real nature of events. Hence he identifies Kotonu's new passiveness with that of the spider who waits for flies to fall into his net; to him Murano is simply a deaf mute tapper, and Professor a crazy, rather frightening old eccentric with a plastic signature. He blames Kotonu's long-standing reluctance to kill dogs for the accident with the masquerader. Ogun must have blood, and those who refuse him dog's blood may have to pay with human:

Kill us a dog Kotonu, kill us a dog.
Kill us a dog before the hungry god
lies in wait and makes a substitute
of me.[2]

Furthest from a real consciousness of death, and hence without any sense of the value of life, are the gang-leader Say Tokyo Kid and his sinister mob of jobless layabouts. Samson is at least dedicated to the life of the road, but these are ready to turn their hands to any casual violence for the sake of a few shillings or a whiff of dagga. They are the instruments of anarchy who were ultimately to destroy the political order which exploited them.

---

1 *Ibid.*, p. 90.   2 *Ibid.*, p. 59.

But for dramatic purposes they are also an infinitely flexible chorus who make possible the play's free movement in time. In Chapter Nine we have seen how Soyinka re-enacts a critical moment of the past as 'a dance of the forests' embedded within the present. This relatively stiff device of the play-within-the-play is rejected in *The Road* in favour of a dramatic moment which continually incorporates other moments, creating a pattern of mutually interacting correspondences within time. Or, to express it otherwise, the apparent sequence of time is marked by certain climacteric moments which simultaneously include all their past and future correspondents. Just as the masquerader communicates with the eternal in the moment of his possession by the god, so the imitation of any past or future action can charge the present with all its terrible and unpredictable energy. The arrival of such a climacteric is often registered by the action of the chorus.

This idea is gently introduced in the early scene when Samson, caught sitting in Professor's chair, confuses everyone's identity by imposing himself upon Professor as a millionaire. It recurs a little later when Samson enacts the Professor in his churchgoing days, bowing at every mention of Jesus Christ and delicately wiping his brow with a succession of clean handkerchiefs. Here the organ music from the church window which dominates the back wall of the stage plays the role of chorus by punctuating the rhythm of the original scene while Samson plays it. Soon after this, the layabouts start dirging:

It's a long long road to heaven[1]

when Samson is muttering to himself about Kotonu's refusal to drive again after the accident. Again, they begin to dirge softly when Samson and Kotonu are recounting the death of Kotonu's truck-pushing father, crushed against his own load of stock-fish by a runaway lorry. On both occasions this dirging underlines the mobility of their function and their ability to change the character of a scene by charging it with the terrible energy of the past.

The funeral service for the passengers killed in a recent accident which Samson and Kotonu have witnessed is mistaken by Murano for the music of evensong which usually

---

1 *Ibid.*, p. 19.

summons him for the evening 'communion service' of palm-wine to the lorry-drivers. Consequently he arrives in daylight and must be hidden by Professor from their profane eyes. The layabouts have just had their heads broken at a political rally and have thus incurred Professor's most bitter rage:

> I offer you a purpose but you take unmeaning risks which means I, I must wait and hope that you return alive to fulfil the course I have drawn for you.[1]

To perish in such a quarrel would be a death without meaning and thus without redemption. Professor's evening service is intended gradually to bring them all to a state of understanding and readiness, for their very trade requires them to live in the constant expectation of death.

Part Two of the play begins with a re-enactment of the accident itself by Samson and Kotonu. A crowded lorry had overtaken them just before a bridge and had thus been the first to go crashing through its rotting timbers, whilst Kotonu's lorry, with a screech of brakes which is now actually heard in the theatre, managed to pull up on the brink. Professor insists that this disaster also was a sacrifice, demanded by the goddess of the river whose waters were running dry:

> Below that bridge, a black rise of buttocks, two unyielding thighs and that red trickle like a woman washing her monthly pain in a thin river. So many lives rush in and out between her legs, and most of it a waste.[2]

This mounting rhythm of interrelated moments prepares us for the most crucial re-enactment of all. Kotonu has been rummaging in the back of the lorry which now serves as his store. Suddenly the tail-board falls with a crash and out falls the mask of the slain masquerader, quickly followed by Kotonu himself. Instantly the stage is flooded with whip-cracking dancers (these would be played by the chorus once again) and we are back in the terrifying moment of the accident itself. The drivers are seeking for their lost god and Kotonu, in order to conceal his death, must deceive them by putting on the mask himself. But it is full of the dead man's blood, which blinds and maddens him. His frenzied efforts to tear it off take on the appearance of a dance of possession which gradually

---

1 *Ibid.*, p. 51. 2 *Ibid.*, p. 58.

brings him to collapse. The drivers, still flogging each other, run off and the stage returns to the uncomplicated present.

Now Samson too must undergo the experience of possession. The policeman Particulars Joe is hunting for the killers of the masquerader. He is about to find the tell-tale mask in the store when someone substitutes the uniform of Sergeant Burma, its former manager, recently killed in yet another motor accident. Samson puts on the uniform and begins to imitate Sergeant Burma for the policeman's benefit, but as the talk moves to the manner of Burma's death the drivers begin to sing his funeral dirge. Samson repeats the frenzied movements of Kotonu as he tears off the uniform in a panic, feeling himself now identified with a dead man.

All these patterns of imitation and possession converge in the closing scene of the play. Now Murano appears upon his proper cue and Professor's evening ritual can begin. It is conducted under the walls of the church in which he has looked for the Word in vain. Only when those walls collapse will the Word perhaps be found among the ruins. In the midst of pouring the wine for the celebrants, Murano's eye falls upon the mask still lying on the stage. Dim memories of his former existence begin to stir in his mind and Professor, intent that everyone shall learn to confront the fear of death, insists that he don it. Murano begins to dance and everyone is transfixed with dread, for death itself is now apparent in their midst and none knows where he will strike. Only Professor is fully ready and, in the course of what appears an accidental scuffle, he is fatally stabbed by Tokyo Kid. Determined that not only his death but his words shall teach his followers, Professor preaches them a final sermon. Kotonu had insisted that the passengers in the ill-fated lorry which passed them near the bridge had no faces, for they were already trans-figured by the imminence of death. Professor reverts to this image in his closing words, for the drivers must learn to cultivate a wise passiveness in the presence of the doomed:

> Dip in the same basin as the man that makes his last journey and stir with one finger, wobbling reflections of two hands, two hands, but one face only. Breathe like the road. Be the road . . .

Meanwhile the mask spins to a stop and falls empty upon the stage, its purpose fulfilled.

The Road is remarkable not only for the economy and flexibility of its dramatic means, as exemplified in the multiple roles of the drivers' chorus, but for the range of language it employs. Soyinka here abandons the rather loose blank verse, occasionally over-rich in its effects, which he favoured in his earlier plays. Instead he offers a sharp-edged and swiftly-moving prose. The language of Professor's speeches is unashamedly metaphysical in its tendencies, but is seasoned with a sometimes startling brutality and directness. Kotonu and Samson range from fairly deep pidgin English and fragments of Yoruba to a speech almost as formal as Professor's own, depending entirely upon the mood and nature of the scene they are playing. Kotonu, for instance, is capable of registering his new-found passivity in these terms:

Much more peaceful to trade in death than to witness it.[1]

Say Tokyo Kid and his gang speak throughout in the Americanized slang of the lorry-parks, whilst Particulars Joe sticks to his stilted policeman's English. The songs themselves are all in Yoruba, since otherwise it would be impossible to give them authentic musical settings making use of Yoruba tones and speech-rhythms. This complexity of linguistic texture is an important source of the play's strength and points the way towards a much greater use of different types and levels of language in African drama. Such modifications as need to be made for production outside Nigeria, which might include some modification of the pidgin and the use of English settings for the songs, are a price well worth paying for the greater authenticity and richness of the original text. A dramatist should write with his ear cocked to his own audience rather than to Broadway or Shaftesbury Avenue, if his plays are to attain the genuine universality of merit.

This liberation of language in Soyinka's later plays has undoubtedly been assisted by the work of Nigeria's popular professional theatre groups, whose influence has greatly increased since the 1950's. Groups like Hubert Ogunde's Theatre Party established that there was an audience—spontaneous, democratic and uninhibited in character—for blood-and-thunder moralities, folk operas and social satire

---

1 *Ibid.*, p. 84.

presented in the vernacular or in pidgin English. At the same time, the use of Yoruba texts for the highly developed drumming, dancing, singing and masking of folk operas like those of Duro Ladipo and H. K. Ogunmola showed how the familiar words could liberate actors, singers and musicians alike, to make possible new developments in Nigerian theatre music that would have been unthinkable upon a basis of English words alone. The kind of freedom exhibited by *The Road* exploits the creative energy released by this music (as evidenced by the many scenes where dramatic action is expressed through dance and song) whilst retaining English as the general language of communication. In the same way, the play exhibits a surface which is accessible to popular enjoyment, such as the many clowning scenes between Samson, Kotonu and Salubi, whilst its full interpretation makes upon the audience demands which we associate with 'intellectual' theatre. *The Road* is complex and profound without being literary in the way that invalidates so many poets' plays.

Certain points in the action are strikingly matched in Soyinka's novel *The Interpreters*, which appeared in the same year. This book divides its attention more or less equally among a group of friends of new professional status who are striving to gain control of their own personalities amid the distracting uproar of modern urban Nigeria. They establish a style of living which is free of the inhibitions which cripple the self-conscious social climbers of Lagos university and government circles, while they treat the corrupt and sinister operators on the fringes of political and journalistic life with a wary contempt. They have thus established a measure of personal freedom, but the pursuit of their own true personalities occupies them right up to the end of the book.

Kola, the painter among the group, is finishing a great canvas in which all his friends figure as gods of the Yoruba pantheon, but he is unable to complete it until he can find a figure who will unite the whole composition. Gradually the friends move towards a recognition of the selves which Kola has rendered for them. Egbo, who has passed up the chance to become a hereditary, reforming chief in his native town and is pursuing a rather desultory career in the Foreign Ministry, finally accepts his identification with Ogun after a terrifying night lying among the boulders of the Ogun River.

Egbo has explored a new world of sensual delight with his mistress Simi and is returning, slack and stale, on the train to Lagos. At the great iron bridge over the Ogun he deserts the train and scrambles down onto the rocks below. Moved by an obscure impulse of refreshment he strips naked, bathes in the river and stretches out upon the rock to hear the train pass overhead. But its confused rumble only increases his fear and helplessness. Waking in the middle of the night, alone with the forest, the river and his nakedness, he tastes fear indeed, but knows also that the god is insisting to be reborn through him. His old self is being used and shattered by the divine thrust towards rebirth:

> So, now, for the first time since his childhood ascent into the gods' domain, Egbo knew and acknowledged fear, stood stark before his new intrusion. For this was no human habitation, and what was he but a hardly ripened fruit of the species, lately celebrated the freeing of the man . . .
>
> And he was remembering the wrung cries of his lovemaking now. . . . In darkness let me lie . . . so now he laughed. In the great yawn of the land the river's run stilled, turned a black choking tongue, he laughed, for the words were hardly dry on his tongue . . . in darkness let me lie. . . .[1]

At the climax of his fear and feminine submission he falls asleep where he lies:

> And morning came, baring lodes in rocks, spanning a grid-iron in the distance; it was a rainbow of planed grey steel and rock-spun girders lifting on pillars from the bowels of the earth. Egbo rose and looked around him, bathing and wondering at life, for it seemed to him that he was born again, he felt night now as a womb of the gods and a passage for travellers . . .
>
> And he made it his preserve, a place of pilgrimage.[2]

Here Egbo seems to sacrifice his old, outworn self in order that he may be made anew, but his renewal is also that of the god who transforms him. Now the bridge is no longer a harsh confusion of girders but 'a rainbow'; specifically that which joins two orders of experience or which unites man with god. Later Egbo returns to the same spot with a girl he barely

---

1 *The Interpreters* (London, Deutsch, 1965) pp. 126–7.
2 *Ibid.*, p. 127.

knows and deliberately takes her virginity on these same rocks, even as he was himself ravished by the god. By sharing his experience in this way he seems to re-establish his link with humanity as well as with divinity.

As Kola's canvas nears completion he succeeds in finding a divine equivalent for all his friends, but he is still searching vainly for a link-figure who will unite the whole canvas and express the covenant between heaven and earth. The group becomes involved with an albino revivalist called Lazarus who claims to have been resurrected from the dead and they find that he too is searching for someone who can express this link for his followers. His choice has lighted upon a young thief whom he has rescued from the mob and christened as Noah:

> 'We baptised him Noah', said Lazarus, 'because the Lord may have forgotten his covenant with earth. Look outside brothers, look out and see the great deluge . . .'[1]

Kola now decides that he will paint Noah at the centre of the canvas and goes back to the lagoon village, accompanied by Egbo, to collect him. But Lazarus has apparently staged some sort of trial by fire to test Noah's will and the boy fails it dismally; imagery of water and fire predominates at this point in the action and Lazarus has already been seen transfigured by the flames of a fire-swallower's torch in a night-club. After Noah's apostasy, Kola transfers his enthusiasm to Lazarus and successfully completes his painting with:

> an arched figure rising not from a dry grave, but from a primordial chaos of gaseous whorls and floodwaters. He is wreathed in nothing but light, a pure rainbow translucence. It was Lazarus, Kola's new dimension to the convenant.[2]

Here the arched figure is expressive not only of Esumare, the rainbow-god, but of the divine boa-constrictor 'bent to kill'. And this side of his nature is perhaps evidenced in the callousness with which Lazarus receives the news of the ensuing death of Noah. This results from an apparently muddled series of events at the end of the novel. Egbo has brought a black ram to be sacrificed in honour of the completion of Kola's canvas (a white ram having earlier been rejected as

---

1 *Ibid.*, p. 173.   2 *Ibid.*, p. 232.

incapable of being truly 'spotless'). Catching sight of himself in the picture, he is affronted to find that Kola has painted him as Ogun the blood-blinded warrior in battle, rather than as Ogun the artist, smith or pathfinder. Kola's selection is in fact a comment upon a vein of recklessness and violence which we still detect in Egbo's character. To express his pique, he takes away his ram and, in a subsequent confusion, leaves the boy Noah alone in Kola's studio with an intolerable American homosexual called Joe Golder. Golder makes his inevitable sexual attempt upon Noah and the terrified boy leaps from the balcony and is killed. His role as a surrogate is specifically referred to by another of the friends, Bandele, who remarks as Egbo subsequently plunges his knife into the ram's throat:

'What do you need the ram for? Haven't you had your sacrifice?'[1]

Bandele, indeed, increasingly dominates the action in the closing pages, and we come to recognize in him the 'guide' who figures in all Soyinka's tragic works. Bandele is perhaps identified with Obatala, the most gentle, passive and inclusive god of the Yoruba pantheon, of whom his praise-songs say:

He rests in the sky like a swarm of bees.

The meaning of Noah's death is related to his status as a reject and an outcast. His death restores him to the under-standing and compassion of the group. But for Golder there is no redemption; his guilt still sets him apart, although Bandele significantly rebukes Egbo for the extremity of his revulsion. As for the lay-figures of the novel, the corrupt politicians, simpering dons and venal doctors, no conceivable sacrifice can redeem them. It is the long-suffering Bandele who ends the book by telling such a group with deadly quietness:

'I hope you all live to bury your daughters'.[2]

No other writer of Anglophone Africa has so pondered the significance of death for the survivors as Soyinka. The depth of this concern in *The Interpreters*, where it coexists with high-spirited satire and life-loving fellowship, places the book squarely in the same area of tragic imagination as *The Road* and much of his recent poetry. It is the refusal of the Ibo

---

1 *Ibid.*, p. 243.   2 *Ibid.*, p. 251.

massacres of October 1966 to yield any meaning except horror and self-disgust which produces the baffled anguish in his poems of that time:

> A host of acorns fell, silent,
> As they were silenced all, whose laughter
> Rose from such indifferent paths, oh God
> They are not strangers all
>
> Whose desecration mocks the word
> of peace—*salaam aleikum*—not strangers any
> Brain of thousands pressed asleep to pig fodder—
> Shun pork the unholy—cries the priest.[1]

These 1966 poems of Soyinka's are a manifestation of that searching concern in recent West African literature which reflects the breakdown of civil order and the military coups and counter-coups of the period 1965–8, culminating, in Nigeria's case, in a wave of massacres and the outbreak of actual civil war. The hope that Africa's new nations would demonstrate in practice the unique humanism which many found in African tradition has not been realized, and there is now a sober reckoning of the cost of this euphoria, in terms of political violence and corruption too long tolerated by the people at large. The temptation to see Africa as uniquely wicked because she has not proved uniquely humane has so far been avoided, but the writers have been far ahead of the politicians in recognizing that human folly and cruelty can flourish on both sides of the line now dividing free black Africa from the garrison-nations to the southward. Soyinka himself has remarked that the African writer must 'free himself from the fascination of the past'.[2] And this new address to the urgency of present concerns has brought West African literature closer to that of Southern Africa, whose struggle has rather been to free itself from the fascination of the immediate.

Nothing could be further from the elaborately-prepared and communally-significant deaths of Professor and Noah, for instance, than the casual flinging of a man's body through a train window, which distracts, for a moment only, the harrassed

---

1 'Massacre' in *Idanre* (Methuen, 1967), p. 52.
2 'The Writer and the Modern African State', Kampala, *Transition* No. 31, 1967.

attention of Johannesburg's morning commuters. The late Can Themba, who has now joined in death the countless victims of *apartheid*, has described the scene in one of his most laconic short stories:

> There is something odd that a knife in a crowd does to various people. Most women go into pointless clamour, sometimes even hugging, round the arms, the men who fight for them. Some men make gangway, stampeding helter-skelter. But with that hulk of a man the sight of the gleaming blade in the *tsotsi's* hand drove him berserk. The splashing people left a sort of arena . . .
>
> Croesus Cemetery flashed past.
>
> Seconds before the impact, the *tsotsi* lifted the blade and plunged it obliquely. Like an instinctual, predatory beast, he seemed to know exactly where the vulnerable jugular was and he aimed for it. The jerk of the train deflected his stroke, though, and the blade slit a big cleavage along the big man's open chest.
>
> With a demoniacal scream, the big man reached out for the boy, crudely and careless now of the blade which made another gash in his arm. He caught the boy by the upper arm with the left hand, and between the legs with the right, he lifted him bodily. Then he hurled him towards me. The flight went clean through the paneless window, and a long cry trailed in the wake of the crushing train.
>
> It was so sudden that the passengers were galvanized into action, darting to the windows; the human missile was nowhere to be seen. It was not a fight proper, not a full-blown quarrel. It was just an incident in the morning Dube train.[1]

The passage has a certain quick effectiveness, a certain shock value. But, like so much South African writing, the story from which it comes is purely descriptive and two-dimensional. The hurry of the train, the street and the police-van communicates itself to the writing, leaving it no time to develop memorability or distinction; 'galvanized into action' is typical of the sort of slackness that results. Lewis Nkosi has complained that South African writing has too often given us only the journalistic fact masquerading as fiction. The incessant tension of South African life, the narrow limits imposed by censorship and the nature of the market, the strong direct influence of jazz and the cinema upon a prose style essentially journalistic

---

1 'The Dube Train', in *Modern African Stories*, ed. Mphahlele and Komey (London, Faber, 1964), pp. 226–7.

in origin; these and a dozen other explanations crowd upon the mind and demand excuse. But it is salutory to remember that, as the next chapter will show, the fascination of the immediate is a hazard to the writer no less acute than the fascination of the past.

Chapter 12

The Claims of the Present

Importunate as rain
the wraiths exhale their woe
over the sirens knuckles boots
my sounds begin again

Dennis Brutus

Lack of 'commitment' has been a favourite reproach of South African intellectuals towards the burgeoning literature of West Africa. Struggling themselves for admission to a fully urbanized and industrialized society, they are impatient of any literary concern centred upon the village, the tribe or the isolated self. Yet not only has their own writing been crippled by the lack of space or breath for reflection, but their impatience has misled them about the real extent of contemporary concern in the literature of the Guinea Coast. The last three or four years have seen a perceptible darkening of tone, notably in Nigerian writing, as the first promise of national independence evaporated in the fierce heat of regional hatred, political intimidation, arson and military violence. And this darkening of tone was to some extent prepared for in works which, though not tragic in overall intention, conveyed in their satiric detail the spirit of critical and creative impatience which was stirring in the young generation of artists. Such books were Wole Soyinka's *The Interpreters* (1965) and Nkem Nwankwo's *Danda* (1964), the first a novel of sophisticated urban life and the second confining itself to an Ibo village setting and placed, perhaps, a decade in the past.

The refreshing irreverence of Danda, hero of Nwankwo's novel, is no more tolerant of modern pretension than it is of traditional pomposity. Danda's profound love of what is creative and exuberant in Ibo culture, expressed in his incessant dancing, singing and flute-playing, enables him to establish a kind of personal independence which offends elders and *arrivistes* alike.

Remembering that anger is not the only nor always the best weapon for attacking arrogance or greed, Nwankwo prefers his hero's peculiar brand of genial ridicule. It is often much more disconcerting to be laughed at than to be sworn at, and the delicious comedy which Danda plays with the jumped-up local man Ndulue Oji at the beginning of the novel cannot be bettered as an active comment upon that particular kind of display.

Ndulue Oji has just entered his native village in a long shiny American car, known in Ibo as a 'land-boat'. Whilst the other villagers are content to stand and stare at their own reflections in the paintwork, Danda is completely uninhibited in his determination to assert a sort of collective ownership for the whole community in the goods secured by any one of them. He steps into the car and defies all comers to remove him. He first brilliantly outmanoeuvres the chauffeur, who is a 'foreigner', and then publicly challenges Oji to behave in a public-spirited manner or take the consequences. Nwankwo evokes to perfection the hollow bonhomie with which the newly-affluent Oji accepts the situation:

'Men of our land,' said Danda, still keeping the sympathy of the crowd, 'did you not tell me that this land-boat belongs to one of my brothers?'

'Therefore it is yours!' roared the herdsman delightedly . . .

The appearance of the owner of the car put an end to further altercation. . . . He saw the people gathered about his car and was pleased. Some ten years ago he had gazed like them at one of the wonders of the white man . . .

'People of our land, I greet you,' he said, with a great laugh, shaking hands with a few. Then he put his hand to the handle of the door of his car but stopped, furious.

'Who is this fellow?' he said glaring at the driver.

'He got in when I went to drink water and I cannot pull him out.'

Ndulue looked more closely, and recognizing the intruder, smiled. 'Ah it is you, brother,' he said. He liked Danda.

'Is it Ndulue's voice I hear?' asked Danda.

'Yes, come out.'

'Take me home in this our land-boat.'

'No, you can ride in it any other day, but not today.'

'Now.'

'No, come out,' said Ndulue, raising his voice slightly.

'Well, if I were you I would listen, Danda', said the herdsman, conciliating Ndulue.

Danda thought for a moment and then said, 'You think you can turn me out of this land-boat?'

'Yes.'

'You are not fit to.'

'Danda is right,' murmured the old woman.

'Does the law say now that when a man has a land-boat he should forget his kindred!'

Ndulue was beaten. . . . So, smiling, he nodded to the driver, got in himself, and sat beside Danda.

The crowd clapped their hands.

'Thank you', said Danda. 'And farewell. Stay on the ground and eat sand. Danda is flying to the land of the spirits on the wings of the eagle.'[1]

But by the same criterion of personal emancipation which rejects the pomposity of Oji, Danda also rejects the painful ordeal of ritual cicatrization which, for him, has lost significance, but which is still the test of manhood accepted by his kin. Wanting the youngest wife of the chief, he simply takes her, thereby bringing his father and family into disgrace. The responsibilities of marriage and farming sit uneasily upon him; he drinks praises but does not know how to earn them. He permits his father to die in bitterness and lie for a whole year without fit burial. Many of these things are forgiven him, especially by the women, because of his abundant vitality and charm. But his reckless disregard for others finally exhausts the reader's patience and lends a bitter-sweet flavour to the closing scene when he returns belatedly to the village to honour his father's ghost. Is *Danda* simply a picaresque novel with a type of vagabond-artist hero new to African fiction? Or does Nwankwo intend him as a personification of all that restlessness, that impatience of constraint and that insistence upon individual self-expression which dooms the traditional order to extinction? We are never quite sure, and this ultimately is a weakness in a book distinguished by its wit and high spirits. But there is no doubt that Danda's refusal to be as other men, his perpetuation of that youthful liberty the others have abandoned, makes him a stimulus and a challenge in a community still bound by custom.

---

1 *Danda* (London, Deutsch, 1964), pp. 8–9.

Danda makes an interesting contrast with the more contemporary Ibo hero of Achebe's *A Man of the People*, Odili
Samulu. Some fifteen years have elapsed since the action of
Danda, and the Ndulue Ojis of Nigeria have climbed, puffing
and wheezing, into the seats of power vacated by imperial
retreat. Chief the Honourable M.A. Nanga M.P., is no longer
simply a village luminary but the occupant of a major office of
state. And the methods of graft, corruption and intimidation
which brought him there are correspondingly swollen in their
scale and effects, until they threaten to shatter the very fabric
of the new nation and plunge it into bankruptcy and chaos.
The practice of feeing bands of unemployed youths to beat
up political opponents, first noted in Nigerian literature in
Cyprian Ekwensi's *Jagua Nana* (1961), has reached such a
scale that the gangs have taken on a life of their own, waylaying
and robbing all wayfarers without discrimination. Similarly,
the corrupt element in every single public contract has so
inflated costs that many projects cannot even be completed.
There is no machinery to combat all this, for there is no-one to
prosecute; and if there were, the courts are probably corrupt-
able also. As Odili (or perhaps Achebe himself) bitterly
remarks, in comparing the new national frauds with the
customary exactions of village chiefs and shopkeepers:

> The owner was the village, and the village had a mind; it could
> say no to sacrilege. But in the affairs of the nation there was no
> owner, the laws of the village became powerless.[1]

The only conceivable 'solution' is a military coup, foreseen in
the closing pages of the novel. But, as the novel also foresees,
such coups are liable to lead to counter-coups, to dreams of
presidential splendour in the breast of every corporal and to a
situation in which the destinies of the nation are decided by
every shift of jealousy and ambition within the closed power-
structure of the army.

The strength of Achebe's portrayal of Nanga is that we can
see him through the eyes of Odili, who is in many respects a
potential Nanga too. The Minister's genial sensuality conceals
a well-developed vein of ruthlessness and cruelty, of which
Odili is only fitfully aware. Having once deplored the savage

---

1 *A Man of the People* (London, Heinemann, 1966), p. 167.

demagogy with which Nanga incited the parliamentary mob against the country's few educated and competent ministers, Odili is happy to swallow his scruples when Nanga invites him to visit his ample villa in the capital. He turns against Nanga again only when the Minister casually, and as of right, takes over his mistress during the night. And the vendetta he then opens against Nanga remains more personal than political until his left-wing friends Max and Eunice persuade him to see things with a rather less heated egotism. His cheap desire to revenge himself on Nanga by seducing the girl who is destined to be the Minister's second wife develops into a genuine love affair, and the real dangers of political intimidation become manifest when they are practised against himself. But the philosophy which sustains Odili through most of the book is essentially no different from Nanga's own and is perfectly expressed in this little exchange with his loose-hilted mistress, Elsie:

> 'Ah! This na the famous Cadillac? I no think say I done see am before.' She was full of girlish excitement. 'Na tough car! Fje-je-je! You think say these people go go another heaven after this?
> 'My sister, I no know-o. Any way make we follow them chop small for dis world.' I opened the door and went in and she helped me close it.[1]

Because the corruption of Nanga's character, and its consequences on the national stage, are viewed throughout by a narrator who is himself made of common clay, Achebe's condemnation of this heedless 'chop today' society is that much more measured and effective. Similarly, his great use of pidgin dialogue in this novel brings out not only the humour and inventiveness of popular speech, its capacity for irreverence and deflation, but also its capacity for registering reactions as naïve and potentially dangerous as those of Odili and Elsie faced with a shiny car and a uniformed chauffeur. Ten years of such half-mocking, half-envious, but essentially tolerant commentary by the populace as its leaders rifled the till and divided the contents among themselves prepared the way for political disintegration, massacre and civil war. These terrible events cast shadows before them in Nigerian writing

---

1 *Ibid.*, p. 65.

from about the end of 1964 onwards. In a poem apparently
written in that year, J. P. Clark had already noted the irony
of the situation in which Nigeria's first and foremost nationalists,
Nnamdi Azikiwe and Obafemi Awolowo, found themselves,
the one powerless President of an independent republic which
he had spent thirty years of his life campaigning to create,
and the other in prison on a political charge. For it is surely
of one of them that Clark writes in his poem 'The Leader',
lamenting the loss not only of a childhood hero but perhaps
perhaps of an ideal of national unity also:

> They have felled him to the ground
> Who announced home from abroad
> Wrestled to a standstill his champion
> Cousin the Killer of Cows. Yes,
> in all that common
> And swamp, pitched piecemeal by storks,
> No iguana during a decade of tongues
> Could throw or twist him round
> While he rallied the race and clan.
> Now like an alligator he lies
> Trussed up in a house without eyes
> And ears:
>   Bit of bamboo
> Flung to laggard dogs by drowning
> Nearest of kin, has quite locked his jaws.[1]

Both men were in reality equally powerless, both equally
muzzled; the one in his prison cell and the other in his presidential palace. What the poem records above all is the collapse
in power and prestige of this first generation of political leaders.
Even martyrdom could scarcely save them now from obscurity.

While *The Times* could lament the overthrow of British-
style democracy in Nigeria by the Army coup of January 1966,
her citizens knew that the event marked no more than the
interment of its putrescent corpse. Throughout the closing
months of 1965 there was a steady decline in public order in
the Western Region. Achebe's remarkable novel was published
in the week of the coup itself, and must have been written at
least a year earlier. Writing in Ibadan in December 1965,

---

1 'The Leader', *A Reed in the Tide* (London, Longmans, 1965) p. 37.

Christopher Okigbo recorded the first massive reverberations of the wrath to come:

> Now that the triumphant march has entered the last street
> corners,
> Remember, O dancers, the thunder among the clouds . . .
>
> Now that the laughter, broken in two, hangs tremulous between
> the teeth,
> Remember, O dancers, the lightning beyond the earth . . .
>
> The smell of blood already floats in the lavender-mist of the
> afternoon . . .
>
> The drowsy heads of the pods in barren farms witness it,
> The homesteads abandoned in this century's brush fire witness it:
> The myriad eyes of deserted corn cobs in burning barns witness it:
> Magic birds with the miracle of lightning flash on their feathers.
>
> The arrows of God tremble at the gates of light,
> The drums of curfew pander to a dance of death;
>
> And the secret thing in its heaving
> Threatens with iron mask
> The last lighted torch of the century . . .[1]

In these last poems of Okigbo's the fine discipline of his earlier, more withdrawn writing comes to his aid in dealing with the onset of events which seem almost to defy the controlled utterance of art. But the few key words in this poem work all the more powerfully because they have behind them all the weight of meaning acquired in his earlier, intensely personal poetry. Now fire and bird, drum and iron mask assume meanings more immediate and overt in a landscape already smouldering into violence, as did the honeybees and the empty stare's nest in Yeat's 'Meditations in Time of Civil War.'

Another of these final poems, dated May 1966, brings back the sinister eagles of 'Fragments out of the Deluge', thereby casting some doubt on any interpretation which would link them too specifically to the original invasions of European colonisers and missionaries. Rather do they appear as general harbingers of hatred, violence and division:

> For the Eagles are now in sight:
> Shadows in the horizon—

---

1 'Come Thunder', in *Black Orpheus*, Vol. 2, No. 1, 1968, p. 7.

THE ROBBERS are here in black sudden steps of showers, of
caterpillars—

THE EAGLES have come again,
The eagles rain down on us—[1]

Writing later in 1966, Wole Soyinka takes up the task of
facing the fact of massacre among his fellow countrymen,
this time on such a scale as to cast doubt on the survival of
Nigeria as a nation. Finding himself by chance far from Africa
in that terrible month of September 1966 when some 30,000
Ibos were indiscriminately slaughtered in the North, Soyinka
charges the European autumn's imagery of death and decay
with the whole force of his outraged humanity, so that even
the acorns beneath his heel explode like the heads severed and
smashed by matchets three thousand miles away:

The lake stayed cold
I swam in an October flush of dying leaves
The gardener's labour flew in seasoned scrolls
Lettering the wind.

Swept from painted craft
A mockery of waves remarked this idyll sham
I trod on acorns; each shell's detonation
Aped the skull's uniqueness.

Came sharper reckoning—
This favoured food of hogs cannot number high
As heads still briefly crop to whirlwinds
I have briefly fled . . .

A host of acorns fell, silent
As they are silenced all, whose laughter
Rose from such indifferent paths, oh God
They are not strangers all . . .

I borrow seasons of an alien land
In brotherhood of ill, pride of race around me
Strewn in sunlit shards. I borrow alien lands
To stay the season of a mind.[2]

Again, it is the control acquired in creating his more rarefied
and reflective works that helps Soyinka to receive and render

1 'Elegy for Alto', *op. cit.*, p. 10.
2 'Massacre, October 1966' in *Idanre* (London, Methuen, 1967), pp. 51–2.

the full shock of these events. While his intellectual honesty demands acceptance of them as facts, only his skill as a poet enables him to render an account of them that goes beyond a mere cry of anguish or despair. In the article already referred to,[1] published during the following year, Soyinka is moved by the course of such events as these to attack the belief in a uniquely African humanism, so often celebrated by the poets of *négritude* and by many African intellectuals. Such thinking, he argues, fails to take account of the extent to which colonialism 'froze' the normal processes of conflict and change; it confuses a temporary lack of the means to do evil with a lack of the will to do it:

> The consideration that brings me, personally, hard to earth is the thought of the Angolan or South African writer either in exile or stretching out his last feeble twitches before the inexorable maul of a desperate regime ends him. . . . And he sees, and he understands for the first time that, given equal opportunity, the black tin-god a few thousand miles north of him would degrade and dehumanize his victim as capably as Vorster or Governor Wallace. This fact has been ever present, this knowledge is not new and the only wonder is that the romancer and the intellectual myth-maker have successfully deleted this black portion of the human equation. And the European intermittent exercises in genocide have been duplicated on the African continent, admittedly on a lower scale, but only because of the temporary lack in scientific organization. We whose humanity the poets celebrated before the proof . . . are now forced by disaster, not foresight, to a reconsideration of our relationship to the outer world and it seems to me that the . . . African writer must have the courage to determine what alone can be salvaged from the recurrent cycle of human stupidity.
>
> The myth of irrational nobility, of a racial essence that must come to the rescue of white depravity, has run its full course. It never in fact existed, for this was not the problem, but the camouflage. . . . It is a remarkable fact that the European writer who had both the leisure and the long history of introspection to ascertain his spiritual needs has not yet sent out a call to the black writer for rescue. Surely the game has become transparent by now, the writer's philosophy does not prescribe for his own society, the enlargement of this commitment conveniently ignores his own inadequacies . . .

1 'The Writer and the Modern African State,' *Transition*, No. 31, p. 13.

Despite the bitter impulse behind these words, Soyinka does not fall into the contrary error of discovering a uniquely African wickedness. He merely argues that Africa, as it resumes control of its own affairs, must inevitably display its full share of the folly and cruelty which belong to all humanity. The same frail barriers against tyranny which have been thrown up in other parts of the world must be attempted here also, and the same sacrifices made in defence of them. In another poem written after the counter-coup of 1966, Soyinka tells with vigorous irony of his sudden encounter with a frightened, excited and heavily-armed soldier, that alarming figure whose every twitch produces death and who stands at the very centre of Africa's tragic decade. For Soyinka death is imminent, but so is life, and life of a quality and intensity his bemused antagonist can never guess at. He hopes, one day, to have the chance to offer life in exchange for that casual threat of annihilation. So, as with 'Telephone Conversation' ten years earlier, he finally gets the best of the encounter. Wraith-like in his improbability at that time and place, he puts on flesh as he recognizes only incomprehension and murderous panic in the eyes of his antagonist:

> I hope some day
> Intent upon my trade of living, to be checked
> In stride by *your* apparition in a trench,
> Signalling, I am a soldier. No hesitation then
> But I shall shoot you clean and fair
> With meat and bread, a gourd of wine
> A bunch of breasts from either arm, and that
> Lone question—do you friend, even now, know
> What it is all about?[1]

The cost to Nigeria's writers of their fearless witness has been bitter already, from the early death of Okigbo to Soyinka's own prolonged imprisonment, for it is but a short step from commitment as a writer to commitment of the more direct kind which they finally attempted. But enough has been said to show that Soyinka was led into a measure of injustice when he accused his fellow West African writers of a lack of concern for the present and immediate world around them. Such a concern has in truth been increasingly evident for the past

---

1 'Civilian and Soldier', *Idanre*, p. 53.

four or five years, and the prevailing mood in African literature cannot be understood without taking this into account. The attempt to retrieve the past did not, I believe, stem from any desire to escape the challenge of today. It was necessary in its time, so that the younger generation of Africans might be offered a place in a world they could recognize as fashioned in part by themselves and their forefathers, rather than falling into a role projected upon them from outside. Now the writer faces a harsher test; he must tell the truth about what is happening in his society today, without falling into despair.

It is the distilled and disciplined passion of such writing as Okigbo's and Soyinka's that has been so often lacking in the work of Southern Africa's black and coloured writers. Perhaps it is the very familiarity and insistence of the brute facts of oppression and loss in their societies which has made these writers believe that the facts themselves are enough. From a documentary point of view this is true, but art demands a more fastidious diet. The fact of death in a Soyinka play or an Achebe novel, for example, is so carefully prepared that its significance is rooted deep in the whole texture of the work. This is equally true of Okonkwo's death in *Things Fall Apart*, of Professor's in *The Road* or of Noah's in *The Interpreters*. It is possible to achieve an effect of poignancy from the very casualness and indifference that surrounds death in a brutal society, but this demands a literary preparation as careful as that bestowed by their creators upon the deeply significant deaths of these characters. Alex la Guma reaches something like this effect in his third book, *The Stone Country* (1967).

This novel is set in a contemporary South African city jail where prisoners of every type are indiscriminately mingled, under the joint tyranny of warders and long-term 'trusties' of the most depraved type. George Adams is a lone political prisoner herded together with a motley gang of criminals which includes the condemned teenage murderer, the Casbah Kid. The approach of death for the Casbah Kid has hung over the whole story since its beginning, and the efforts of George Adams, the hero, have been bent precisely upon wringing some meaning from this apparently random act of cruelty, one of thousands enacted every day up and down South Africa. He makes these efforts as much on his own account as on that of the Kid, for the latter might find it easier to die in the dulled, indifferent

201

state in which he comes to the prison, but Adams would find it more difficult to live on, if he had made no effort to reach another human heart lying so close to his and in such peril.

This youth, who has known nothing in his life but squalor and brutality, has even managed to commit another murder during his few weeks in prison awaiting execution, though he has managed to escape detection for this last act of defiance. Adams, who has made one or two futile attempts at human communication with him, is standing at the door of his own cell when the guards finally come to take the Casbah Kid away for execution:

> The Casbah Kid stepped coldly out of the cell to join the guards. He felt uncomfortable in the stiff new uniform, and the hard edge of the collar scratched his neck. He looked expressionlessly at the faces of the men who waited to take him downstairs. He paused for a second, and then brushed past them, going down to the cell where George Adams waited.
>
> George Adams saw the boy come up. The guards made no move to stop him, and George Adams saw him on the other side of the wire screen, and for an infinitesimal instant there was a flicker of light in the cold, grey eyes, like a spark of faulty electricity. The bitter mouth cracked slightly into one of its rare grins.
>
> 'So long, mister,' the Casbah Kid said.
>
> George Adams nodded. He said,
>
> 'So long, mate.'
>
> Then the boy turned and went back to the guards . . .[1]

The monosyllabic terseness of this description stems from the belief, so common among South African writers, that bare description is enough. And so it is, for the purposes of political rapportage, but not for the purposes of fiction. In *The Stone Country* la Guma comes closer than ever before to presenting internal development, development in the relationship of human beings and their discovery of one another, in place of a brilliantly precise but entirely external reporting of actions and events. The latter is essentially a short story technique and it was as a short story writer that la Guma, like so many South African authors, first became known. The conditions of the market, as well as the tension and hurry of location life, have

---

1 *The Stone Country* (Berlin, Seven Seas, 1967), p. 168.

made for a constant striving after the quick effect. At its best this column and short story writing of the old *Drum* tradition is excellent journalism, sustained by a sharp wit and an electric sense of prose rhythm which makes it as intensely urban as Damon Runyon or Simenon. But it is unlikely to prove more durable than such journalism elsewhere, and the shortness of literary breath which it encourages often makes sustained literary endeavour especially difficult. Typical of these qualities, and of the sense of strain that underlies them, is this passage from a sketch of Casey Motsisi's:

> I'm still racking my brainpan on the major problem of how the world can rid itself of editors and still run smoothly when who should walk into this fly-ful Hotela Bantu but this character called Kid Nice. Now the gang calls this character Kid Nice on account each time he wants to get drunk he says, 'I wanna get nice, man, nice.' Kid Nice spots me the same time as I spot him and he walks over to where I'm sitting and sipping soda water. . . ·
> Before I can tell Kid Nice why for I'm committing the unpardonable sin of drinking soda water while vines still grow, he says to me we should go and get nice seeing as his ship is in. Now Kid Nice is one tough character who never takes no for an answer . . .[1]

Motsisi clearly feels that, given the nature of his audience, he cannot afford to flag to a moment. We are kept skating desperately over the surface of life, under a hail of wisecracks and liquor-shots. And in many South African stories the pressure is almost as relentless as in a magazine-piece such as this. Here is Richard Rive opening a story in a style that sounds more like a hastily-compiled film scenario:

> Rain poured down, blotting out all sound with its sharp and vibrant tattoo. Dripping neon signs reflecting lurid reds and yellows in mirror-wet streets. Swollen gutters. Water overflowing and squelching onto pavements. Gurgling and sucking at storm-water drains. Table Mountain cut off in a grey film of mist and rain. A lost City Hall clock trying manfully to chime nine over an indifferent Cape Town. Baleful reverberations through a spluttering all-consuming drizzle. . . .
> Solly himself in shirt-sleeves, sweating, vulgar and moody. Bellowing at a dripping woman who had just come in.
> 'Shut 'e damn door. Think you live in a tent?'

---

1 'Editors' in *Modern African Stories* (Faber, 1964), p. 127.

'Ag, Solly.'
'Don't ag me. You Coloured people never shut blarry doors.'[1]

To grasp the prevailing difference of tempo between South and West African writing, we need only compare the crude energy of this with the opening of a story by the gifted young Ghanaian writer Ama Ata Aidoo. Writing of a community which is itself unhurried and, within the limits of its familiar environment, secure, Miss Aidoo can afford to take her time. Here even urgent news must be forced to accommodate itself, to the pace of village assimilation. Yet, as their slow words filter into the reader's mind, her characters reveal themselves more deeply and fully than those of any other African short story writer except Luis Bernardo Honwana of Mozambique. In her hands the short story moves away from pure narrative and description towards insight and exploration:

'Look here, my sister, it should not be said but they say they opened her up.'
'They opened her up?'
'Yes, opened her up.'
'And the baby removed?'
'Yes, baby removed.'
'I say!...'
'They do not say, my sister.'

—Have you heard it?
—What
'This and this and this...'
'A-a-ah! that is it...'
'Meewuo!'
'They don't say meewuo...'
'And how is she?'
'Am I not here with you? Do I know the highway which leads to Cape Coast?'
'Hmm...'
'And anyway how can she live? How is it like even giving birth with a stomach which is whole... eh?... eh?... I am asking you. And if you are always standing on the brink of death who go to war with your stomach whole, then how would she do whose stomach is open to the winds?'[2]

---

1 'Rain,' *ibid.*, p. 201.
2 'The Message', *African Writing Today*, ed. Ezekiel Mphahlele (Penguin, 1967), p. 87.

In comparison with such writing, the bulk of African short stories have a curiously archaic air, all bones and no flesh. Attempting too little, they refuse to move beyond the ephemeral.

No black South African has published a novel in English since the war, and the only substantial body of work produced by a coloured writer in this medium has been that of Peter Abrahams, written entirely in exile. It is this which makes the development of la Guma as a writer so important, for his is a style and world of experience acquired entirely in South Africa, whereas Abrahams left the country for good at the age of twenty, before his serious activity as a writer had even begun. Writers as talented as Can Themba, Todd Matshikiza and Nat Nakasa have died leaving nothing behind them but a bundle of sketches and articles, and one fragment of auto-biography[1] which is inferior to Matshikiza's best work in libretto and journalism. *Drum* and the mass-circulation news-papers of South Africa were a hard professional school, but scarcely an ideal one for the training of novelists or poets.

Autobiography of the 'threshold' variety, marking the moment of the hero's definitive departure from South Africa, has been the field in which the most substantial work has so far been achieved. The first such autobiography was Peter Abrahams's *Tell Freedom*, published in 1954. It is conventionally told, insofar as Abrahams offers a sequential account of his life, from recollections of early childhood onwards to the point where he determines to sail to England and become a writer. This book is often eloquent, painful and honest, but it has the element of artificiality that is almost inseparable from such a treatment; for the author feels bound to keep some balance between events which seem objectively important and those which happen to be most deeply marked on his memory. The duty of 'presenting' a life in this way often leads to the elabora-tion of events which are in reality scarcely remembered, and sometimes to the elimination of others which do not seem, as narrative, to justify the brilliance with which they are actually recalled. Since we do not in fact experience the recollection of our past sequentially, but rather in a series of flashes, pools and

---

1 *Chocolates for My Wife*, Todd Matchikiza (London, Hodder & Stoughton, 1961).

exploding lines irradiating darkness, the art of unofficial autobiography seems nowadays to demand the development of new narrative forms. One of the first of such experiments was Joyce's attempt in *Portrait of the Artist as a Young Man* to place himself inside the skin of his infant self, rather than recalling it, with a certain avuncular solicitude, from the safe and lofty distance of adult life. But writers were generally slow to see how completely Joyce's work had revolutionized the art of autobiography.

The next important South African autobiography was Ezekiel Mphahlele's *Down Second Avenue*, in which the author cuts across a more or less sequential narrative by inserting freely-associative and directly-recalled flashes of experience here and there in the story. These 'Interludes', as he calls them, are written in a more jagged and immediate style than the main stream of the narrative; they recreate instants of experience, whilst the narrative reconstructs a series of events. Here Mphahlele moves from an account of how he came to teach in Basutoland (having been banned from teaching in the Union) to an evocation of his bitter restlessness when he reached there:

> I did more thinking in Basutoland than I have ever done. I had toyed with the idea of making it my home. But life was stagnant; people apathetic; the civil servants looked miserably bogged down.... And then I had become thoroughly urbanized and couldn't feel happy in such a country.

> **Interlude**

> I went to Basutoland in search of something. What it was I didn't know. But it was there, where it wasn't, inside me. Perhaps it was hate, maybe love, or both; or sordidness; maybe it was beauty.... I stood one night a few yards away from the foot of a hill. You find solid palpable darkness in Basutoland. I tried to rip the dark with the razor edge of my desire; but I found nothing to ease the heaviness of my soul. I scoured the sky with my eyes; in my fancy I raked the stars together, leaving a sieve in the velvet sky. Then I collected them and splashed the sky with them. Some of the stars were pulverized in transit and chalked the blue with a milky way. You know, it reminded me of the powder of an exhausted moth killer ...[1]

---

1 *Down Second Avenue* (London, Faber, 1959), pp. 183–4.

It will be seen that the Interludes provide Mphahlele with an outlet for the baffled energy and frustration which are not fully expressed in the main narrative. Yet the final effect of this counterpointing of styles is perhaps more stimulating than satisfying: the Interludes contain what the narrative refuses to assimilate. The finished work lacks unity of style, but it does have organization, and the great problem of the 'free' auto-biography is to devise some structure which will sustain the reader's interest. This is perhaps more easily seduced by a purely chronological sequence of events than by any freer association of memories, regrets and desires; for the writer's difficulty with the latter is to make the patterns of association seem as significant to the reader as they do to himself. Hence the free autobiography which breaks away altogether from chronology demands very high qualities of eloquence, selection and control. Probably the writer must still 'doctor' his acutest memories to some extent because, quite apart from the limits which even candour imposes on itself, it is unlikely that his skill can always convey the full sweetness or pain of episodes apparently trivial in themselves.

It is a freedom of this nature that the South African writer Bloke Modisane attempts in his autobiography *Blame Me on History*. Once more, this is a book of the 'threshold' type, which does not attempt to take us beyond the point in 1959 when Modisane decided to quit South Africa, rather than submit himself to the gradual erosion of his humanity by hatred and violence. Modisane develops his structure like a series of concentric rings moving out from a central point of entry, this point being his last visit to Sophiatown just before his final departure. By this time the bulldozers of the Group Areas Act had already largely ruined that violent and vital township where he had spent the first thirty-five years of his life. Starting in this way, he is able to make every broken wall and desolate eyeless building yield memories and asso-ciations which stretch back through his youth and child-hood, yet to keep some part of the reader's attention still focused upon Sophiatown in its last agonies of futile protest and eviction. Thus his own imminent departure from South Africa is seen as an extension of a common deprivation, for the destruction of Sophiatown marks the end of an era for all its inhabitants. The old life is dead for ever, as much for those who remain in South Africa as for those who leave it:

> My Sophiatown was a blitzed area which had suffered the vengeance of political conquest . . .; my world was falling away, Martha Maduma's shebeen was gone, she had moved her business to Meyer Street, but the new shebeen lacked the colour and smell of the long passage, the stench from the puddles of urine. I walked through the passage, the puddles were dried up and the smells were gone; and at the end of it was the door into Martha's shebeen, but she was not there.
>
> Across the door over the corrugated iron fence was destruction, the tenement houses were razed to the ground; and somewhere among the ruins was the room of Neme, a boyhood friend, who had grown up to be a murderer doing a seven-year term of imprisonment. He would never see his room again or the woman he lived with. I hurried away from the scene, through the long passage and back to Good Street, past Aly's fish and chip shop which always smelt of old dripping. I stopped at the Odin cinema to look at stills . . .
>
> Over the street facing the cinema was one of those enormous communal yards accommodating thirty-two families in thirty-two rooms. . . . On the walls of two of the rooms were slogans painted, perhaps hurriedly, and the paint bled down from the letters:
>
> 'WE WON'T MOVE,' 'ONS POLA HIER,' 'HANDS OFF SOPHIA TOWN.' . . .[1]

Writing in this way Modisane is able, like Auden's poet, to rummage among the ruins and fetch

> the images out
>
> That hurt and connect.

Among the most painful of these is the necessity to admit the cringing and clowning which are forced upon even the most militant African when he wants to avoid trouble with a posse of armed white bruisers. All the truths that wound the soul most deeply are here. Modisane traces the growth of that self-contempt which can gradually spread to all one's most intimate relationships and poison them at source. Thus the young boy is permanently estranged from his father when that lonely, difficult man fails to defy an insulting mob of policemen who break into his house during a pass-raid. His feeling for his black wife Fiki is gradually distorted by his

---

[1] *Blame Me on History* (London, Thames & Hudson, 1963), p. 6.

increasing obsession with cross-colour affairs with all their overheated significance in a legally divided society. He recounts the drunken sexual orgies and 'nice-times' which acquire such importance where so much else is forbidden and where early death or imprisonment snatch so many away. The words 'black' and 'white' chequer the page until they create a kind of sick refrain that carries the whole burden of alternating hate and hope, rejection and aspiration, desire to kill, desire to be accepted. And it is this painful truth-telling which has caused resentment among so many South African readers of the book, and much facile disapproval by readers elsewhere who lack the imagination to place themselves within this life and this experience. We should all like to behave heroically in a tense and perilous situation, but only those who have lived permanently with tension and peril know that it is impossible to be a hero all the time.

Yet *Blame Me on History* probably suffers from one hazard that is almost inseparable from this mode of composition; there is no structural compulsion to read the whole book. How many times do we persevere with a mediocre novel merely in order to find out 'what happens next'? A conventional auto-biography often imposes a rather similar constraint upon the reader, whereas the experimenter must hold us by the force and brilliance of his style alone, leading us through a pattern which cannot be apparent to the reader until it is complete. The association of events with one another must seem as significant to the reader as it does to the autobiographer, although it may in fact be a random one. The technique, therefore, demands a sustained level of performance throughout, for once the reader's attention is lost, he is likely to throw the book aside for good. Nevertheless it seems likely that an ordering of events which owes much to the cinema and to the psychology of perception will become more and more common in literary autobiography, in Africa and elsewhere.

The lack of black South African achievement in the novel is thus counterbalanced to some extent by a creative handling of the memoir. In poetry a necessary discipline has been attained in two ways. One is dependence upon the imagery and modes of expression of Southern Bantu poetry. Not only is there an immense canon of traditional poetry in this region of Africa, with its countless paeans in praise of cattle and warriors, its love songs and elegies for the dead, but there is also a considerable body of Bantu poetry written and published during the first quarter of this century, when the afterglow of Cape liberalism witnessed a great flowering of vernacular literature. Working now in English, certain poets have been able to draw upon that tradition for phrases which can bear the weight of their own anguish and at the same time relate it to the ancient suffering of the race. The most successful of these poets is Mazisi Kunene of Zululand, whose 'Elegy' employs phrases which might be found in a traditional funeral song but which gain their resonance today from the fact that there is now so much more than a bad harvest or a drought for which to reproach the ancestors; for it was they who lost Africa to the invaders:

> We count a million
> Strewn in the dust of ruined capitals
> The bull tramples us on an anthill
> We are late in our birth
> Accumulating violent voices
> Made from the lion's death
> You whose love comes from the stars
> Have mercy on us!
> Give us the crown of thunder
> That our grief may overhang the earth.[1]

Without such assistance, the poet faces the task of giving back to English words their full burden of meaning and emotion in an environment where everyone has been to some extent dulled to the full impact of cruelty and injustice by sheer familiarity. Though he must be angry, he must never be shrill. His must be a quiet voice where there is already too much shouting. For it is not so much the call to action that he is uniquely qualified to give, as the call to see, to hear and to know. The coloured poet Dennis Brutus has measured the difficulty of this task; starting with a tendency towards a certain lushness and over-elaboration of language, he has achieved in some poems a control which masters horror without diminishing its impact:

> Patrols uncoil along the asphalt dark
> hissing their menace to our lives,

---

1 'Elegy', *Modern Poetry from Africa* (London, Penguin, 1968 edn.), pp. 208-9.

most cruel, all our land is scarred with terror,
rendered unlovely and unlovable;
sundered are we and all our passionate surrender

but somehow tenderness survives.[1]

Here the lunge and hiss of tyranny do not shatter the texture
of the poem, leaving us again face-to-face with 'the journalistic
fact'. And poetry interposes itself, not to diminish our pain,
but to remind us that even in this extremity man can be something more than an object or a fugitive. In another poem,
Brutus lets the night-sounds of a South African city yield their
own secretion of terror, yet the single word 'my' which qualifies
them in the last stanza, by bringing the living and suffering
poet directly into the poem, somehow diminishes that terror
just a little; it makes the impact of the sounds more intimate
and almost humanizes them. For to assert ownership of anything in a system that denies your humanity is to assert that
humanity also:

The sounds begin again;
the siren in the night
the thunder at the door
the shriek of nerves in pain.

Then the keening crescendo
of faces split by pain
the wordless, endless wail
only the unfree know.

Importunate as rain
the wraiths exhale their woe
over the sirens, knuckles, boots
my sounds begin again.[2]

It is the very refusal of these lines to become a scream that
makes them tensile. Unlike the tortured prisoner, the poet
may talk, but at least he will not squeal.

Thus from many parts of Africa writers are showing an
ability to match the grim visage of the times with a control of
language that can contain both anger and compassion, both
grief and a refusal to despair. In the process English has been

---

1 'Somehow we survive', *Sirens, Knuckles, Boots* (Ibadan, Mbari, 1963).
2 *Ibid.*

stripped of those associations which might appear to tie it to colonialism, or to its mirror-image and opposite, the nationalist struggle for independence. Whatever the future may hold for the literary development of one or several African languages, the present shows us a continent which can bend and shape this chosen tongue so that it becomes once more the vehicle through which a young nation can explore the limits of its strength, heal its wounds and grope painfully for the real bases of its unity. It can, as always, be snatched up by those seeking only to express hatred, fanaticism or the justifications of the tyrant. But the best of the work explored here shows that English, whether in Africa or the Caribbean, has not yet lost its capacity to enshrine the hopes as well as the fears of men. For those of us who also use that tongue, nothing protects us from the responsibility of knowing what these men are saying to us, and to each other.

The Chosen Tongue

Sources of the superscriptions to chapters

Chapter 1 'As John to Patmos', *In a Green Night*, p. 12 (Jonathan Cape, 1962).

Chapter 2 'The Emigrants', *Rights of Passage*, p. 51 (OUP, 1967).

Chapter 3 Caribbean Artists Movement, Newsletter No. 2, 1967.

Chapter 4 *The Whole Armour*, p. 108 (Faber, 1963).

Chapter 5 *Eternity to Season* (British Guiana, 1954).

Chapter 6 *Rights of Passage*, p. 39 (OUP, 1967).

Chapter 7 *The Lonely Londoners* (Mayflower Edition), p. 123.

Chapter 8 *Children of Sisyphus*, p. 118 (New Authors, 1964).

Chapter 9 *Five Plays*, Wole Soyinka, pp. 40–1 (OUP, 1964).

Chapter 10 Limits III, *Limits* (no page nos.) (Ibadan, Mbari, 1964).

Chapter 11 *The Road*, p. 11 (OUP, 1965).

Chapter 12 'My sounds begin again', *Sirens, Knuckles, Boots* (no page nos.) (Ibadan, Mbari, 1963).

Index